Communications in Computer and Information Science   1610

More information about this series at https://link.springer.com/bookseries/7899

Ludovico Boratto · Stefano Faralli ·
Mirko Marras · Giovanni Stilo (Eds.)

Advances in Bias and Fairness in Information Retrieval

Third International Workshop, BIAS 2022
Stavanger, Norway, April 10, 2022
Revised Selected Papers

Editors
Ludovico Boratto (iD)
University of Cagliari
Cagliari, Italy

Mirko Marras (iD)
University of Cagliari
Cagliari, Italy

Stefano Faralli (iD)
Sapienza University of Rome
Rome, Italy

Giovanni Stilo (iD)
University of L'Aquila
L'Aquila, Italy

ISSN 1865-0929   ISSN 1865-0937 (electronic)
Communications in Computer and Information Science
ISBN 978-3-031-09315-9   ISBN 978-3-031-09316-6 (eBook)
https://doi.org/10.1007/978-3-031-09316-6

This Springer imprint is published by the registered company Springer Nature Switzerland AG
The registered company address is: Gewerbestrasse 11, 6330 Cham, Switzerland

Advances in Bias and Fairness in Information Retrieval: Preface

The Third International Workshop on Algorithmic Bias in Search and Recommendation (BIAS 2022) was held as part of the 43rd European Conference on Information Retrieval (ECIR 2022) on April 10, 2022. BIAS 2022 was held in Stavanger, Norway, with support for remote attendance. The workshop was jointly organized by the University of Cagliari (Italy), the Sapienza University of Rome (Italy), and the University of L'Aquila (Italy). It was supported by the ACM Conference on Fairness, Accountability, and Transparency (ACM FAccT) Network.

This year, the workshop received 34 submissions from authors based in a number of different countries. All submissions were double-blind peer-reviewed by at least three internal Program Committee members, ensuring that only high-quality work was included in the final workshop program. The pool of reviewers has been strengthened, integrating both new and accomplished researchers in the field from industry and academia. The final program included nine full papers and four short papers (38% acceptance rate).

The workshop day included interesting paper presentations and a final discussion to highlight open issues, research challenges, and briefly summarize the outcomes of the workshop. The collected novel contributions fell into two main topics: biases on preference distribution and biases on fairness dimensions. The first topic included presentations on popularity bias in collaborative filtering multimedia recommender systems; users' behavior effect on choice's distribution and quality within recommender systems; issues (e.g., due to the sequential nature of data gathering); perspectives (e.g., dynamic aspects of bias and beyond-accuracy measures); methods (e.g., crowd-sourcing) emerging in the evaluation process; and the limits of bias mitigation approaches. The second topic covered studies on unfairness issues caused by popularity biases; methods to enhance fairness in classification and search tasks; and group recommendation. More than 50 participants participated in the workshop in person or online.

In addition to the paper presentations, the program included a keynote talk given by Ebrahim Bagheri from Ryerson University (Canada). Ebrahim first showed the extent to which stereotypical gender biases are prevalent in information retrieval gold standard relevance judgment datasets, which then get picked up and acted upon by deep learning-based neural rankers. His talk then featured some recent works that attempt to de-bias traditional frequency-based retrieval methods as well as neural rankers. Finally, Ebrahim presented a range of works focused on de-biasing gold standard information retrieval datasets, showing how they could lead to less biased retrieval outcomes.

This workshop greatly confirmed the success of the two previous editions, with an increasing level of engagement thanks to the return to an in-person event. BIAS 2022 served to strengthen the community working on algorithmic bias and fairness in information retrieval, representing a key event where ideas and solutions for the current challenges were discussed. This success motivates us to organize the fourth edition of the workshop next year. The organizers would like to thank the authors, the reviewers for helping to shape an interesting program, and the attendees for their participation.

May 2022

Ludovico Boratto
Stefano Faralli
Mirko Marras
Giovanni Stilo

Organization

Workshop Chairs

Ludovico Boratto	University of Cagliari, Italy
Stefano Faralli	Sapienza University of Rome, Italy
Mirko Marras	University of Cagliari, Italy
Giovanni Stilo	University of L'Aquila, Italy

Program Committee

Mehwish Alam	FIZ Karlsruhe and Karlsruhe Institute of Technology, Germany
Marcelo Gabriel Armentano	National University of Central Buenos Aires, Argentina
Ashwathy Ashokana	University of Nebraska Omaha, USA
Alejandro Bellogin	Universidad Autónoma de Madrid, Spain
Iván Cantador	Universidad Autónoma de Madrid, Spain
Evgenia Christoforou	CYENS Centre of Excellence, Cyprus
Giordano D'Aloisio	University of L'Aquila, Italy
Danilo Dessì	University of Cagliari, Italy
Francesco Fabbri	Universitat Pompeu Fabra, Spain
Saeed Farzi	K. N. Toosi University of Technology, Iran
Eduard Fosch-Villaronga	Leiden University, The Netherlands
Nina Grgic-Hlaca	Max Planck Institute for Software Systems, Germany
Alan Hanjalic	Delft University of Technology, The Netherlands
Frank Hopfgartner	University of Sheffield, UK
Bill Howe	University of Washington, USA
Bipin Indurkhya	AGH University of Science and Technology, Poland
Toshihiro Kamishima	National Institute of Advanced Industrial Science and Technology, Japan
Karrie Karahalios	University of Illinois, USA
Arvind Karunakaran	McGill University, Canada
Aonghus Lawlor	University College Dublin, Ireland
Sandy Mayson	University of Georgia, USA
Rishabh Mehrotra	Spotify Research, UK
Joanna Misztal-Radeckaa	AGH University of Science and Technology, Poland

Contents

Popularity Bias in Collaborative Filtering-Based Multimedia Recommender Systems

Dominik Kowald[1,2]([✉]) and Emanuel Lacic[1]

[1] Know-Center GmbH, Graz, Austria
{dkowald,elacic}@know-center.at
[2] Graz University of Technology, Graz, Austria

Abstract. Multimedia recommender systems suggest media items, e.g., songs, (digital) books and movies, to users by utilizing concepts of traditional recommender systems such as collaborative filtering. In this paper, we investigate a potential issue of such collaborative-filtering based multimedia recommender systems, namely popularity bias that leads to the underrepresentation of unpopular items in the recommendation lists. Therefore, we study four multimedia datasets, i.e., Last.fm, MovieLens, BookCrossing and MyAnimeList, that we each split into three user groups differing in their inclination to popularity, i.e., LowPop, MedPop and HighPop. Using these user groups, we evaluate four collaborative filtering-based algorithms with respect to popularity bias on the item and the user level. Our findings are three-fold: firstly, we show that users with little interest into popular items tend to have large user profiles and thus, are important data sources for multimedia recommender systems. Secondly, we find that popular items are recommended more frequently than unpopular ones. Thirdly, we find that users with little interest into popular items receive significantly worse recommendations than users with medium or high interest into popularity.

Keywords: multimedia recommender systems · collaborative filtering · popularity bias · algorithmic fairness

1 Introduction

Collaborative filtering (CF) is one of the most traditional but also most powerful concepts for calculating personalized recommendations [22] and is vastly used in the field of multimedia recommender systems (MMRS) [11]. However, one issue of CF-based approaches is that they are prone to popularity bias, which leads to the overrepresentation of popular items in the recommendation lists [2,3]. Recent research has studied popularity bias in domains such as music [15,16] or movies [3] by comparing the recommendation performance for different user groups that differ in their inclination to mainstream multimedia items. However, a comprehensive study of investigating popularity bias on the item and user level across several multimedia domains is still missing (see Sect. 2).

L. Boratto et al. (Eds.): BIAS 2022, CCIS 1610, pp. 1–11, 2022.
https://doi.org/10.1007/978-3-031-09316-6_1

In the present paper, we therefore build upon these previous works and expand the study of popularity bias to four different domains of MMRS: music (Last.fm), movies (MovieLens), digital books (BookCrossing), and animes (MyAnimeList). Within these domains, we show that users with little interest into popular items tend to have large user profiles and thus, are important consumers and data sources for MMRS. Furthermore, we apply four different CF-based recommendation algorithms (see Sect. 3) on our four datasets that we each split into three user groups that differ in their inclination to popularity (i.e., LowPop, MedPop, and HighPop). With this, we address two research questions (RQ):

- **RQ1:** To what extent does an item's popularity affect this item's recommendation frequency in MMRS?
- **RQ2:** To what extent does a user's inclination to popular items affect the quality of MMRS?

Regarding **RQ1**, we find that the probability of a multimedia item to be recommended strongly correlates with this items' popularity. Regarding **RQ2**, we find that users with less inclination to popularity (LowPop) receive statistically significantly worse multimedia recommendations than users with medium (MedPop) and high (HighPop) inclination to popular items (see Sect. 4). Our results demonstrate that although users with little interest into popular items tend to have the largest user profiles, they receive the lowest recommendation accuracy. Hence, future research is needed to mitigate popularity bias in MMRS, both on the item and the user level.

2   Related Work

This section presents research on popularity bias that is related to our work. We split these research outcomes in two groups: (i) work related to recommender systems in general, and (ii) work that focuses on popularity bias mitigation techniques.

Popularity Bias in Recommender Systems. Within the domain of recommender systems, there is an increasing number of works that study the effect of popularity bias. For example, as reported in [8], bias towards popular items can affect the consumption of items that are not popular. This in turn prevents them to become popular in the future at all. That way, a recommender system is prone to ignoring novel items or the items liked by niche users that are typically hidden in the "long-tail" of the available item catalog. Tackling these long-tail items has been recognized by some earlier work, such as [10,20]. This issue is further investigated by [1,2] using the popular movie dataset MovieLens 1M. The authors show that more than 80% of all ratings actually belong to popular items, and based on this, focus on improving the trade-off between the ranking accuracy and coverage of long-tail items. Research conducted in [13] illustrates a comprehensive algorithmic comparison with respect to popularity bias. The authors analyze multimedia datasets such as MovieLens, Netflix, Yahoo!Movies and BookCrossing, and find that recommendation methods only consider a small fraction of the available item spectrum. For instance, they find that KNN-based techniques focus mostly on high-rated items and factorization models lean towards recommending popular items. In our work, we analyze an even larger set of multimedia domains and study popularity bias not only on the item but also on the user level.

Popularity Bias Mitigation Techniques. Typical research on mitigating popularity bias performs a re-ranking step on a larger set of recommended candidate items. The goal of such post-processing approaches is to better expose long-tail items in the recommendation list [2,4,6]. Here, for example, [7] proposes to improve the total number of distinct recommended items by defining a target distribution of item exposure and minimizing the discrepancy between exposure and recommendation frequency of each item. In order to find a fair ratio between popular and less popular items, [24] proposes to create a protected group of long-tail items and to ensure that their exposure remains statistically indistinguishable from a given minimum. Beside focusing on post-processing, there are some in-processing attempts in adapting existing recommendation algorithms in a way that the generated recommendations are less biased toward popular items. For example, [5] proposes to use a probabilistic neighborhood selection for KNN methods, or [23] suggests a blind-spot-aware matrix factorization approach that debiases interactions between the recommender system and the user. We believe that the findings of our paper can inform future research on choosing the right mitigation technique for a given setting.

3   Method

In this section, we describe (i) our definition of popularity, (ii) our four multimedia datasets, and (iii) our four recommendation algorithms based on collaborative filtering as well as our evaluation protocol.

3.1   Defining Popularity

Here, we describe how we define popularity (i) on the item level, and (ii) on the user level. We use the item popularity definition of [3], where the item popularity score Pop_i of an item i is given by the relative number of users who have rated i, i.e., $Pop_i = \frac{|U_i|}{|U|}$. Based on this, we can also define $Pop_{i,u}$ as the average item popularity in the user profile I_u, i.e., $Pop_{i,u} = \frac{1}{|I_u|} \sum_{i \in I_u} Pop_i$. Additionally, we can also define an item i as popular if it falls within the top-20% of item popularity scores. Thus, we define $I_{u,Pop}$ as the set of popular items in the user profile.

On the user level, we also follow the work of [3] and define a user u's inclination to popularity Pop_u as the ratio of popular items in the user profile, i.e., $Pop_u = \frac{|I_{u,Pop}|}{|I_u|}$. As an example, $Pop_u = 0.8$ if 80% of the items in the user's item history are popular ones. We use this definition to create the LowPop, MedPop and HighPop user groups in case of MovieLens, BookCrossing and MyAnimeList.

Table 1. Statistics of our four datasets, where $|U|$ is the number of users, $|I|$ is the number of media items, $|R|$ is the number of ratings, sparsity is defined as the ratio of observed ratings $|R|$ to possible ratings $|U| \times |I|$, and R-range is the rating range.

Dataset	$|U|$	$|I|$	$|R|$	$|R|/|U|$	$|R|/|I|$	Sparsity	R-range
Last.fm	3,000	352,805	1,755,361	585	5	0.998	[1–1,000]
MovieLens	3,000	3,667	675,610	225	184	0.938	[1–5]
BookCrossing	3,000	223,607	577,414	192	3	0.999	[1–10]
MyAnimeList	3,000	9,450	649,814	216	69	0.977	[1–10]

In case of Last.fm, we use a definition for Pop_u especially proposed for the music domain, which is termed the mainstreaminess score [9]. Here, we use the $M_{R,APC}^{global}$ definition, which is already provided in the dataset[1] published in our previous work [16]. Formally, $M_{R,APC}^{global}(u) = \tau(ranks(APC), ranks(APC(u)))$, where APC and $APC(u)$ are the artist play counts averaged over all users and for a given user u, respectively. τ indicates the rank-order correlation according to Kendall's τ. Thus, u's mainstreaminess score is defined as the overlap between a user's item history and the aggregated item history of all Last.fm users in the dataset. Thus, the higher the mainstreaminess score, the higher a user's inclination to popular music. Please note that we cannot calculate the mainstreaminess score for the other datasets, since we do not have multiple interactions per item (i.e., play counts) in these cases (only one rating per user-item pair).

To get a better feeling of the relationship between average item popularity scores in the user profiles (i.e., $Pop_{u,i}$) and the user profile size (i.e., $|I_u|$), we plot these correlations for our four datasets and per user group in Fig. 1. Across all datasets, we see a negative correlation between average item popularity and user profile size, which means that users with little interest in popular items tend to have large user profiles. This suggests that these users are important consumers and data sources in MMRS, and thus, should also be treated in a fair way (i.e., should receive similar accuracy scores as users with medium or high interest in popular items).

3.2 Multimedia Datasets

For our study, we use four datasets containing rating data of users for media items. The statistics of our datasets can be found in Table 1, and we provide the datasets via Zenodo[2]. The users in each of our four datasets are split into three equally-sized user groups: (i) LowPop, i.e., the 1,000 users with the least inclination to popular items, (ii) MedPop, i.e., 1,000 users with medium inclination to popular media items, and (iii) HighPop, i.e., the 1,000 users with the highest inclination to popular media items. This sums up to $|U| = 3,000$ users per

---

[1] https://zenodo.org/record/3475975.
[2] https://zenodo.org/record/6123879.

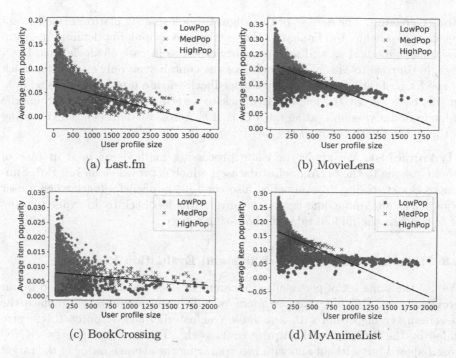

Fig. 1. Relationship between average item popularity scores in the user profiles (i.e., $Pop_{u,i}$) and user profile size (i.e., $|I_u|$). We see that users with little interest in popular items tend to have large user profiles.

dataset. Next, we describe our four datasets and how we split the user groups based on the popularity definitions given before:

Last.fm. For the music streaming platform Last.fm, we use the dataset published in our previous work [16], which is based on the LFM-1b dataset[3]. Here, a user is assigned to one of the three groups LowPop, MedPop and HighPop based on the user's mainstreaminess score [9], which we defined earlier (i.e., $M_{R,APC}^{global}$). Additionally, in this Last.fm dataset, the listening counts of users for music artists are scaled to a rating range of [1–1,000]. When looking at Table 1, Last.fm has the largest number of items $|I| = 352,805$ and the largest number of ratings $|R| = 1,755,361$ across our four datasets.

MovieLens. In case of the movie rating portal MovieLens, we use the well-known MovieLens-1M dataset[4]. We extract all users with a minimum of 50 ratings and a maximum of 2,000 ratings. We assign these users to one of the three user groups LowPop, MedPop and HighPop based on the ratio of popular items in the user profiles [3] as described earlier (i.e., Pop_u). Table 1 shows that MovieLens is the least sparse (i.e., most dense) dataset in our study and also has the highest number of ratings per items ($|R|/|I|$).

---

[3] http://www.cp.jku.at/datasets/LFM-1b/.
[4] https://grouplens.org/datasets/movielens/1m/.

BookCrossing. The dataset of the (digital) book sharing platform BookCrossing was provided by Uni Freiburg[5]. We use the same popularity definitions, group assignment method as well as rating thresholds as in case of MovieLens. However, in contrast to MovieLens, BookCrossing contains not only explicit feedback in the form of ratings but also implicit feedback when a user bookmarks a book. In this case, we set the implicit feedback to a rating of 5, which is the middle value in BookCrossing's rating range of [1–10]. Across all datasets, BookCrossing is the dataset with the highest sparsity.

MyAnimeList. We apply the same processing methods as used in case of BookCrossing to the MyAnimeList dataset, which is provided via Kaggle[6]. Similar to BookCrossing, MyAnimeList also contains implicit feedback when a user bookmarks an Anime, and again we convert this feedback to an explicit rating of 5, which is the middle value in the rating range.

3.3   Recommendation Algorithms and Evaluation Protocol

We use the same set of personalized recommendation algorithms as used in our previous work [16] but since we focus on CF-based methods, we replace the UserItemAvg algorithm with a scalable co-clustering-based approach [12] provided by the Python-based Surprise framework[7]. Thus, we evaluate two KNN-based algorithms without and with incorporating the average rating of the target user and item (UserKNN and UserKNNAvg), one non-negative matrix factorization variant [19] (NMF) as well as the aforementioned CoClustering algorithm. In most cases, we stick to the default parameter settings as suggested by the Surprise framework and provide the detailed settings in our GitHub repository[8].

We also follow the same evaluation protocol as used in our previous work [16] and formulate the recommendation task as a rating prediction problem, which we measure using the mean absolute error (MAE). However, instead of using only one 80/20 train-set split, we use a more sophisticated 5-fold cross-validation evaluation protocol. To test for statistical significance, we perform pairwise t-tests between LowPop and MedPop as well as between LowPop and HighPop since we are interested if LowPop is treated in an unfair way by the MMRS. We report statistical significance for LowPop only in cases in which there is a significant difference between LowPop and MedPop as well as between LowPop and HighPop for all five folds.

4   Results

We structure our results based on our two research questions. Thus, we first investigate popularity bias on the item level by investigating the relationship

[5] http://www2.informatik.uni-freiburg.de/~cziegler/BX/.
[6] https://www.kaggle.com/CooperUnion/anime-recommendations-database.
[7] http://surpriselib.com/.
[8] https://github.com/domkowald/FairRecSys.

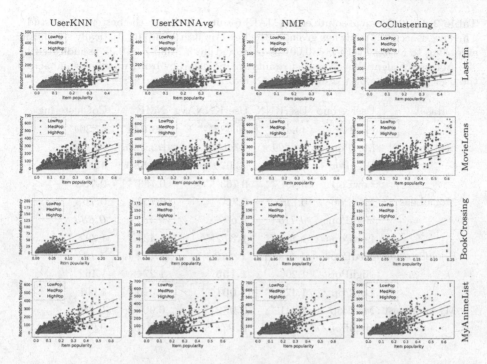

Fig. 2. RQ1: Relationship between item popularity and recommendation frequency of four CF-based algorithms for Last.fm, MovieLens, BookCrossing and MyAnimeList. In all 16 cases, we see that popular media items have a higher probability of being recommended than unpopular ones.

between item popularity and recommendation frequency (**RQ1**). Next, we investigate popularity bias on the user level by comparing the recommendation performance for our three user groups (**RQ2**).

4.1 RQ1: Relationship Between Item Popularity and Recommendation Frequency

Figure 2 shows the relationship between item popularity and recommendation frequency for the four CF-based algorithms UserKNN, UserKNNAvg, NMF and CoClustering on all five folds of our four multimedia datasets Last.fm, MovieLens, BookCrossing and MyAnimeList. The solid lines indicate the linear regression between the two variables for the three user groups.

In all 16 plots, and all three user groups, we observe a positive relationship between an item's popularity and how often this item gets recommended (**RQ1**). However, for NMF applied to Last.fm, the maximum recommendation frequency is much lower as in case of the other algorithms. Thus, only in case of NMF applied to Last.fm, we see a weak relationship between popularity and recommendation frequency, while in all other cases, we see a strong relationship

Table 2. RQ2: Mean absolute error (MAE) results (the lower, the better) of our study. The lowest accuracy is always given for the LowPop user group (statistically significant according to a t-test with $p < 0.001$ as indicated by *** and $p < 0.05$ as indicated by **). Across the algorithms, the best results are indicated by **bold numbers** and across the user groups, the best results are indicated by *italic numbers*.

Dataset	User group	UserKNN	UserKNNAvg	NMF	CoClustering
Last.fm	LowPop	49.489***	46.483***	**39.641****	47.304***
	MedPop	*42.899*	*37.940*	***32.405***	*37.918*
	HighPop	45.805	43.070	**38.580**	42.982
MovieLens	LowPop	0.801***	0.763***	0.753***	**0.738***
	MedPop	0.748	0.727	0.722	**0.705**
	HighPop	*0.716*	*0.697*	*0.701*	***0.683***
BookCrossing	LowPop	1.403***	**1.372***	1.424***	1.392***
	MedPop	*1.154*	***1.122***	*1.214*	*1.134*
	HighPop	1.206	**1.155**	1.274	1.162
MyAnimeList	LowPop	1.373***	**1.001***	1.010***	1.001***
	MedPop	1.341	**0.952**	0.968	*0.956*
	HighPop	*1.311*	***0.948***	*0.951*	0.975

between these variables. This is in line with our previous related work investigating popularity bias in Last.fm [16]. When comparing the three user groups, we see the weakest relationship between the variables for LowPop and the strongest relationship for HighPop. We will refer to this finding when investigating **RQ2**.

4.2   RQ2: Relationship Between Users' Inclination to Popular Items and Recommendation Accuracy

Table 2 shows the MAE estimates for the aforementioned CF-based recommendation algorithms (UserKNN, UserKNNAvg, NMF, and CoClustering) on the four multimedia datasets (Last.fm, MovieLens, BookCrossing, and MyAnimeList) split in three user groups that differ in their inclination to popularity (LowPop, MedPop, and HighPop). Additionally, we indicate statistically significant differences between both LowPop and MedPop, and LowPop and HighPop according to a t-test with $p < 0.001$ using *** and with $p < 0.05$ using ** in the LowPop lines.

Across all datasets, we observe the highest MAE estimates, and thus lowest recommendation accuracy, for the LowPop user groups. The best results, indicated by *italic numbers*, are reached for the MedPop group in case of Last.fm and BookCrossing, and for the HighPop group in case of MovieLens and MyAnimeList. For Last.fm this is in line with our previous work [16]. Across the algorithms, we see varying results: for Last.fm, and again in line with our previous work [16], the best results are reached for NMF. For MovieLens, we get the best results for the CoClustering approach, and for BookCrossing and MyAnimeList the highest accuracy is reached for the UserKNN variant UserKNNAvg. We plan to investigate these differences across the user groups and the algorithms in our future research, as outlined in the next section.

Taken together, users with little inclination to popular multimedia items receive statistically significantly worse recommendations by CF-based algorithms than users with medium and high inclination to popularity (**RQ2**). When referring back to our results of **RQ1** in Fig. 2, this is interesting since LowPop is the group with the weakest relationship between item popularity and recommendation frequency. However, this suggests that recommendations are still too popular for this user group and an adequate mitigation strategy is needed.

5   Conclusion

In this paper, we have studied popularity bias in CF-based MMRS. Therefore, we investigated four recommendation algorithms (UserKNN, UserKNNAvg, NMF, and CoClustering) for three user groups (LowPop, MedPop, and HighPop) on four multimedia datasets (Last.fm, MovieLens, BookCrossing, and MyAnimeList). Specifically, we investigated popularity bias from the item (**RQ1**) and user (**RQ2**) perspective. Additionally, we have shown that users with little interest into popular items tend to have large profile sizes, and therefore are important data sources for MMRS.

With respect to **RQ1**, we find that the popularity of a multimedia item strongly correlates with the probability that this item is recommended by CF-based approaches. With respect to **RQ2**, we find that users with little interest in popular multimedia items (i.e., LowPop) receive significantly worse recommendations than users with medium (i.e., MedPop) or high (i.e., HighPop) interest in popular items. This is especially problematic since users with little interest into popularity tend to have large profile sizes, and thus, should be treated in a fair way by MMRS.

Future Work. Our results demonstrate that future work should further focus on studying this underserved user group in order to mitigate popularity bias in CF-based recommendation algorithms. We believe that our findings are a first step to inform the research on popularity bias mitigation techniques (see Sect. 2) to choose the right mitigation strategy for a given setting.

Additionally, as mentioned earlier, we plan to further study the differences we found with respect to algorithmic performance for the different user groups and multimedia domains. Here, we also want to study popularity bias in top-n settings using ranking-aware metrics such as nDCG (e.g., as used in [18]). Finally, we plan to work on further bias mitigation strategies based on cognitive-inspired user modeling and recommendation techniques (e.g., [14,17,21].

Acknowledgements. This research was funded by the H2020 project TRUSTS (GA: 871481) and the "DDAI" COMET Module within the COMET - Competence Centers for Excellent Technologies Programme, funded by the Austrian Federal Ministry for

Transport, Innovation and Technology (bmvit), the Austrian Federal Ministry for Digital and Economic Affairs (bmdw), the Austrian Research Promotion Agency (FFG), the province of Styria (SFG) and partners from industry and academia. The COMET Programme is managed by FFG.

References

1. Abdollahpouri, H., Burke, R., Mobasher, B.: Controlling popularity bias in learning-to-rank recommendation. In: Proceedings of the Eleventh ACM Conference on Recommender Systems, pp. 42–46 (2017)
2. Abdollahpouri, H., Burke, R., Mobasher, B.: Managing popularity bias in recommender systems with personalized re-ranking. In: The Thirty-second International Flairs Conference (2019)
3. Abdollahpouri, H., Mansoury, M., Burke, R., Mobasher, B.: The unfairness of popularity bias in recommendation. In: RecSys Workshop on Recommendation in Multistakeholder Environments (RMSE) (2019)
4. Abdollahpouri, H., Mansoury, M., Burke, R., Mobasher, B., Malthouse, E.: User-centered evaluation of popularity bias in recommender systems. In: Proceedings of the 29th ACM Conference on User Modeling, Adaptation and Personalization, pp. 119–129 (2021)
5. Adamopoulos, P., Tuzhilin, A.: On over-specialization and concentration bias of recommendations: probabilistic neighborhood selection in collaborative filtering systems. In: Proceedings of the 8th ACM Conference on Recommender Systems, pp. 153–160 (2014)
6. Adomavicius, G., Kwon, Y.: Improving aggregate recommendation diversity using ranking-based techniques. IEEE Trans. Knowl. Data Eng. **24**(5), 896–911 (2011)
7. Antikacioglu, A., Ravi, R.: Post processing recommender systems for diversity. In: Proceedings of the 23rd ACM SIGKDD International Conference on Knowledge Discovery and Data Mining, pp. 707–716 (2017)
8. Baeza-Yates, R.: Bias in search and recommender systems. In: Fourteenth ACM Conference on Recommender Systems, p. 2 (2020)
9. Bauer, C., Schedl, M.: Global and country-specific mainstreaminess measures: definitions, analysis, and usage for improving personalized music recommendation systems. PLoS One **14**(6), e0217389 (2019)
10. Brynjolfsson, E., Hu, Y.J., Smith, M.D.: From niches to riches: anatomy of the long tail. Sloan Manage. Rev. **47**(4), 67–71 (2006)
11. Deldjoo, Y., Schedl, M., Cremonesi, P., Pasi, G.: Recommender systems leveraging multimedia content. ACM Comput. Surv. (CSUR) **53**(5), 1–38 (2020)
12. George, T., Merugu, S.: A scalable collaborative filtering framework based on co-clustering. In: Fifth IEEE International Conference on Data Mining (ICDM 2005), p. 4. IEEE (2005)
13. Jannach, D., Lerche, L., Kamehkhosh, I., Jugovac, M.: What recommenders recommend: an analysis of recommendation biases and possible countermeasures. User Model. User Adapt. Interact. **25**(5), 427–491 (2015). https://doi.org/10.1007/s11257-015-9165-3
14. Kowald, D., Lex, E.: The influence of frequency, recency and semantic context on the reuse of tags in social tagging systems. In: Proceedings of Hypertext 2016, pp. 237–242. ACM, New York, NY, USA (2016)

15. Kowald, D., Muellner, P., Zangerle, E., Bauer, C., Schedl, M., Lex, E.: Support the underground: characteristics of beyond-mainstream music listeners. EPJ Data Sci. **10**(1), 1–26 (2021). https://doi.org/10.1140/epjds/s13688-021-00268-9
16. Kowald, D., Schedl, M., Lex, E.: The unfairness of popularity bias in music recommendation: a reproducibility study. In: Jose, J.M., et al. (eds.) ECIR 2020. LNCS, vol. 12036, pp. 35–42. Springer, Cham (2020). https://doi.org/10.1007/978-3-030-45442-5_5
17. Lacic, E., Kowald, D., Seitlinger, P.C., Trattner, C., Parra, D.: Recommending items in social tagging systems using tag and time information. In: Proceedings of the 1st Social Personalization Workshop co-located with the 25th ACM Conference on Hypertext and Social Media, pp. 4–9. ACM (2014)
18. Lacic, E., Kowald, D., Traub, M., Luzhnica, G., Simon, J.P., Lex, E.: Tackling cold-start users in recommender systems with indoor positioning systems. In: Poster Proceedings of the 9th ACM Conference on Recommender Systems. Association of Computing Machinery (2015)
19. Luo, X., Zhou, M., Xia, Y., Zhu, Q.: An efficient non-negative matrix-factorization-based approach to collaborative filtering for recommender systems. IEEE Trans. Indust. Inform. **10**(2), 1273–1284 (2014)
20. Park, Y.J., Tuzhilin, A.: The long tail of recommender systems and how to leverage it. In: Proceedings of the 2008 ACM Conference on Recommender Systems, pp. 11–18 (2008)
21. Seitlinger, P., Kowald, D., Kopeinik, S., Hasani-Mavriqi, I., Lex, E., Ley, T.: Attention please! a hybrid resource recommender mimicking attention-interpretation dynamics. In: Proceedings of WWW 2015 companion, pp. 339–345. ACM (2015)
22. Shi, Y., Larson, M., Hanjalic, A.: Collaborative filtering beyond the user-item matrix: a survey of the state of the art and future challenges. ACM Comput. Surv. **47**(1), 3:1–3:45 (2014)
23. Sun, W., Khenissi, S., Nasraoui, O., Shafto, P.: Debiasing the human-recommender system feedback loop in collaborative filtering. In: Companion Proceedings of The 2019 World Wide Web Conference, pp. 645–651 (2019)
24. Zehlike, M., Bonchi, F., Castillo, C., Hajian, S., Megahed, M., Baeza-Yates, R.: Fa*ir: A fair top-k ranking algorithm. In: Proceedings of the 2017 ACM on Conference on Information and Knowledge Management, pp. 1569–1578 (2017)

The Impact of Recommender System and Users' Behaviour on Choices' Distribution and Quality

Naieme Hazrati[✉] and Francesco Ricci

Free University of Bozen-Bolzano, Bolzano, Italy
{nhazrati,fricci}@unibz.it

Abstract. Recommender Systems (RSs) research has become interested in assessing the system effect on the actual choices of their users: the distribution and the quality of the choices. By simulating users' choices, influenced by RSs, it was shown that algorithmic biases, such as the tendency to recommend popular items, are transferred to the users' choices.

In this paper we conjecture that the effect of an RS on the quality and distribution of the users' choices can also be influenced by the users' tendency to prefer certain types of items, i.e., popular, recent, or highly rated items. To quantify this impact, we define alternative Choice Models (CMs) and we simulate their effect when users are exposed to recommendations. We find that RS biases can also be enforced by the CM, e.g., the tendency to concentrate the choices on a restricted number of items. Moreover, we discover that the quality of the choices can be jeopardised by a CM. We also find that for some RSs the impact of the CM is less prominent and their biases are not modified by the CM. This study show the importance of assessing algorithmic biases in conjunction with a proper model of users' behaviour.

Keywords: Choice model · Recommender system · Simulation

1 Introduction

The research on Recommender Systems' (RSs) biases, such as the tendency to recommend popular items (popularity bias), has focused on the empirical analysis of the system generated recommendations [9]. However, in practice, users are never passively choosing the recommended items; they evaluate them before making a choice. Hence, real users' choices are determined by the combined effect of an RS and the specific users' choice behaviour. For instance, one can reasonably conjecture that users' choices overall distribution and quality can also be determined by users' tendency to choose items with specific properties, such as, those more popular or recent [17].

In this paper, with the aim of understanding the effects of users' choice behaviour on the distribution and quality of the produced choices, we operationalise alternative choice models (CMs) that, as we tested in a correlation

L. Boratto et al. (Eds.): BIAS 2022, CCIS 1610, pp. 12–20, 2022.
https://doi.org/10.1007/978-3-031-09316-6_2

analysis, appear to be adopted by real users (Amazon Apps and Games ratings data sets). Then, we use these CMs in a study where users are simulated to repeatedly choose items during a long time span, among those recommended by an RS. In order to build the CMs, we consider three item properties that users may consider as criteria for making a choice: item popularity, item rating and item age, which is the time difference between the choice and when the chosen item was first available in the system. These three specific properties have been chosen because they have already been studied in the literature [1,2,14] and are often influencing users in their choices. Additionally, item age, rating and popularity are easily derived from user-item interactions data sets. To quantify the existence of a dependency of users' choices on these properties in the considered data sets, we have performed a correlation test. The result of a point biserial correlation test between a boolean variable representing the presence/absence of a user's choice for an item and the considered item properties, has shown that, for a large proportion of the users, there is a strong correlation between choice and the considered item properties: more popular, recent and higher rated items are preferred by the users.

Accordingly, we design three corresponding CMs (Popularity-CM, Rating-CM, and Age-CM) that may be adopted by users that have the tendency to prioritise in their choices items that excel in being: popular, high rating or more recent. We also define a fourth choice model, Base-CM, where the simulated users always select the top recommended item. Base-CM is used to measure the sole effect of the RS and to differentiate the effect of the RS from that of the CM. In our empirical analysis we have found interesting properties of the distribution and quality of the users' choices, hence showing the importance of studying the combined effect of a CM and an RS:

1. *The CM can have a significant impact on the distribution and quality of the the users' choices.* For instance, when users tend to choose more popular items (Popularity-CM) the choices become even more concentrated over a small set of items. While choosing newer items (i.e., adopting Age-CM) can lead to more diverse choices but with lower quality. Moreover, we observe that Age-CM and Rating-CM can slightly mitigate the concentration bias of a popular RS such as the Factor Model.

2. *Some important properties and biases of the RS, and how they affect the distribution and quality of the choices, are not influenced by the CM.* Hence, in these cases the RS has an unavoidable effect that cannot be mitigated by any CM. For instance, non-personalised RSs create a strong concentration of the choices over a small set of items, and none of the considered CMs can moderate this effect.

The obtained results enlighten the not yet analysed, but significant, effect of the users' choice model. We clearly show that it is essential to understand the implications of the target users adopting a particular CM, when the goal is to anticipate the long term effect of an RS on these users' choices.

2   Related Works

2.1   Impact of Recommender System on Users' Choice Distribution

Recommender systems have drawn the attention of researchers and practitioners for their ability to support online users of almost any web portal in their decision making process. Recently, some RSs studies leveraged simulation methods to better understand their users' behaviour as well as the evolution of the system performance. In particular, some researches focused on analysing the impact of the RS on users' choice behaviour [3, 6, 10]. In such simulations, users' repeated choices are simulated while alternative RSs suggest items to them. Then, the simulated choices are analysed in order to quantify the effect of the simulated RSs on users' choice behaviour. A seminal research is described in [6], where the effect of an RS on the diversity of users choices is measured. The authors designed a simulation framework where the users select items iteratively among a small set of products according to a probabilistic multinomial-logit choice model (CM). The model is based on a randomly generated utility function of the users, hence, their preferences are not supposed to be similar to those of any real RS users' population. Each user is assumed to choose from a (fictitious) catalogue of items, and if an item is recommended to a user, then the probability that the user selects that item is increased. The authors discovered that common RSs, namely CF algorithms, produce a choice concentration bias. Another simulation-based analysis was performed in [3] on the news domain, where the aim of the study was to understand how recommendations affect the diversity of news consumption. The authors adopted a framework similar to that introduced in [6], but they considered two additional diversity metrics: long-tail diversity and unexpectedness [18]. They found that the more the users choose popular topics, the less unexpected the recommendations become. More recently, in [4] the authors have performed another simulation analysis and they have found that RSs increase the concentration of the choices over a narrow set of items and create a richer-get-richer effect for popular items. Moreover, they have discovered that choices' homogeneity reduces the utility of the RSs as it hinders the user-item match, which was previously noted also in [5].

2.2   Impact of Choice Model on Users' Choice Distribution

In another line of research, some authors aimed at understanding the effect of specific users' choice behaviours on the resulting choice distribution, when users are exposed to an RS. In general, choice modelling refers to a set of theoretical attempts to model individual decision making among discrete alternatives, where alternatives vary in their attributes and features [15]. Choice models aim at being faithful descriptions of the expected behaviour of individuals and they are widely used to understand the aggregated users' behaviour.

In [17] the authors analysed the conjoint impact of an RS and the users' choice model. They conducted a simulation of the users' choices under different choice models, while users are exposed to recommendations. The authors refer to a choice model as the combination of a recommendation set and simple criteria adopted by the user to select an item among the recommendations, i.e., they do not distinguish the two concepts, as we propose. Even in this study, the simulated users are iteratively exposed to recommendations (generated by a matrix factorization [7] RS), and they make simulated choices among the recommended items, on the base of a simple deterministic or probabilistic criteria. The authors discovered that with a CM where all the users choose the same number of items randomly among the recommended items, the choices do not necessarily become more uniform and their mean rating decreases.

In a more recent study [19] several user choice models, referred to as "consumption strategies" are simulated. The study aims at understanding the effect, of varying the users' reliance on recommendations, on the performance of a recommender system. The authors discovered a phenomenon called the "performance paradox", i.e., when a strong reliance on recommendations leads to suboptimal performance of the RS in the long run. Additionally, they modeled other scenarios, such as, when users consume items among personalised and popularity-based recommendations (hybrid consumption). The authors found that the hybrid consumption strategy improves the relevance of consumed items over time, mainly because RSs popularise the good quality items that are preferred by a large number of users. While this study focuses primarily on choice models that simulate different levels of reliance of users on the recommendations, the CMs considered in our study are meant to simulate and predict the choices of users that tend to prefer items with certain properties. In addition, while in [19] only one RS (which is sometimes combined with a popularity-based RS) is considered, we study the combined effect of six alternative RSs and four CMs.

3   Simulation of Users' Choices

The logical schema of the adopted simulation approach is shown in Fig. 1. We simulate the iterative process of users' choice making for items in an RS. Users choices for items are simulated in monthly time intervals. We use the observed choices in a data set, up to a certain time point t_0, as the starting point of the simulation. We use this initial data set to train the RS, and then we simulate the choices in successive months. At the end of each month, the RS is re-trained by considering also the simulated choices of that month as real signals of users' preferences. Six rather different RSs are studied in our simulation.

1. Popularity-based Collaborative Filtering (PCF) is a nearest neighbourhood collaborative filtering (CF) RS that suggests the most popular items among the choices of nearest neighbour users [6].
2. Low Popularity-based Collaborative Filtering ($LPCF$) is similar to PCF, but it penalises the ranking score of popular items, computed by PCF, by multiplying it with the inverse of their popularity.
3. Factor Model (FM) is a CF RS based on matrix factorization [13].

4. Neural network-based Collaborative Filtering (NCF) leverages a multi-layer perceptron to learn the user-item interaction function that is used to recommend top-k items to the target user [12].
5. Popularity-based (POP) is a non-personalised RS that recommends the same most popular items to all the users.
6. Average Rating (AR) is another non-personalised RS that recommends items with the highest average ratings.

We note that we assume that a user does not choose (buy) an item twice; hence, if an item is chosen once, then the RS excludes it from the future recommendations.

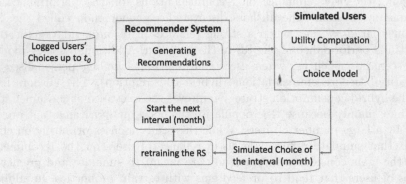

Fig. 1. Schema of the simulation process.

When a simulated user is given the chance to make a choice among the recommended items she is supposed to use a multinomial-logit CM [6]. Namely, the user u is supposed to choose an item j among those in the recommendation set S_u, with the following probability:

$$p(u \; chooses \; j) = \frac{e^{v_{uj}}}{\sum_{k \in S_u} e^{v_{uk}}}$$

where v_{uj} is the utility of the item j for user u, and S_u is the set of recommendations for u ($|S_u| = 50$ in our experiments). Clearly, items with a larger utility are more likely to be chosen, but users do not necessarily maximise utility.

Four alternative CMs, based on the same multinomial-logit model are here considered. They differ in how the item's utility is assumed to be assessed by the user before making a choice:

– **Rating-CM**: the utility of item j for user u is equal to the best available rating prediction, $\hat{r}_{uj}$, i.e., obtained by using all the ratings in the considered data set. This may be considered the standard choice model: users are supposed to prefer items with larger ratings [10,17]. We use Inverse Propensity Score Matrix Factorization model (IPS-MF) [16] to debias the rating prediction and compute a reliable estimation of the ratings.

- **Popularity-CM:** the utility of the item j is equal to:

$$v_{uj} = k_f * f_j \tag{1}$$

where f_j is the item popularity of j (at the time of the user choice), i.e., the number of times j has been chosen in n days prior to the simulated choice, divided by n ($n = 90$). This kind of choice behaviour has been extensively studied in [1,20], and can be easily quantified in any user-item interaction data set. In order to make a fair comparison of the considered CMs, as well as between the considered data sets, we use the parameter k_f to adjust the impact of popularity on the utility so that v_{uj} always ranges between 1 and 5, which is the default set of values of the Rating-CM's utility (five stars rating).

- **Age-CM:** here the utility of item j is equal to:

$$v_{uj} = k_a * (m - a_j) \tag{2}$$

where a_j is the age of item j (at the simulated choice time). Age is the time difference between the choice time and the release date of the item j and m is the maximum item age in the entire data set. Similarly to k_f, k_a adjusts the impact of the item age on the utility so that v_{uj} ranges between 1 and 5. Here, more recent items have a larger utility, hence they tend to be preferred by the simulated users. Such a choice behaviour has been observed in some domains [2,8]. To calculate the age of an item at rating time, we searched the *Amazon* website for the original release date of each rated item. Accordingly, we developed a web crawler to fetch *Amazon* item pages, and we extracted the release date field.

- **Base-CM:** here the user is assumed to select always the top recommended item. To force this choice, we manually set the value of $e^{v_{uj}}$ to 1 if j is the first recommended item and 0 otherwise. This CM is interesting because its analysis will show the aggregated behaviour of a population of users that faithfully adopt the RS; hence, in practice it will reveal the sole effect of the RS on the user choices.

With six RSs and four CMs, there are 24 distinct scenarios where we simulate users' choices when users are recommended by a given RS. The source code of the implemented simulation will be shared upon request.

4   Experimental Analysis

We use two *Amazon* collection's data sets to conduct the simulation: *Apps* and *Games* [11]. They contain timestamped users' ratings for items, distributed over several months. Here, ratings signal actual choices, as they are typically provided after the purchase. We simulate choices performed in the last ten months of the recorded data, and we use the previous months' data to bootstrap the simulation (RSs initial training data) with the required observations.

We analyse the simulated choices (after 10 months) by considering two metrics that are computed on the these choices: (a) the *Gini index* of the chosen items [6], where a higher value of Gini signal a lower diversity of the choices over items; and (b) *Choice's Rating* which is the average predicted rating (by our IPS-MF debiased model) of the choices, which signals the quality of the choices.

In the following tables we present the Gini index and the Choice's Rating calculated over all of the simulated choices for the 24 mentioned combinations of CM and RS. To better compare the effect of RSs as well as the CM, the tables also present the average values over all the CMs (last column) and all the RSs (last row). We briefly discuss in the following the obtained results.

Table 1. Gini index: Gini index calculated over all of the simulated choices.

Data set	RS ↓	Choice Model				
		Base	Age	Popularity	Rating	RS Average
Apps	PCF	0.94	0.93	0.98	0.93	0.94
	LPCF	0.77	0.91	0.96	0.90	0.89
	FM	0.98	0.94	0.98	0.95	0.96
	NCF	0.95	0.95	0.98	0.94	0.96
	POP	0.99	0.99	0.99	0.99	0.99
	AR	0.99	0.99	0.99	0.99	0.99
CM Average		0.94	0.95	0.98	0.95	
Games	PCF	0.96	0.94	0.97	0.95	0.96
	LPCF	0.92	0.92	0.93	0.91	0.92
	FM	0.99	0.96	0.99	0.96	0.97
	NCF	0.96	0.95	0.97	0.95	0.96
	POP	0.99	0.99	0.99	0.99	0.99
	AR	0.99	0.99	0.99	0.99	0.99
CM Average		0.97	0.96	0.98	0.96	

The CM can have a significant impact on the distribution and quality of the users' choices. In Table 1 it is shown that when Popularity-CM is adopted, the Gini index is always larger (choice diversity is lower) compared to when other CMs are used. Conversely, when users adopt the Age-CM the Gini index decreases, but there is also a negative effect on users' satisfaction: Choice's Rating is the lowest with this CM (see Table 2). We can also observe here that Age-CM and Rating-CM can slightly mitigate the concentration bias of FM, i.e., when the users adopt one of these CMs, Gini index is actually lower than when users adopt the Base-CM. This result suggests that the measured bias of an RS in reality, i.e., when the system is actually used, can be lower than that offline estimated (by using the Base-CM). It is also interesting to note that LPCF tends to produce smaller values of Choice's Rating and Gini index by its own, i.e., when Base-CM is used (see Table 2 and 1). However, when users adopt any of the other three CMs, the Choice's Rating and the Gini index increase. This, again, suggests that the actual performance of an RS, i.e., measured in a user study, may be rather different from that estimated without taking into account the possibly even complex choice behaviour of the users.

Table 2. Choice's Rating: average predicted ratings of the chosen items over all of the simulated choices.

Data set	RS ↓	Choice Model				
		Base	Age	Popularity	Rating	RS Average
Apps	PCF	3.94	3.80	4.02	4.01	3.94
	LPCF	3.68	3.77	3.93	3.96	3.83
	FM	3.68	3.69	3.74	3.81	3.73
	NCF	3.88	3.84	4.01	4.07	3.95
	POP	4.18	4.02	4.08	4.23	4.13
	AR	4.18	4.23	4.27	4.36	4.26
CM Average		3.92	3.89	4.01	4.07	
Games	PCF	4.20	4.13	4.21	4.25	4.20
	LPCF	4.01	4.03	4.07	4.12	4.06
	FM	4.09	4.03	4.08	4.09	4.07
	NCF	4.15	4.11	4.24	4.24	4.19
	POP	4.39	4.33	4.34	4.45	4.37
	AR	4.72	4.63	4.61	4.63	4.65
CM Average		4.26	4.21	4.26	4.30	

Certain biases of the RS are independent from the CM. It is important to note that certain biases of the RS are so strong that remain visible in the choices, irrespectively of the CM. In fact, one can look again at Table 1 and note that the non personalised RSs (POP and AR) do have a very large value of Gini index, which is not influenced by the CM. It is also interesting to note that LPCF, which is an RS that tries explicitly to suggest unpopular items and clearly has the lowest Gini index, still produces not much more diverse choices, compared with the other RSs, when the effect of a CM is considered (Age-CM, Popularity-CM and Rating-CM).

5   Conclusion

In this paper we have analysed, by a properly defined simulation approach, the impact of alternative users' choice behaviours in the presence of an RS. We have found several interesting facts related to the combined impact of the CM and the RS on the quality and diversity of the users' choices. We believe that our approach contributes to the start of a new line of research where the impact of recommendation technologies can be studied with respect to alternative decision making approaches, which are actually followed by real users. In the future it will be interesting to extract even more sophisticated CMs from observed data, in order to generate simulations that can faithfully anticipate long term consequences of RSs.

References

1. Abdollahpouri, H., et al.: Beyond personalization: Research directions in multi-stakeholder recommendation. arXiv preprint arXiv:1905.01986 (2019)

2. Bartels, J., Reinders, M.J.: Consumer innovativeness and its correlates: a proposi-
tional inventory for future research. J. Bus. Res. **64**(6), 601–609 (2011)
3. Bountouridis, D., Harambam, J., Makhortykh, M., Marrero, M., Tintarev, N.,
Hauff, C.: Siren: a simulation framework for understanding the effects of recommender systems in online news environments. In: Proceedings of the Conference
on Fairness, Accountability, and Transparency, pp. 150–159. ACM (2019)
4. Chaney, A.J., Stewart, B.M., Engelhardt, B.E.: How algorithmic confounding in
recommendation systems increases homogeneity and decreases utility. In: Proceedings of the 12th ACM Conference on Recommender Systems, pp. 224–232 (2018)
5. Ciampaglia, G.L., Nematzadeh, A., Menczer, F., Flammini, A.: How algorithmic
popularity bias hinders or promotes quality. Sci. Rep. **8**(1), 1–7 (2018)
6. Fleder, D., Hosanagar, K.: Blockbuster culture's next rise or fall: the impact of
recommender systems on sales diversity. Manage. Sci. **55**(5), 697–712 (2009)
7. Funk, S.: Netflix update: try this at home (2006)
8. Gravino, P., Monechi, B., Loreto, V.: Towards novelty-driven recommender systems. Comptes Rendus Physique **20**(4), 371–379 (2019)
9. Gunawardana, A., Shani, G.: A survey of accuracy evaluation metrics of recommendation tasks. J. Mach. Learn. Res. **10**(Dec), 2935–2962 (2009)
10. Hazrati, N., Ricci, F.: Recommender systems effect on the evolution of users'
choices distribution. Inf. Process. Manage. **59**(1), 102766 (2022)
11. He, R., McAuley, J.: Ups and downs: modeling the visual evolution of fashion trends
with one-class collaborative filtering. In: Proceedings of the 25th International
Conference On World Wide Web, pp. 507–517 (2016)
12. He, X., Liao, L., Zhang, H., Nie, L., Hu, X., Chua, T.S.: Neural collaborative
filtering. In: Proceedings of the 26th International Conference on World Wide
Web, pp. 173–182 (2017)
13. Hu, Y., Koren, Y., Volinsky, C.: Collaborative filtering for implicit feedback
datasets. In: 2008 Eighth IEEE International Conference on Data Mining, pp.
263–272. IEEE (2008)
14. Kowald, D., Schedl, M., Lex, E.: The unfairness of popularity bias in music recommendation: a reproducibility study. In: Jose, J.M., et al. (eds.) ECIR 2020. LNCS,
vol. 12036, pp. 35–42. Springer, Cham (2020). https://doi.org/10.1007/978-3-030-
45442-5_5
15. Levin, J., Milgrom, P.: Introduction to choice theory (2004). http://web.stanford.
edu/$~$jdlevin/Econd/20202
16. Schnabel, T., Swaminathan, A., Singh, A., Chandak, N., Joachims, T.: Recommendations as treatments: debiasing learning and evaluation. arXiv preprint
arXiv:1602.05352 (2016)
17. Szlávik, Z., Kowalczyk, W., Schut, M.: Diversity measurement of recommender systems under different user choice models. In: Fifth International AAAI Conference
on Weblogs and Social Media (2011)
18. Vargas, S.: Novelty and diversity evaluation and enhancement in recommender systems. Ph.D. thesis, Ph.D. Dissertation. Universidad Autónoma de Madrid (2015)
19. Zhang, J., Adomavicius, G., Gupta, A., Ketter, W.: Consumption and performance:
understanding longitudinal dynamics of recommender systems via an agent-based
simulation framework. Inf. Syst. Res. **31**(1), 76–101 (2020)
20. Zhu, Z., Wang, J., Caverlee, J.: Measuring and mitigating item under-
recommendation bias in personalized ranking systems. In: Proceedings of the 43rd
International ACM SIGIR Conference on Research and Development in Information Retrieval, pp. 449–458 (2020)

Sequential Nature of Recommender Systems Disrupts the Evaluation Process

Ali Shirali[✉][iD]

University of California, Berkeley, CA, USA
shirali_ali@berkeley.edu

Abstract. Datasets are often generated in a sequential manner, where the previous samples and intermediate decisions or interventions affect subsequent samples. This is especially prominent in cases where there are significant human-AI interactions, such as in recommender systems. To characterize the importance of this relationship across samples, we propose to use adversarial attacks on popular evaluation processes. We present sequence-aware boosting attacks and provide a lower bound on the amount of extra information that can be exploited from a confidential test set solely based on the order of the observed data. We use real and synthetic data to test our methods and show that the evaluation process on the MovieLense-100k dataset can be affected by ~1% which is important when considering the close competition. Codes are publicly available (https://github.com/alishiraliGit/augmented-boosting-attack).

Keywords: Sequential Decision Making · Sequential Recommender System · Evaluation Mechanisms · Missing-Not-At-Random

1 Introduction

Datasets are frequently generated in a sequential manner, where there is substantial shared information between samples. Particularly, in settings where there are significant human-AI interactions, decisions made by algorithms often take place sequentially based on observed feedback from previous decisions. Through this process, algorithms can learn more about individuals they are interacting with and indirectly also learn about other similar individuals. For example, consider a patient whose response to a current drug provides information about the specific disease the patient had and what may provide better treatment for similar individuals in the future. Similarly, how a user rates a movie informs recommender systems about that individual's interest and other users in the same demographic group.

Despite the ubiquity of sequentially-generated datasets, there remains room for understanding how significant of a challenge this sequential nature presents to the pipeline of training and evaluating a model. In this work, we specifically focus on the evaluation process and show how it might be distorted by samples that are not independently generated.

L. Boratto et al. (Eds.): BIAS 2022, CCIS 1610, pp. 21–34, 2022.
https://doi.org/10.1007/978-3-031-09316-6_3

In a general prediction task, we train and evaluate a predictor by setting aside a part of the data as the *holdout* or *test* set, and train the predictor on the rest of the data (*training* set). We then evaluate the trained model using *empirical risk* on the test set as a proxy for the true risk. When samples in the test set are independently and identically distributed (i.i.d), this empirical risk will be close to the true risk with high probability. But this no longer holds if the samples are not i.i.d, which is the case in sequentially-generated datasets. We focus on the gap between this empirical risk on the test set and the true risk to show the extent our evaluation might be disrupted.

To characterize the role of sequential information in the evaluation process, we propose to use *adversarial* attacks on the test set with and without the knowledge of the data generation order. Generally, an adversarial attacker tries to reveal the test set by sending many queries to the evaluation system and adaptively designing new predictions. Such an attacker is blind to the training set and cannot do better than random in terms of the true risk. What if, however, the attacker was given sequential information?

We explore this question using recommender systems (RS), where sequentially-generated datasets are commonplace. In fact, the major benchmark datasets of recommendation were collected when another RS, *logging* RS, was frequently interacting with users. As the logging RS tried to offer favorable items to users while learning their preference, the collected samples are neither complete random drawn from user-item space nor independent of each other. First of all, observed ratings are often positively biased. In other words, users are exposed to recommendations that are more likely to be in their favor compared to a set of random recommendations. This effect is studied under the Missing-Not-At-Random (MNAR) problem [7,9]. Second, the order of observation informs us beyond just being likely to be positive. Change or consistency in the category of recommended items over time can be a sign of dislike or like. For example, if a horror movie is recommended to a user after a comedy movie, we may infer that the user was not interested in comedies. Here, the observation order matters because the opposite conclusion could be drawn if the comedy movie was recommended after the horror.

To exploit the information hidden in the order of observed data, we need full knowledge of the logging RS algorithm. However, this knowledge is unlikely to be openly available. We, therefore, propose a simple k-NN RS to approximate the logging RS. The k-NN RS is simple compared to the state-of-the-art algorithms, but we will show it effectively approximates a real logging RS.

Although we have focused on adversarial attacks trying to reveal the test set, information leakage might naturally happen when an adaptive algorithm tries to improve its predictions after observing the performance of previous predictions. This adaptation harms the predictor's generalization ability and disrupts the relative performance evaluation of multiple algorithms (for example, in a competition). As a response, a natural evaluation mechanism, the Ladder [1], is suggested which for any new submission reports empirical risk on the test set only if the risk is improved. The ladder blocks too much information leakage due to multiple submissions. We will study the importance of sequential information under conventional and ladder evaluation mechanisms.

In the following, after reviewing related works and introducing the notation, we first formalize the evaluation process and adversarial attacks in Sect. 2. We then study recommender systems as sequential decision-makers and introduce k-NN RS in Sect. 3. We propose two sequence-aware boosting attacks in Sect. 4. The experiments and results are then discussed in Sect. 5.

1.1   Related Works

The human-RS interaction gets more complicated when we consider the sequential nature of human decision-making. Human decisions might be directed towards a goal. This leads to *complementary* preference over items. For example, a user searching for an airplane ticket will probably look for a hotel as well. Various methods are proposed to capture complementary preference over items, including but not limited to Markov chains [2,4,12], sequence-aware factorization machines [10], and Recurrent Neural Networks (RNN) [6,14]. We distinguish the complexity of sequential decision-making of humans from the complexity of sequential decisions of RS. In the given example, we might study flight and hotel recommenders separately. Note that the recommendation process for the selected topic is still sequential because the recommender is learning the user's preference.

The logging RS attempts to recommend favorable items, resulting in positively biased ratings. This problem is generally studied under Missed-Not-At-Random (MNAR) problem [7,9]. Training a model on MNAR data usually yields overly optimistic predictions over unseen ratings. A direct way to address MNAR is to treat the recommendation problem as missing-data imputation of the rating matrix based on the joint likelihood of the missing data model and the rating model [5]. This leads to sophisticated methods. Alternatively, Inverse Propensity Scoring (IPS) has been shown to effectively debias training and evaluation on MNAR data [11,13]. In IPS, each term of the empirical risk corresponding to an observed rating will be normalized by the inverse of the probability they would have been observed (aka propensity). Existing works typically estimate propensities as outputs of a simple predictor such as logistic regression or naive Bayes [11] or more recently reconstruct it under low nuclear norm assumption [8]. In none of these works, sequential information is exploited. However, we will show that sequential information is effective and important in the rating prediction task and consequently can be used for better propensity estimation.

1.2   Notation and Definitions

We use lowercase, bold-faced lowercase, and bold-faced uppercase letters to represent scalars, vectors, and matrices.

Focusing on the binary classification task, we represent i^{th} sample by its *feature* vector $x^{(i)} \in \mathbb{R}^d$ and *label* $y^{(i)} \in \{0, 1\}$. For any set S of samples, we can put together feature vectors as rows of a matrix and labels as elements of a vector to obtain $\boldsymbol{X}_S \in \mathbb{R}^{|S| \times d}$ and $\boldsymbol{y}_S \in \{0,1\}^{|S|}$, respectively. We use $\mathcal{D}$ to refer to the training data $(\boldsymbol{X}_{train}, \boldsymbol{y}_{train})$.

Unless otherwise stated, we use zero-one *loss* function as the performance indicator of a prediction: $loss(\hat{y}, y) = 1_{\hat{y}=y}$. The empirical risk of a classifier $f : \mathbb{R}^d \to \{0,1\}$ over samples S is defined as $R_S[f] = \frac{1}{|S|} \sum_{i \in S} loss(f(\boldsymbol{x}^{(i)}), y^{(i)})$. Assuming features and labels are drawn from a joint distribution P, the (true) risk of a classifier is defined as $R[f] = \mathbb{E}_{\boldsymbol{x}, y \sim P}[loss(f(\boldsymbol{x}), y)]$. We sometimes explicitly refer to the empirical and true risk of predicted labels $\hat{\boldsymbol{y}}$ as $R_S[\hat{\boldsymbol{y}}]$ and $R[\hat{\boldsymbol{y}}]$, respectively.

2   Evaluation Systems and Adaptation

Generally, we can define three interacting components in the evaluation process of a classification task: data, evaluator, and algorithm as shown in Fig. 1. In the holdout method, data is divided into training ($\mathcal{D}$) and test (holdout) sets, while labels corresponding to the test set ($\boldsymbol{y}_{test}$) are secured in the evaluator and hidden to the algorithm. At each time step t, the evaluator compares the input predictions $\hat{\boldsymbol{y}}_t$ to $\boldsymbol{y}_{test}$ and reports a performance indicator R_t. For example, the *Kaggle* mechanism reports the empirical risk $R_{test}[\hat{\boldsymbol{y}}_t]$ with 10^{-5} precision. The evaluator can have a state and might not necessarily report the empirical risk.

A non-adaptive algorithm trains a classifier f_t on $\mathcal{D}$ regardless of the previously reported performances. If samples in the test set are generated i.i.d, applying Hoeffding's bound and union bound implies the empirical risk on the holdout set is close to the true risk with high probability:

$$P(\exists t \leq T : |R_{test}[f_t] - R[f_t]| > \epsilon) \leq 2T \exp\left(-2\epsilon^2 n_{test}\right) \qquad (1)$$

where n_{test} is the number of samples in the test set. However, even when samples are i.i.d., an adaptive algorithm might use the performance on the previous predictions in training phase to design a new predictor:

$$f_t = \mathcal{A}(\mathcal{D}, \{(\hat{\boldsymbol{y}}_{t'}, R_{t'})\}_{t'<t}). \qquad (2)$$

In this case, f_t is a function of all samples in the test set, so $loss(\hat{y}_t^{(i)}, y^{(i)})$ is not independent of other losses and Hoeffding's bound is not applicable. Consequently, the bound from Eq. 1 is no longer valid and empirical risk on the test set might be very far from the true risk [1].

2.1   Ladder Mechanism

The Ladder mechanism [1] keeps the best (smallest) empirical risk so far achieved as its state. As long as new predictions do not improve the best seen risk, it refuses to report their empirical risks. Formally, the Ladder's state at time t is R_t^{best}. Let $[.]_\eta$ operator rounds the input to the nearest integer multiple of η. For any new classifier f_t, Ladder returns $R_t^{best} = [R_{test}[f_t]]_\eta$ if $R_{test}[f_t] < R_{t-1}^{best} - \eta$ and $R_t^{best} = R_{t-1}^{best}$ otherwise. Even when classifiers are trained adaptively, at

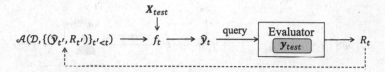

Fig. 1. Training and evaluation process of an adaptive classifier.

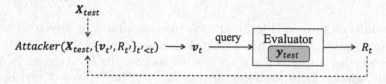

Fig. 2. A general attacker might use X_{test} and previous risks and queries for the new guess.

any time t, R_t^{best} will remain close to the best empirical risk observed so far (Theorem 3.1 of [1]) which means R_t^{best} is unlikely to diverge significantly from $\min_{t' \leq t} R[f_{t'}]$.

2.2 Adversarial Attacks

An attacker tries to reveal y_{test} by many queries to the evaluator without actually learning anything about the patterns of data. A well-known randomized attack is *boosting attack* where at each time step t the attacker

1. Query evaluator with a random vector $v_t \sim unif(\{0,1\}^{n_{test}})$.
2. If R_t returned by the evaluator is better than random and better than the best risk observed so far, add v_t to the set of informative vectors $\mathcal{I}$.

The final prediction of the attacker is the elementwise majority vote of all informative vectors: $v^* = majority(\{v_t \mid t \in \mathcal{I}\})$.

Queries are generally random, but they might also depend on previous queries (Fig. 2). For example, queries of the boosting attack are generated uniformly at random, regardless of the previous queries. However, in the random window boosting attack we propose in Sect. 4.1, the distribution of a new query depends on the queries and risks observed so far.

Attackers do not use the training data, as they would otherwise be real learners, but they might use X_{test}. For example, the boosting attack is unaware of X_{test}, but the sequence-aware attackers we propose in Sect. 4 use X_{test} to elicit information about observation order.

3 Recommender Systems as Sequential Decision Makers

Generally, an RS consists of a set of users $(\mathcal{U})$ and items $(\mathcal{I})$. We assume a user (an item) can be represented by a vector $u \in \mathcal{U}$ $(i \in \mathcal{I})$. During the

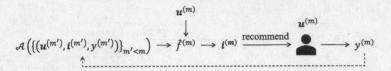

Fig. 3. The process of recommendation for a general RS.

recommendation process (Fig. 3), at each time m, a random user $\boldsymbol{u}^{(m)}$ asks for a recommendation. The RS has a trained classifier $\hat{f}^{(m)} : \mathcal{U} \times \mathcal{I} \to \{1,0\}$, which predicts whether a user will like an item or not. So, the RS suggests item $\boldsymbol{i}^{(m)}$ randomly selected from all items that satisfy $\hat{f}^{(m)}(\boldsymbol{u}^{(m)}, \boldsymbol{i}) = 1$ and observes the user's feedback $y^{(m)} = f(\boldsymbol{u}^{(m)}, \boldsymbol{i}^{(m)}) \in \{1,0\}$. Here, we assumed feedback is completely determined by $(\boldsymbol{u}, \boldsymbol{i})$ and is time-invariant. This assumption implicitly means user preferences do not change over time and the vector representations of users and items are enough to determine the feedback. In practice, these assumptions are only valid with approximation. Based on the observed feedback, RS updates its classifier $\hat{f}^{(m+1)} = \mathcal{A}(\{\boldsymbol{u}^{(m')}, \boldsymbol{i}^{(m')}, y^{(m')}\}_{m'<m})$. So, how a user responded to the previous recommendations impacts future recommendations.

3.1 k-NN Recommender System

The k-NN RS is a simple RS we use to approximate a real logging RS. For any pair of user-item $(\boldsymbol{u}, \boldsymbol{i})$, the k-NN RS uses a k-NN classifier to assign a label to $(\boldsymbol{u}, \boldsymbol{i})$ based on the majority of feedback already observed from k nearest user-items.

Formally, let $\mathcal{N}_k^{(m)}(\boldsymbol{u}, \boldsymbol{i})$ be the set of k time stamps $\{m'\}$ corresponding to $\{(\boldsymbol{u}^{(m')}, \boldsymbol{i}^{(m')})\}$, which have the shortest distance to $(\boldsymbol{u}, \boldsymbol{i})$ among all the ratings already observed till time m $(m' < m)$. We measure distance by $\|\boldsymbol{u} - \boldsymbol{u}^{(m')}\|_2^2 + \|\boldsymbol{i} - \boldsymbol{i}^{(m')}\|_2^2$. Then

$$\hat{f}^{(m)}(\boldsymbol{u}, \boldsymbol{i}) = majority(\{y^{(m')} \mid m' \in \mathcal{N}_k^{(m)}(\boldsymbol{u}, \boldsymbol{i})\}). \tag{3}$$

To control the level of divergence from being i.i.d., we introduce a new parameter named *exploration* $\in [0,1]$. For any new user $\boldsymbol{u}^{(m)}$, we define $\mathcal{I}_+^{(m)} = \{i \in \mathcal{I} \mid \hat{f}^{(m)}(\boldsymbol{u}^{(m)}, \boldsymbol{i}) = 1\}$ and $\mathcal{I}_-^{(m)} = \{i \in \mathcal{I} \mid \hat{f}^{(m)}(\boldsymbol{u}^{(m)}, \boldsymbol{i}) = 0\}$, where we assume $|\mathcal{I}|$ is finite. Then RS suggests an item i from $\mathcal{I} = \mathcal{I}_+^{(m)} \cup \mathcal{I}_-^{(m)}$ such that

$$\frac{P(i \in \mathcal{I}_-^{(m)})}{P(i \in \mathcal{I}_+^{(m)})} = exploration \times \frac{|\mathcal{I}_-^{(m)}|}{|\mathcal{I}_+^{(m)}|} \tag{4}$$

So, *exploration* $= 1$ corresponds to having no preference over $\mathcal{I}_-^{(m)}$ and $\mathcal{I}_+^{(m)}$, and recommendations are perfectly random. In contrast, *exploration* $= 0$ corresponds to the case where only items predicted to receive positive feedback will be recommended.

Finally, putting in the context of a classification problem, $y^{(m)}$ is the label for feature vector $\boldsymbol{x}^{(m)} = (\boldsymbol{u}^{(m)}, \boldsymbol{i}^{(m)}, m)$. We explicitly include time m in the feature vector to investigate the value of this extra information later.

4   Sequence-Aware Adversarial Attacks

This section proposes two augmented boosting attacks specifically targeted for sequential data. The boosting attack queries the evaluator with completely random vectors from $\{0,1\}^{n_{test}}$ because it doesn't have any prior on the labels of the test set. However, if samples are generated sequentially, and the order of their generation is accessible, we can update our prior and design better queries.

We incorporate order information in two different ways, resulting in the following algorithms. The first algorithm (Sect. 4.1) is a model-free algorithm based on the intuition that initial recommendations to a user are less likely than the following recommendations to receive positive feedback. So, over time, there is a distribution shift that the proposed random window boosting attack (*WBoost*) tries to learn. In contrast to the boosting attack, the next query in this method depends on the previous queries and responses.

The second proposed algorithm (Sect. 4.2) is a model-based algorithm that considers k-NN RS as an approximation of the logging RS. Based on the order of the observed data, it calculates the posterior probability over the test set's labels. Compared to the boosting attack, this method samples queries according to this posterior probability rather than uniform distribution, which significantly increases the chance of guessing the correct labels.

4.1   Random Window Boosting Attack (WBoost)

In this method, we try to compensate for the distribution shift of labels over time. The discussed boosting attack is blind to this shift because it simply samples query from $\boldsymbol{v} \sim unif(\{0,1\}^{n_{test}})$ without considering that elements of $\boldsymbol{y}_{test}$ are recommended at different times.

Without loss of generality, we assume labels in $\boldsymbol{y}_{test}$ are ordered in time (the order that items are recommended is available in $\boldsymbol{X}_{test}$ so we can rearrange elements of $\boldsymbol{y}_{test}$ chronologically). We define the state of the attacker at time t with $\boldsymbol{b}_t \in [0,1]^{n_{test}}$ where $b_t^{(m)}$ (m^{th} element of $\boldsymbol{b}_t$) is the attacker's estimation from $P(y_{test}^{(m)} = 1)$. The algorithm starts with $\boldsymbol{b}_1 = \frac{1}{2}\boldsymbol{1}$ (a vector of all 0.5) at time $t = 1$. At odd time t, it generates $\boldsymbol{v}_t$ according to $\boldsymbol{b}_t$. At even time t, it selects a random window with length w from $\boldsymbol{v}_{t-1}$, assigns the value of all elements under the window to the their minority value, and draws the rest of the elements from $\boldsymbol{b}_{t-1}$. Then by observing R_t from the evaluator, the attacker updates $\boldsymbol{b}_t$. Figure 4 shows an example of this process.

Here is the updating rule: let $\mathcal{W}_t$ be elements under the window at even time t. As elements outside of the window in both $\boldsymbol{v}_{t-1}$ and $\boldsymbol{v}_t$ are selected according to $\boldsymbol{b}_{t-1}$, in expectation, they don't have any effect on $R[\boldsymbol{v}_t] - R[\boldsymbol{v}_{t-1}]$. Let's assume the actual probability of $P(y_{test}^{(m)} = 1)$ is B^* for all $m \in \mathcal{W}_t$, then:

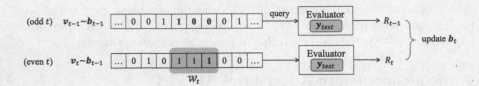

Fig. 4. An example from the WBoost updating procedure

$$\mathbb{E}[R[\boldsymbol{v}_t] - R[\boldsymbol{v}_{t-1}]] = \frac{1}{n_{test}} \sum_{m \in \mathcal{W}_t} P(y_{test}^{(m)} = 1)(1 - v_t^{(m)}) + P(y_{test}^{(m)} = 0)v_t^{(m)}$$

$$- \frac{1}{n_{test}} \sum_{m \in \mathcal{W}_t} P(y_{test}^{(m)} = 1)(1 - v_{t-1}^{(m)}) + P(y_{test}^{(m)} = 0)v_{t-1}^{(m)}$$

$$= \frac{1 - 2B^*}{n_{test}} \sum_{m \in \mathcal{W}_t} v_t^{(m)} - v_{t-1}^{(m)} \tag{5}$$

where expectation is taken w.r.t elements outside of the $\mathcal{W}_t$. Using R_t and R_{t-1} returned by the evaluator as a proxy for $\mathbb{E}[R[\boldsymbol{v}_t]]$ and $\mathbb{E}[R[\boldsymbol{v}_{t-1}]]$ we can estimate B^* and update $\boldsymbol{b}$:

$$b_t^{(m)} = \begin{cases} (1 - \alpha)b_{t-1}^{(m)} + \alpha\frac{1}{2}\left(1 - n_{test}\frac{R_t - R_{t-1}}{\sum_{m \in \mathcal{W}_t} v_t^{(m)} - v_{t-1}^{(m)}}\right) & m \in \mathcal{W}_t \\ b_{t-1}^{(m)} & o.w. \end{cases} \tag{6}$$

where $\alpha \in (0, 1]$ controls the speed of the convergence.

4.2 k-NN Posterior Boosting Attack (PostBoost)

In this method, we approximate the logging RS with a k-NN RS and calculate a posterior probability over the unseen test set's labels based on available test set's features: $P(\boldsymbol{y}_{test} = \boldsymbol{v} \mid \boldsymbol{X}_{test})$. Again, we presume elements of $\boldsymbol{y}_{test}$ and $\boldsymbol{v}$ are ordered chronologically (o.w. we rearrange them).

As defined in Sect. 3, let $\mathcal{N}_k^{(m)}(\boldsymbol{u}, \boldsymbol{i})$ be the set of k nearest neighbours of $(\boldsymbol{u}, \boldsymbol{i})$ from $\{(\boldsymbol{u}^{(m')}, \boldsymbol{i}^{(m')})\}_{m' < m}$. We define $\mathcal{N}_k^{(m)}(\boldsymbol{u}, all) = \bigcup_{i \in \mathcal{I}} \mathcal{N}_k^{(m)}(\boldsymbol{u}, \boldsymbol{i})$ as the set of all previous recommendations which are important in determining the next recommendation to user $\boldsymbol{u}$. At any time m, for a given observed ratings $\{y^{(m')} = v^{(m')}\}_{m' < m}$, we can find the RS's classifier ($\hat{f}^{(m)}$) from Eq. 3. Then we can calculate the likelihood that $\boldsymbol{i}^{(m)}$ is recommended next according to Eq. 4:

$$P_m = P\left(\boldsymbol{i}^{(m)} \mid \boldsymbol{u}^{(m)}, \{(\boldsymbol{u}^{(m')}, \boldsymbol{i}^{(m')}, y^{(m')} = v^{(m')}) \mid m' \in \mathcal{N}_k^{(m)}(\boldsymbol{u}^{(m)}, all)\}\right)$$

$$= \begin{cases} \frac{exploration}{exploration \times |\mathcal{I}_-^{(m)}| + |\mathcal{I}_+^{(m)}|} & \hat{f}^{(m)}(\boldsymbol{u}^{(m)}, \boldsymbol{i}^{(m)}) = 0 \\ \frac{1}{exploration \times |\mathcal{I}_-^{(m)}| + |\mathcal{I}_+^{(m)}|} & \hat{f}^{(m)}(\boldsymbol{u}^{(m)}, \boldsymbol{i}^{(m)}) = 1 \end{cases}. \tag{7}$$

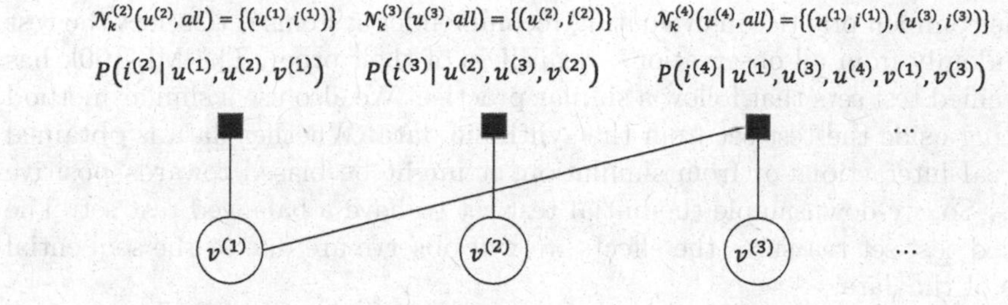

$$\mathcal{N}_k^{(2)}(u^{(2)}, all) = \{(u^{(1)}, i^{(1)})\} \quad \mathcal{N}_k^{(3)}(u^{(3)}, all) = \{(u^{(2)}, i^{(2)})\} \quad \mathcal{N}_k^{(4)}(u^{(4)}, all) = \{(u^{(1)}, i^{(1)}), (u^{(3)}, i^{(3)})\}$$

$$P(i^{(2)}|\, u^{(1)}, u^{(2)}, v^{(1)}) \quad P(i^{(3)}|\, u^{(2)}, u^{(3)}, v^{(2)}) \quad P(i^{(4)}|\, u^{(1)}, u^{(3)}, u^{(4)}, v^{(1)}, v^{(3)})$$

$v^{(1)}$ $v^{(2)}$ $v^{(3)}$ $\cdots$

Fig. 5. An example factor graph utilized in calculating posterior probability over test set's labels.

So, we can calculate the likelihood

$$P(\{\boldsymbol{i}^{(m)}\}_{m=1}^{n_{test}} \mid \{\boldsymbol{u}^{(m)}\}_m, \boldsymbol{y} = \boldsymbol{v}) = \prod_{m=1}^{n_{test}} P_m. \tag{8}$$

for any $\boldsymbol{v}$. Without loss of generality, we assume data is balanced and the prior $P(v^{(m)}) = 0.5$. Now, we can find the posterior $P(\boldsymbol{y} = \boldsymbol{v} \mid \{(u^{(m)}, i^{(m)})\}_{m=1}^{n_{test}}) = P(\boldsymbol{y} = \boldsymbol{v} \mid \boldsymbol{X}_{test})$ from the likelihood of Eq. 8. Here, we utilize a factor graphical model, with elements of $\boldsymbol{v}$ as variable vertices and P_ms as factor vertices. The marginal joint distribution of variable vertices, will be our desired $P(\boldsymbol{y} = \boldsymbol{v} \mid \boldsymbol{X}_{test})$. An example of this graph is depicted in Fig. 5.

Approximate Posterior Calculation. When n_{test} is large, finding the posterior probability over the test set's labels is not computationally feasible. So, we propose to cluster ratings into equal size groups and find the posterior probability for each cluster separately. In order to do a sequence-aware clustering, we start by $\mathcal{C}_0 = [n_{test}]$ and iteratively find clusters. For a desired cluster size z, at each iteration $t \geq 1$, we

1. Draw a random m from $\mathcal{C}_{t-1}$.
2. Select $z - 1$ members from $\mathcal{N}_k^{(m)}(\boldsymbol{u}^{(m)}, \boldsymbol{i}^{(m)}) \cap \mathcal{C}_{t-1}$ randomly.
3. Form a new cluster with m and the selected $z - 1$ neighbours.
4. Remove the new cluster's members from $\mathcal{C}_{t-1}$ and obtain $\mathcal{C}_t$.

5   Experiments

To investigate the importance of sequential information in real scenarios, we use MovieLense-100k (ML-100k) [3], a well-known benchmark dataset for rating prediction. What makes ML-100k interesting for us is the availability of timestamps for samples. Besides ML-100k, we also use synthetic data to study the effectiveness of the proposed methods in a controlled environment with the desired level of divergence from randomness.

The common practice in evaluating recommender systems is to select the test set randomly from all observations, regardless of their order. The ML-100k has prespecified test sets that follow a similar practice. We also use a similar method in setting aside the test set from the synthetic data. Whether data is obtained from real interactions or from simulation, it might be biased towards positive ratings. So, we downsample the initial test set to have a balanced test set. The balanced test set reassures the effects we will observe are due to the sequential nature of the data.

In all experiments, attackers do not have access to any training data and labels. So, the true risk of an attacker cannot be better than the chance level, which is 0.5 in our balanced design. Therefore, the difference of the attacker's average loss on the test set with 0.5 reflects the amount of information leaked about the test set. As the boosting attack is unaware of the sequential nature of the data, the gap between a sequence-aware attacker and the boosting attack shows the extent that sequential information can disrupt the evaluation. The level of disruption might vary based on the evaluation mechanism. Notably, we compare two natural mechanisms, Kaggle and Ladder, in this regard.

Synthetic Data Simulation. In simulating ratings, we assume that the user's feedback function (f) follows a similar structure as Eq. 3 and specify it with ground truth centers and labels: $\mathcal{C}_* = \{(\boldsymbol{u}_*^{(l)}, \boldsymbol{i}_*^{(l)})\}_l$ and $\mathcal{Y}_* = \{y_*^{(l)}\}_l$. For any pair of user and item $(\boldsymbol{u}, \boldsymbol{i})$, let $\mathcal{N}_k^*(\boldsymbol{u}, \boldsymbol{i})$ be the set of k closest $(\boldsymbol{u}_*^{(l)}, \boldsymbol{i}_*^{(l)}) \in \mathcal{C}_*$ to $(\boldsymbol{u}, \boldsymbol{i})$. Then the label of $(\boldsymbol{u}, \boldsymbol{i})$ will be

$$f^*(\boldsymbol{u}, \boldsymbol{i}) = majority(\{y_*^{(l)} \mid l \in \mathcal{N}_k^*(\boldsymbol{u}, \boldsymbol{i})\}). \qquad (9)$$

Given the feedback function f^*, we run another k-NN RS as the logging RS to obtain samples: at each time m, a random user $\boldsymbol{u}^{(m)}$ queries the logging RS and receives $\boldsymbol{i}^{(m)}$. The user's response to $\boldsymbol{i}^{(m)}$ will be determined by $f^*(\boldsymbol{u}^{(m)}, \boldsymbol{i}^{(m)})$.

5.1 Evaluation on Synthetic Data

We simulate synthetic data consisting of 1000 balanced samples obtained by a 1-NN logging RS to investigate how well the random window boosting attack (WBoost) can exploit the sequential information. Figure 6 shows the empirical risk on the test set while the attackers send more and more queries to the evaluator. Here we have repeated data simulation and attacks and plotted average results. Note that the value on the y-axis (empirical risk or equivalently average loss) is not accessible to attackers; what attackers observe depends on the evaluation mechanism (e.g., Kaggle reports the empirical risk with a limited precision). One can see that WBoost gradually learns the distribution shift over time when the evaluator is Kaggle; however, the Ladder mechanism effectively blocks it.

We simulate a very smaller data consisting of only 10 balanced samples to observe the full capability of k-NN posterior boosting attack (PostBoost). The computational complexity of PostBoost limits the number of samples it can infer

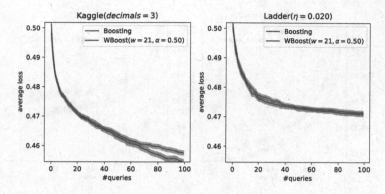

Fig. 6. Empirical risk on the test set of synthetic data with 1000 samples while WBoost sends more queries to evaluators.

about. Although the approximate PostBoost explained in Sect. 4.2 solves this difficulty, for now we only focus on the exact version to see the maximum capability of the method. Figure 7 shows the empirical risk on the test vs. the number of submissions to evaluators. Here we assumed PostBoost is enjoying the complete knowledge of the logging k-NN RS model, including the vector representations of users and items. There are a few takeaways: PostBoost can consistently disrupt the evaluation process by ~5% whether the evaluation mechanism is Kaggle or Ladder. Even on the first query, when no feedback from the evaluator is reported, PostBoost can guess the test set's labels better than the chance level. This gap exactly shows the value of the sequential information hidden in the test set.

It should be noted, that in both experiments with WBoost and PostBoost, we selected evaluation parameters manually to make the difference of Kaggle and Ladder mechanisms clear. We also reported results for the special case of 1-NN RS with *exploration* = 0.1. However, similar results can be obtained by a wide range of k and *exploration*.

5.2   Evaluation on ML-100k

The ML-100k ratings to movies range from 1 to 5. To use the ratings as binary labels, we associated ratings larger than 2 with positive labels. Then we downsampled the prespecified test sets to a balanced test set consisting of 1000 samples, preserving the time order of samples. In order to use k-NN posterior boosting attack, we need user and item vector representations. For simplicity, we used side information available for users and items as their representations. Specifically, we represent users with a three-dimensional vector of normalized age, sex, and occupation and represent items with a zero-one vector of genres.

Figure 8 shows the empirical risk on the test set while increasing the number of queries. To make the PostBoost computationally feasible, we used its approximate version here. Although we didn't know the actual algorithm behind the ML-100k collection, our k-NN PostBoost attacker can still exploit sequential

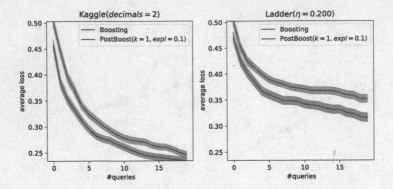

Fig. 7. Empirical risk on the test set of synthetic data with 10 samples while k-NN posterior boosting attacker (PostBoost) sends more queries to evaluators.

information and disrupt the evaluation for relatively ∼1%. Roughly speaking, this is a significant number as the performance of state-of-the-art methods on the ML-100k over the last 5 years has only been improved for ∼3%. So, disruption in the evaluation due to sequential information can change the leaderboard[1]. One can also see that WBoost is able to outperform the boosting attack by submitting more and more queries when the evaluation mechanism is Kaggle. This shows the distribution shift over time exists in real data and is informative about the test set. Finally, we should mention similar results hold for a wide range of k and *exploration*, and we only chose current values for demonstration.

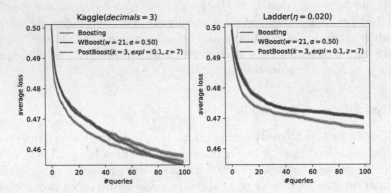

Fig. 8. Empirical risk on the ML-100k's test sets while increasing the number of queries.

---

[1] https://paperswithcode.com/sota/collaborative-filtering-on-movielens-100k.

6   Discussion

In any dataset obtained through interactions, the knowledge of the purpose of that interaction (e.g., recommending favorable items) can inform us about the data we should expect. This extra knowledge can challenge the evaluation process. In this study, we focused on recommender systems as one of the most widely applied interactive systems and showed sequential information at the test time can be exploited to disrupt the evaluation process in both real and synthetic datasets.

This study has multiple implications. First, as our k-NN posterior boosting attacker suggests, samples of a sequence are not equally likely to be positive; some samples are harder to predict. This opens a question on the correct practice in evaluating two algorithms on sequential data. Second, although we focused on the evaluation process and test sets, the train sets also suffer from similar problems. Sequence-aware attackers can be used to obtain a joint distribution over training samples and this distribution can be utilized in unbiasing the training process. Finally, we used a simple k-NN RS to approximate the actual logging RS in real data to show that the sequential information matters. Future works can propose to learn the logging RS from the order of observations to extract more of this information.

References

1. Blum, A., Hardt, M.: The ladder: a reliable leaderboard for machine learning competitions. In: International Conference on Machine Learning, pp. 1006–1014. PMLR (2015)
2. Garcin, F., Dimitrakakis, C., Faltings, B.: Personalized news recommendation with context trees. In: Proceedings of the 7th ACM Conference on Recommender Systems, pp. 105–112 (2013)
3. Harper, F.M., Konstan, J.A.: The movielens datasets: history and context. ACM Trans. Interact. Intell. Syst. (TIIS) 5(4), 1–19 (2015)
4. He, R., McAuley, J.: Fusing similarity models with Markov chains for sparse sequential recommendation. In: 2016 IEEE 16th International Conference on Data Mining (ICDM), pp. 191–200. IEEE (2016)
5. Hernández-Lobato, J.M., Houlsby, N., Ghahramani, Z.: Probabilistic matrix factorization with non-random missing data. In: International Conference on Machine Learning, pp. 1512–1520. PMLR (2014)
6. Hidasi, B., Karatzoglou, A., Baltrunas, L., Tikk, D.: Session-based recommendations with recurrent neural networks. arXiv:1511.06939 (2015)
7. Little, R.J., Rubin, D.B.: Statistical Analysis With Missing Data, vol. 793. John Wiley & Sons, Hoboken (2019)
8. Ma, W., Chen, G.H.: Missing not at random in matrix completion: The effectiveness of estimating missingness probabilities under a low nuclear norm assumption. arXiv:1910.12774 (2019)
9. Pradel, B., Usunier, N., Gallinari, P.: Ranking with non-random missing ratings: influence of popularity and positivity on evaluation metrics. In: Proceedings of the Sixth ACM Conference on Recommender Systems, pp. 147–154 (2012)

10. Rendle, S., Freudenthaler, C., Schmidt-Thieme, L.: Factorizing personalized markov chains for next-basket recommendation. In: Proceedings of the 19th International Conference on World Wide Web, pp. 811–820 (2010)
11. Schnabel, T., Swaminathan, A., Singh, A., Chandak, N., Joachims, T.: Recommendations as treatments: debiasing learning and evaluation. In: International Conference on Machine Learning, pp. 1670–1679. PMLR (2016)
12. Shani, G., Heckerman, D., Brafman, R.I., Boutilier, C.: An MDP-based recommender system. J. Mach. Learn. Res. **6**(9), 1 (2005)
13. Wang, X., Zhang, R., Sun, Y., Qi, J.: Doubly robust joint learning for recommendation on data missing not at random. In: International Conference on Machine Learning, pp. 6638–6647. PMLR (2019)
14. Wu, C.Y., Ahmed, A., Beutel, A., Smola, A.J., Jing, H.: Recurrent recommender networks. In: Proceedings of the Tenth ACM International Conference on Web Search and Data Mining, pp. 495–503 (2017)

Towards an Approach for Analyzing Dynamic Aspects of Bias and Beyond-Accuracy Measures

Julia Neidhardt[✉] and Mete Sertkan

Christian Doppler Laboratory for Advancing the State-of-the-Art of Recommender
Systems in Multi-domain Settings, Research Unit E-Commerce,
TU Wien, Wien, Austria
{julia.neidhardt,mete.sertkan}@tuwien.ac.at
https://recsys-lab.at

Abstract. The quality of recommender systems has traditionally only
been assessed using accuracy measures. Research has shown that accuracy is only one side of the medallion and that we should also consider
quality features that go beyond accuracy. Recently, also fairness-related
aspects and bias have increasingly been considered as outcome dimensions in this context. While beyond-accuracy measures including diversity, novelty and serendipity and bias in recommendation have been subject to the research discourse, their interrelation and temporal and group
dynamics are clearly under-explored. In this position paper, we propose
an approach that groups users based on their behaviors and preferences
and that addresses beyond-accuracy needs of those groups while controlling for bias. Further, we consider the analysis of long-term dynamics
of different interrelated beyond-accuracy measures and bias as crucial
research direction since it helps to advance the field and to address societal issues related to recommender systems and personalization.

Keywords: Bias · Beyond-accuracy Measures · Long-term Dynamics

1 Introduction

In recent years, recommender systems and personalization have been gaining
more and more attention in academia, industry, and society. The number of websites, social media platforms, and online systems that support the information
needs and product search of their users by providing personalized suggestions
has been increasing rapidly [21].

With the growing prevalence of artificial intelligence and machine learning-
based systems, there has also been an increasing discussion about their role and
impact. The extensive public discourse about filter bubbles, echo chambers, fake
news, micro-targeting, and related web-based phenomena during recent elections

Supported by the Christian Doppler Research Association (CDG).

L. Boratto et al. (Eds.): BIAS 2022, CCIS 1610, pp. 35–42, 2022.
https://doi.org/10.1007/978-3-031-09316-6_4

and referendums shows strong societal interest in this topic. For a number of these problems, personalization and recommender systems can be blamed – at least to some extent. A recent example is misinformation about COVID, vaccines, and the US 2020 elections recommended by the Instagram algorithm to the users of that platform as a new study of the Center for Countering Digital Hate reveals [7].

Many traditional recommendation techniques are geared towards predicting accuracy, i.e., they aim to estimate how a user rated certain items in the past. As a consequence, recommendations by these systems presented to a specific user tend to resemble products bought or consumed by that user before. Thus, the accuracy of these systems often is rather high, i.e., the recommendations made by the system are correct, but people are not really surprised by what is proposed to them [16]. Just looking at accuracy could lead, moreover, to bias (e.g., to filter bubbles and related phenomena) [23]. In general, it has been increasingly recognized that the quality of a recommender system clearly goes beyond measuring accuracy only. Thus, other aspects are more and more considered [6, 13]. Nowadays, in particular, researchers try to evaluate their methods also based on beyond-accuracy measures such as novelty, diversity, serendipity, or coverage. In essence, these measures aim to assess whether the provided list of recommendations contains new items, how diverse the items in this list are, whether the list contains surprising items, and what fraction of items are recommended by the system [17]. Although there are certain improvements, many crucial challenges are still unsolved; e.g., an in-depth understanding of how accuracy is affected by optimizing for beyond-accuracy is missing [16]. Furthermore, very simple user models in static settings are typically considered, and beyond-accuracy solutions are not adapted to the needs or preferences of specific users or groups of users nor to different domains (e.g., news vs. tourism). However, studies indicate that these aspects should be taken into account [17].

In addition, questions about the fairness of machine learning systems have received tremendous attention lately. Typically classification tasks in static environments are considered, whereas in the context of personalized recommendations, fairness-aware measurements and methodologies are under-researched [10]. However, there are a number of emerging approaches that aim to capture fairness-related questions in recommender systems, e.g., how bias mitigation strategies can look like or how unfairness for different groups of stakeholders can be avoided [2]. Measurement to capture fairness for customers or providers are increasingly deployed to assess the quality of recommender systems in addition to considering accuracy and other outcome dimensions [4].

Although capturing different concerns, there are, in fact, close relations between some fairness-related concepts and diversity, novelty and coverage [25]. Coverage, in particular, helps to capture subject fairness, which aims to make sure that the items to be recommended are fairly represented [5]. In the discussion of fairness, bias plays a major role, in particular popularity bias. Certain measurements have been introduced to capture bias in the context of recommendation (e.g., popularity rate, Gini Index, etc.) [2,17]; but typically investigations are based on offline experiments and only consider static settings.

Moreover, new approaches emerge that capture the impact of bias on different groups. However, in the literature, groups are typically distinguished based on specific features such as gender [24]. There is some very recent work that assesses the impact of popularity bias on groups based on user preferences [1], but the groups are constructed in a rather simple manner and serve illustration purposes.

Finally, there is a lack of research investigating the evolution of bias over time [11]. Only very recently a few studies looking at such long-term effects have been published [12,22], and there is still a great need for an in-depth investigation of dynamic aspects of bias and other outcome dimensions.

2 Understanding Long-Term Dynamics

With all of this in mind, we see an urgent need for examining the relationships between beyond-accuracy measures and fairness-aware measures for different groups of users over time. Specifically, we consider it absolutely necessary to pursue the following two objectives:

1. Developing novel recommendation approaches that better adapt to different groups of users and different domains while revealing bias;
2. Analyzing long-term dynamics of different interrelated dimensions (i.e., accuracy, diversity, serendipity and novelty) as well as bias.

As mentioned above, there are more and more attempts to study bias with respect to user groups that are characterized based on the preferences of the group members. This perspective has proven to be promising as it clearly reveals differences in the relevance of the recommended items between the determined user groups [1]. However, we propose to pursue a more comprehensive group construction process to get deeper insights into the groups and their specifics. Here, theories from the social sciences including Bourdieu's theory of habitus [3] and social network analysis [26] should be considered. Both approaches allow to model individual preferences as a result from both individual disposition and social context and describe ways to identify groups with similar behaviors and preferences. Combining advanced data mining techniques and social sciences helps to define user groups that are formed based on the preferences and behavior of the users in a specific domain. This will lead to more persistent user models that help to study beyond-accuracy measures more systematically and also assess the long-term effects of bias. The insights that are gained and their implications will form the basis to develop more adaptive recommender systems. However, literature suggests that user needs for beyond-accuracy measures depends on the items' domain [17]. Thus, also this aspect has to be considered.

A distinctive feature of recommender systems is the feedback loop that they cause, i.e., by presenting the results to a user they typically influence the perception and behavior of that user. However, most of the research considers static settings and neither explores how bias develops over time nor how this dynamics affects a recommender system [8]. In particular, a broader understanding of the relationships between bias, beyond-accuracy measures and accuracy is absolutely missing. A thorough investigation of these dynamics is clearly related to various challenges, e.g., how the feedback loop and its implication can be modeled and how a dynamic evaluation can look like [11]. Here, recommendation approaches that utilize reinforcement learning [9] should specifically be considered. As a starting point, however, we advocate observational studies of real systems over time that capture the different outcome dimensions and their co-evolution with the help of advanced statistical methods including time-series analysis with generalized additive models [14] and time-series clustering techniques [15]. In this context, we propose a case study as a first step into the outlined directions and describe it in the following.

3   Case Study

To model and compare beyond-accuracy needs of users in different domains and to capture the dynamic aspects of bias and beyond-accuracy measures we will conduct a systematic analysis using real-world data. In a first step, multi-facet feature sets from different domains (i.e., news, lifestyle, e-commerce, and fashion) will be extracted and will be used to learn – separably for each domain – a representation of the users as well as of the items in a joint user-item vector-space [19]. Based on these embeddings, clustering will be performed to identify the user groups. As mentioned in Sect. 2 also frameworks from the social sciences (e.g., social network analysis [26], which allows to systematically capture the impact of social relations on preferences, and geometric data analysis [18], which operationalized Bourdieu's theory of habitus [3]) will be considered to better define and characterize the groups.

In this case study, we plan to consider two types of bias, i.e., popularity bias and bias related to item categories [24], and aim to develop strategies to mitigate these biases while controlling for diversity, novelty, and serendipity. Thus, we introduce another dimension that aims to reflect the system's overall behavior over time. As mentioned above, these dynamic settings have only been covered extremely rarely in the literature.

Various methods have been introduced to enhance the diversity, serendipity, or novelty of a list of recommendations [17]. Overall, there are two main approaches. One is based on re-ranking the candidate recommendations provided by any recommender approach. The other approach requires introducing beyond-accuracy objectives into the recommender model itself. In our case study, we will use re-ranking, as it allows us to control the trade-off between accuracy and beyond-accuracy measures explicitly. Thus, it is better comparable and easier to interpret.

Similarly, two approaches can be followed to increase the fairness of a recommender system [4]: The first is to integrate fairness directly into the recommendation approach, e.g., as an optimization constraint. The second is applying a post-processing procedure such as personalized fairness-aware re-ranking [20]. Again, we will apply the post-processing approach in the proposed study to influence the behavior of bias.

The research will be realized in collaboration with two companies sharing their data and integrating the models into their systems. The first one is a Viennese publisher. Its online platform provides comprehensive information for politics, culture, media and lifestyle in Vienna (i.e., it comprises multiple domains). It contains, in particular, all articles from the weekly newspaper FALTER as well as a web shop selling books and music. Furthermore, the platform provides up-to-date details on events, restaurants and cinemas in Vienna. The second company is an Austrian start-up that incorporates social relations into the recommendation process by connecting web stores with private chats. Within this collaboration, the focus will be on the fashion domain. In both cases, data capturing user interactions with the platform and metadata of the users will be provided.

Based on these real-world settings, different evaluation strategies are possible. We aim to do offline evaluations to test the models empirically based on well-established performance measures. Furthermore, multi-objective evaluations should be conducted to assess different goals simultaneously (e.g., accuracy and diversity or accuracy and bias) to find out whether there is a trade-off between the measures [17]. Since there is the specific aim to examine the differences between user groups, measurements that capture bias on a group level (such as user popularity deviation for user groups [1]) should be particularly considered.

In order to draw conclusions and to put the gained insights into practice, the results for different domains as well as for different groups of users will be analyzed and compared in detail. Furthermore, statistical models including time-series analysis with generalized additive models and time-series clustering techniques for analyzing the co-evolution of different measurements over time will be employed (see Sect. 2). These models will be evaluated (e.g., based on their goodness-of-fit and predictive power) and integrated into a framework to monitor the dynamics over time.

To summarize, we propose the following procedure (see Fig. 1):

1. **Embedding users and items:** end-to-end (E2E) learning based on multimodal content (i.e., textual information, meta data, pictures, etc.) trained by users' log history; joint user-item vector space
2. **Retrieving:** scoring function to rank candidate items for a user based on dot product or other similarity measure
3. **Post-processing:** re-ranking candidate items to control trade-off between accuracy and beyond-accuracy measures, also considering user groups and assessing bias
4. **User Groups:** clustering of user embeddings, taking also explicit relationships between the users into account; frameworks from social sciences (e.g., social network analysis, geometric data analysis)
5. **Evaluation:** offline evaluation, qualitative user studies and A/B tests
6. **Meta-analysis and bias detection**: Statistical analysis to compare different groups of users and domains, co-evolution of different measures over time

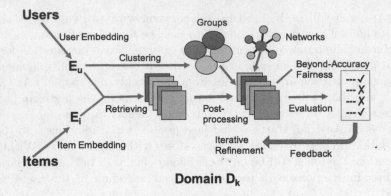

Fig. 1. Overview of the proposed case study.

4   Conclusion

In this position paper, we argue that there is an urgent need for modeling and understanding the long-term dynamics of outcome dimensions of recommender systems (such as accuracy, novelty, diversity, and serendipity) and their relation to bias. Since there is evidence that answers may depend on the domain (e.g., books, news) as well as on characteristics of users and groups of users, we propose to focus on all these aspects. As a first step into the outlined directions, we propose a case study in a real-worlds setting.

References

1. Abdollahpouri, H., Mansoury, M., Burke, R., Mobasher, B., Malthouse, E.: User-centered evaluation of popularity bias in recommender systems. In: Proceedings of the 29th ACM Conference on User Modeling, Adaptation and Personalization, pp. 119–129 (2021)
2. Boratto, L., Marras, M.: Advances in bias-aware recommendation on the web. In: Proceedings of the 14th ACM International Conference on Web Search and Data Mining, pp. 1147–1149 (2021)
3. Bourdieu, P.: Distinction: A Social Critique of the Judgement of Taste. Harvard University Press. Cambridge (1984)
4. Burke, R., Sonboli, N., Ordonez-Gauger, A.: Balanced neighborhoods for multi-sided fairness in recommendation. In: Conference on Fairness, Accountability and Transparency, pp. 202–214. PMLR (2018)
5. Burke, R.D., Mansoury, M., Sonboli, N.: Experimentation with fairness-aware recommendation using librec-auto: hands-on tutorial. In: Proceedings of the 2020 Conference on Fairness, Accountability, and Transparency, pp. 700 (2020)
6. Castells, P., Hurley, N.J., Vargas, S.: Novelty and diversity in recommender systems. In: Ricci, F., Rokach, L., Shapira, B. (eds.) Recommender Systems Handbook, pp. 881–918. Springer, Boston, MA (2015). https://doi.org/10.1007/978-1-4899-7637-6_26

7. Center for Countering Digital Hate, CCDH: Malgorithm how Instagram's algorithm publishes misinformation and hate to millions during a pandemic (2021). https://tinyurl.com/2um6fxpk. Accessed 13 Mar 2021

8. Chen, J., Dong, H., Wang, X., Feng, F., Wang, M., He, X.: Bias and debias in recommender system: a survey and future directions. arXiv preprint arXiv:2010.03240 (2020)

9. Chen, X., Yao, L., McAuley, J., Zhou, G., Wang, X.: A survey of deep reinforcement learning in recommender systems: A systematic review and future directions. arXiv preprint arXiv:2109.03540 (2021)

10. Chouldechova, A., Roth, A.: A snapshot of the frontiers of fairness in machine learning. Commun. ACM **63**(5), 82–89 (2020)

11. Ekstrand, M.D., Das, A., Burke, R., Diaz, F.: Fairness and discrimination in information access systems. arXiv preprint arXiv:2105.05779 (2021)

12. Ge, Y., et al.: Towards long-term fairness in recommendation. In: Proceedings of the 14th ACM International Conference on Web Search and Data Mining, pp. 445–453 (2021)

13. Gunawardana, A., Shani, G.: Evaluating recommender systems. In: Ricci, F., Rokach, L., Shapira, B. (eds.) Recommender Systems Handbook, pp. 265–308. Springer, Boston, MA (2015). https://doi.org/10.1007/978-1-4899-7637-6_8

14. Hastie, T.J., Tibshirani, R.J.: Generalized Additive Models. Routledge, London (2017)

15. Hyndman, R.J., Athanasopoulos, G.: Forecasting: principles and practice. OTexts (2018)

16. Jannach, D., Resnick, P., Tuzhilin, A., Zanker, M.: Recommender systems-beyond matrix completion. Commun. ACM **59**(11), 94–102 (2016)

17. Kaminskas, M., Bridge, D.: Diversity, serendipity, novelty, and coverage: a survey and empirical analysis of beyond-accuracy objectives in recommender systems. ACM Trans. Interact. Intell. Syst. **7**(1), 2 (2017)

18. Le Roux, B., Rouanet, H.: Geometric Data Analysis: From Correspondence Analysis to Structured Data Analysis. Springer, Dordrecht (2004).https://doi.org/10.1007/1-4020-2236-0

19. Lian, J., Zhang, F., Xie, X., Sun, G.: Towards better representation learning for personalized news recommendation: a multi-channel deep fusion approach. In: IJCAI, pp. 3805–3811 (2018)

20. Liu, W., Burke, R.: Personalizing fairness-aware re-ranking. In: FATRec Workshop on Responsible Recommendation, pp. 1–6 (2018)

21. Meinl, R.: Recommender systems: the most valuable application of machine learning, towards data science. https://tinyurl.com/5csbkuyl (2020). Accessed 11 Feb 2021

22. Morik, M., Singh, A., Hong, J., Joachims, T.: Controlling fairness and bias in dynamic learning-to-rank. In: Proceedings of the 43rd International ACM SIGIR Conference on Research and Development in Information Retrieval, pp. 429–438 (2020)

23. Nguyen, T.T., Hui, P.M., Harper, F.M., Terveen, L., Konstan, J.A.: Exploring the filter bubble: the effect of using recommender systems on content diversity. In: Proceedings of the 23rd International Conference on World Wide Web, pp. 677–686 (2014)

24. Tsintzou, V., Pitoura, E., Tsaparas, P.: Bias disparity in recommendation systems. In: Proceedings of the ACM Workshop on Recommendation in Multi-stakeholder Environments (RMSE) 2019. vol. 2440. CEUR-WS (2019)

25. Verma, S., Gao, R., Shah, C.: Facets of fairness in search and recommendation. In: Boratto, L., Faralli, S., Marras, M., Stilo, G. (eds.) BIAS 2020. CCIS, vol. 1245, pp. 1–11. Springer, Cham (2020). https://doi.org/10.1007/978-3-030-52485-2_1
26. Wasserman, S., Faust, K.: Social Network Analysis: Methods and Applications, vol. 8. Cambridge University Press, London (1994)

A Crowdsourcing Methodology to Measure Algorithmic Bias in Black-Box Systems: A Case Study with COVID-Related Searches

Binh Le[1] , Damiano Spina[1]([✉]) , Falk Scholer[1] , and Hui Chia[2]

[1] RMIT University, Melbourne, Australia
{binh.le,damiano.spina,falk.scholer}@rmit.edu.au
[2] The University of Melbourne, Melbourne, Australia
chia.h@unimelb.edu.au

Abstract. Commercial software systems are typically opaque with regard to their inner workings. This makes it challenging to understand the nuances of complex systems, and to study their operation, in particular in the context of fairness and bias. We explore a methodology for studying aspects of the behavior of black box systems, focusing on a commercial search engine as a case study. A crowdsourcing platform is used to collect search engine result pages for a pre-defined set of queries related to the COVID-19 pandemic, to investigate whether the returned search results vary between individuals, and whether the returned results vary for the same individual when their information need is instantiated in a positive or a negative way. We observed that crowd workers tend to obtain different search results when using positive and negative query wording of the information needs, as well as different results for the same queries depending on the country in which they reside. These results indicate that using crowdsourcing platforms to study system behavior, in a way that preserves participant privacy, is a viable approach to obtain insights into black-box systems, supporting research investigations into particular aspects of system behavior.

Keywords: Crowdsourcing · Algorithmic bias · Search engines

1 Introduction

"Should I get vaccinated for COVID-19?" is a question that many people may ask a web search engine or an intelligent assistant nowadays. Would users find the same information if they ask the same question in the negative form, e.g., "Should I avoid getting vaccinated for COVID-19?" Anyone who expects the retrieval

This work has been partially supported by the Australian Research Council (ARC) Centre of Excellence for Automated Decision-Making and Society (ADM+S, CE200100005). Damiano Spina is the recipient of an ARC DECRA Research Fellowship (DE200100064).

system to be fair and unbiased might expect that overall, the key information that is returned would allow them to ultimately draw the same conclusion.

Beyond specific nuances of how a search query is phrased, modern web search engines combine query matching and ranking functions together with multiple signals, including a user's search history, click behavior, and location, so as to maximize the likelihood of retrieving search results or answers to satisfy that specific user's information need. As a consequence of personalizing the user experience, different individuals may get different search results for the same queries. In some scenarios, e.g., health or security-related queries, this can have undesirable implications, as different people may be exposed to information with different content, or inconsistent levels of reliability and trustworthiness. Moreover, the phenomenon of *echo chambers* – where information access systems such as search engines or recommender systems reinforce existing preferences of users in a feedback loop [1, 5, 8, 9] – is particularly problematic in this context. In this work we consider a commercial web search engine and health-related queries. This is especially relevant in the context of the COVID-19 pandemic, where health information has been highly politicized, and echo chambers of false information regarding COVID-19 have been found on social media platforms such as Twitter [7] or YouTube [2].

The aim of this study was to investigate whether individuals receive different search results for health information queries, based upon a difference in opinion as expressed in the wording of the query. For instance, if a person was more inclined to get vaccinated, they are more likely to search "Should I get vaccinated"; whereas if a person is already less inclined to get vaccinated, they may be more likely to search "Should I avoid getting vaccinated". This is within the context of online misinformation and politicization of health information surrounding the COVID-19 pandemic, where the spread of scientifically inaccurate misinformation has emerged as a risk to public health and safety [11, 13, 16].

The rationale underlying this study is that search engines have an ethical obligation to give all individuals equal access to credible health information from authoritative sources, regardless of the individual's current opinion on that health topic. The personalization of Search Engine Result Pages (SERPs) is generally acceptable for most topics, as it can improve the user experience and usually does not cause harm. However, the personalization of SERPs when it comes to critical information such as regarding health may cause direct harm to the community, if it leads to some individuals receiving less credible information. Thus, we sought to identify whether a person's current viewpoint about controversial topics related to the COVID-19 pandemic, tested by expressing the same query posed in negative or positive terms, would impact the quality of their search results from authoritative sources.

In this setting, we consider the following questions:

– Do different individuals get the same or different search results for the same queries?
– Do results vary between positive and negative query formulations for the same person?

We tested the feasibility of using a crowdsourcing methodology to quantify algorithmic bias when treating the underlying information access and retrieval system as a black-box, which is the case with commercial web search engines that keep their ranking processes as tightly controlled corporate secrets. Using Amazon Mechanical Turk, we asked 50 crowd workers to submit a set of 10 queries related to the COVID-19 pandemic – including both positive and negative forms of expressing the same information needs – to a commercial web search engine (i.e., Google) and to upload the de-identified Search Engine Results Page (SERP) that they obtained.[1]

Our results demonstrate that different individuals can indeed receive different search results for the same queries, based on factors such as the country in which the searcher is located. While this is not an unexpected result, it validates the sensitivity of the proposed method. More surprisingly, we also found that results can vary substantially between positive and negative query formulations.

2   Preliminaries

2.1   Auditing Algorithmic Bias

Friedman and Nissenbaum [4] defined a biased system as one that systematically treats specific individuals or groups differently from others, providing either unfair advantages or disadvantages. As computer applications and their development processes become more complex, the definition of bias became multifaceted. To understand a black-box system and whether its workings exhibit possible bias, a range of approaches are available. A number of studies have investigated the advantages and disadvantages of these different methods for auditing the fairness of systems [12,14].

Five approaches for the auditing of systems, as described by Sandvig et al. [14], are:

Code Audit (Algorithm Transparency): With this method, one simply looks directly at the source code of an algorithm. However, algorithms are commonly trade secrets and highly protected by the owning company, whose competitiveness and revenue may be directly impacted by the effectiveness of their system. Furthermore, given the complexity of modern systems, it's very challenging for third parties to audit source code directly, line by line, without a tremendous amount of effort, often including needing explanations from the developer.

Noninvasive User Audit: This approach is conducted by surveying users of the platform, rather than examining the platform itself. This, however, is not easy when it comes to getting a representative sample, and the results may themselves suffer from a high degree of bias due to the limitations of human memory and emotions related to the users' experience of the platform.

---

[1] The data collection process for this work was reviewed and approved by RMIT University's Human Research Ethics Committee (project number 23588).

Scraping Audit: This method is more programmatic, and involves writing automated scripts that make use of a system's API services, or directly download and process system outputs (e.g. raw HTML markup from a web page). The downside of this approach is that it does not reflect the way normal users would interact with system in an everyday context. Another major challenge of this approach is legal; under the US Computer Fraud and Abuse Act (CFAA), a researcher who attempts to do this might open themselves to legal action, with penalties possibly including jail terms.

Sock Puppet Audit: Instead of involving real users, the researcher creates a software program that behaves like one. If the platform cannot distinguish between the program and a real user, this method can provide useful data.

Crowdsourced Audit/Collaborative Audit: This method differs from the previous methods in that it gets real humans to work on a task as designed by the researchers. With this method, the platform has to treat the request as if it comes from real humans, as they are real humans.

2.2 Auditing Platforms and Search Engines

In recent years, watchdog organizations such as AlgorithmWatch[2] [10,15] or initiatives such as Ad Observer,[3] part of the NYU Cybersecurity for Democracy project, have proposed *data donation* methodologies to investigate the transparency and accountability of automated decision-making (ADM) systems deployed in online platforms such as recommender systems on Instagram or advertising engines on Facebook. These initiatives ask volunteers to donate the data they observe in a platform or a search engine by installing a plugin in their browser. The ADM+S Australian Search Experience project[4] uses a similar methodology to understand to what extent the SERPs retrieved using a common set of search queries (e.g., 'federal elections') differ across different users aged 18 or older and currently residing in Australia.

2.3 Crowdsourcing Platform: Amazon Mechanical Turk

Amazon Mechanical Turk[5] (MTurk) launched in 2005 as a crowdsourcing platform for tasks that cannot be completed by a machine and require human contribution, including identifying and characterizing objects, voices, images, etc. [12]. The system brings together *requesters* and *workers*: the former set up and publish series of work tasks (often called HITs or human intelligence tasks) to be done, and the latter browse and choose from a list of available tasks that they can complete at their convenience.

---

[2] https://algorithmwatch.org/en/.
[3] https://adobserver.org/.
[4] https://www.admscentre.org.au/searchexperience/.
[5] https://www.mturk.com/.

MTurk work requests can come from different countries, as can workers (i.e., participants in work tasks). However, it is known that most of the MTurk workers reside in the United States, followed by India [3,6].

The actual demographics of particular participants in a given MTurk project may vary substantially, for a range of reasons including the nature of the work, the amount of reward (money) offered, or even the time of day at which a task is launched. Requesters can place restrictions on workers, including for example setting limits on countries, past worker performance, and so on.

2.4 Measuring Similarity Among SERPs

We consider two similarity metrics to compare SERPs: Rank-Biased Overlap (RBO), which considers the order of individual search results in a SERP; and, Jaccard similarity, which compares SERPs as sets (i.e., without considering the ranking order or individual results).

Rank-Biased Overlap. Rank-biased overlap (RBO), introduced by Webber et al. [17], is a metric to quantify the similarity of two lists, with the ability to determine the relative weighting of earlier and later items in the list. RBO allows us to compare two sets of Google search results based on the websites they returned, and their order. RBO scores between two lists range from 0 to 1, with 1 indicating that the lists are identical and 0 indicating no similarity at all. The RBO function includes a parameter p that models the *persistence* of a user inspecting a SERP. In practice, the parameter p adjusts the weight given to earlier results. By default, p has a value of 1, meaning that the weights applied to the items in the list become arbitrarily flat, and the evaluation becomes arbitrarily deep, i.e., the user would inspect all the search results in the SERP. A lower value of p gives more weight to top results, when p is 0, only the highest-ranked item in the list is considered. RBO can be calibrated to an expected stopping depth $n = \frac{1}{(1-p)}$. For instance, if we want to model the scenario where the users would pay most attention to the top three search results on a SERP, we would set the stopping depth to $n = 3$, which corresponds to RBO with $p = 0.\overline{6}$.

Jaccard Similarity. Jaccard similarity is a popular similarity metric to measure the overlap between two sets. Given two sets A and B, Jaccard similarity is defined as the cardinality of the intersection divided by the cardinality of the union of the two sets:

$$\text{Jaccard}(A, B) = \frac{|A \cap B|}{|A \cup B|}$$

Both RBO and Jaccard similarity metrics range between 0 and 1, and higher scores indicate higher similarity. In our setting, a score of 0 is obtained when two SERPs have no overlap in the search results they contain, while 1 represents identical SERPs.

3   Methodology

In this section we describe the overall process used to collect data via crowd-sourcing. We also detail the configuration of the crowdsourcing task, the queries included in our study, and the process to de-identify the collected data.

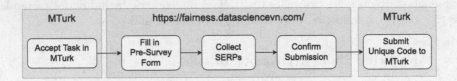

Fig. 1. Overall process used for collecting data via MTurk.

3.1   Crowdsourcing Search Engine Result Pages

The Amazon Mechanical Turk (MTurk) service was used to collect Search Engine Reult Pages (SERPs) from crowd workers. The data collection process consisted of five steps, illustrated in Fig. 1.

1. **Accept the Task.** The crowdsourcing task is listed in MTurk, where workers can view a brief introduction to the task and the amount of reward obtained by completing the task. The workers then can decide if they are willing to participate. Once they start the survey, participants receive a link to our experiment.
2. **Fill in Pre-Survey Form.** Participants start by filling a pre-task questionnaire to collect demographic information such as gender, age, country of residence, and level of education. The pre-task questionnaire can be viewed at: https://fairness.datasciencevn.com/survey/start (Accessed: 21 Feb 2022).
3. **Collect SERPs.** Participants are directed to the perform the main task of our study, requiring them to:
   (a) Manually run a provided query using Google search
   (b) Save the SERP as a HTML file, and
   (c) Upload the file into our web application.
   For data verification purposes, we configured our system to analyse the content of the HTML file and determine whether the query in the file exactly matches the query that the participant is required to upload at that stage. For example, the participant could be required to upload HTML search results for "should i not get tested for covid", however, either due to confusion or laziness, they may attempt to upload the results for a different query. In this case, the system rejects the uploaded file and asks the participant to upload again. For convenience, we created a YouTube video[6] to explain the process to participants.
   Participants repeat this process for each of the 10 search queries described below, one query at a time. We shuffle the order of queries displayed to participants, to minimize possible ordering effects.

---

[6] https://www.youtube.com/watch?v=RucW_Ok7EdQ (Accessed: 21 Feb 2022).

The HTML file submitted by the participants may contain information about the participant's Google profile, such as profile image and e-mail address, if they are signed in while submitting a query. To protect participant anonymity, as soon as each HTML file is submitted to the web application, the system automatically runs a data de-identification process: JavaScript code is run in the client side of the web application, which automatically removes all personal information (if present) and then saves the de-identified version of the HTML file. Therefore, only the de-identified version of the HTML is stored at the server-side for later analysis.

4. **Confirm Submission.** At the end of the task, the MTurk workers receive a unique code generated by our system.

5. **Submit Unique Code to MTurk.** Workers are redirected back to MTurk to submit the unique code. This code is then used to verify the submission of the worker and accept the valid tasks. Once the tasks are approved, MTurk automatically pays the workers for their completed tasks.

Crowdsourcing Setup. Participants were compensated for completing the task by a payment of US$1.20, based on the average estimated completion time of 10 min. In total, 50 workers were recruited to complete the task. Each worker could submit only one task. The maximum task completion time was set to 1 h, allowing participants to take short breaks if needed, but encouraging them to focus and complete the task in a constrained block of time.

3.2 Queries

For our experiment, we devised a set of queries relating to public health considerations and beliefs around COVID-19, including testing, facemasks, and controversial treatments such as hydroxychloroquine.

Table 1 shows the queries included in our study. The queries are grouped into five semantically related pairs, one representing an information need in a *positive* form, and the other representing the information need in a *negative* form with the use of negation. We intentionally explored different ways of representing negation in queries. For Queries 2, 4, and 8 we used 'not'; for Query 6 we used 'avoid'; and for Query 10 we used the prefix 'in'.

4   Results and Discussion

4.1   Collected Data

We initially requested 50 crowdsourcing tasks to be completed. One participant submitted an incorrect validation code; therefore, only one survey needed to be republished. The average time the participants took to complete both the pre-task questionnaire and the task itself was 23 min 37 s. We launched the crowdsourcing tasks on October 5, 2020 and all the 50 valid tasks were completed by October 7, 2020.

Table 1. Queries included in our experiment, organized in pairs consisting of positive and negative expressions of an information need.

ID	Query	Pair
1	should i get tested for covid	Pair 1
2	should i not get tested for covid	
3	should i get flu shot	Pair 2
4	should i not get flu shot	
5	should i get vaccinated	Pair 3
6	should i avoid get vaccinated	
7	should i wear facemask	Pair 4
8	should i not wear facemask	
9	is hydroxychloroquine effective for covid	Pair 5
10	is hydroxychloroquine ineffective for covid	

A total of 500 SERPs (10 per participant) were obtained, resulting in a total of 4,692 items (accounting for repetition). Most of the SERPs consist of 9 or 10 items/search results. The amount of organic search results vary depending on the layout of the first page; Google search may include additional information (e.g., common questions related to COVID-19), leaving less room for organic search results. The dataset and source code used for our analysis are publicly available at https://github.com/rmit-ir/crowdsourcing-algorithmic-bias (Accessed: 21 Feb 2022).

4.2   Demographics

The crowdsourcing task was carried out by a total of 50 crowd workers residing in different countries: US (34), India (9), Brazil (5), Germany (1), and Spain (1). This is broadly in-keeping with the population of workers who use the MTurk platform [6].

Participants reported their gender as female (12), male (11), other (13), or preferred not answer this question (14). In terms of age, participants were skewed towards younger ages: 18–24 (1), 25–34 (29), 35–44 (12), 45–54 (6), 55–64 (1), and 65+ (1). For level of education, the participants reported: College degree/bachelor's degree (32); Some college (some community college, associate's degree) (7); Postgraduate or professional degree, including master's, doctorate, medical or law degree (6); Some postgraduate or professional schooling, no postgraduate degree (4); High school graduate or GED (includes technical/vocational training that does not count towards college credit) (1).

4.3   Do Different Participants Get Different Search Results for the Same Queries?

First we compared the SERPs obtained by the participants for the 10 queries included in our experiment. Given the set of participants $\mathcal{W} = \{w_1, \ldots, w_{50}\}$

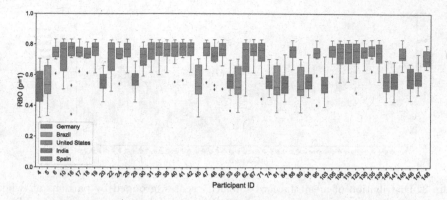

Fig. 2. Distribution of mean RBO ($p = 1$) scores, grouped by participant, when the full URL is considered to compare items in SERPs. Colors indicate the country of residence as indicated by participants.

and the set of queries $\mathcal{Q} = \{q_1, \ldots, q_{10}\}$, we compare the SERP for a given query $q \in \mathcal{Q}$ seen by participant w_i against the SERPs seen by the rest of the participants $w_j \neq w_i \in \mathcal{W}$ for the same query q, i.e., a *between participant* analysis. We then compute the arithmetic mean of the similarity scores obtained for a given query q. This process is repeated for all queries $q \in Q$, resulting in 10 similarity scores per participant.

Individual results in SERPs can be compared at two levels: considering the full URL of the item, or considering only the domain of the item (e.g., vic.gov.au). Given that we have two similarity measures (RBO, and Jaccard) this results in four combinations for comparison. Figure 2 shows the results for RBO considering full URLs of items in the compared SERPs. The trends for the other three configurations where highly similar, and are not included due to space limitations.

Overall, independently of the similarity metric (RBO or Jaccard) and the granularity (full URL or domain) used, different participants may see different search results when they submit the same query to a web search engine such as Google. Even in the setting most tolerant to differences (Jaccard similarity of sets of domains and not taking rank position into account, Fig. 3), we found that distribution of similarity scores cover a wide range of scores for many of the participants. Participants that indicated the country of residence as Germany, Brazil, India, or Spain, are more likely to see different SERPs that those obtained by the majority of participants residing in the US.[7] This suggests that submitting the same query may lead to different search results, depending on the location from which the query is submitted. Note that, Even though we provided a link to

---

[7] The participant with ID 140 who indicated US as country of residence had substantially lower similarity scores than the other participants residing in the US. However, we do not have sufficient data to better understand the reason behind this difference, and note that the self-reported location may be inaccurate.

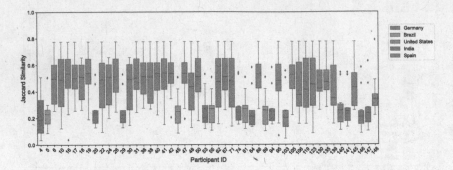

Fig. 3. Distribution of mean Jaccard similarity scores, grouped by participant, when the domain is used to compare items in SERPs. Colors indicate country of residence as indicated by participants.

submit the queries to the same search engine's domain (i.e., `google.com`), the search engine automatically redirects requests to the region-specific endpoint (based on user's IP), unless a specific region is manually set in the settings.

In addition, we analyzed the results using RBO with a persistence parameter of $p = 0.67$, which corresponds to a scenario where attention is focused on the top-3 search results, and observed similar trends.

5 Do Results Vary Between Positive and Negative Query Formulations?

We performed a *within participant* analysis to investigate whether participants would see different SERPs when issuing queries in positive or negative formulations, e.g., "should i get flu shot" vs. "should i *not* get flu shot". From our data, for each query pair we have 50 similarity scores, one per participant. Figures 4 and 5 show the distribution of RBO ($p = 1$) scores when comparing the SERPs obtained by each participant for each query pairs, when full URLs and domain are considered to compare items, respectively.

When full URLs are considered in the measurements (Fig. 4), RBO scores are relatively low, indicating that participants tend to obtain different answers depending on the wording used to formulate the query. At the domain level, for query pairs 1–3, the returned search results are more similar in terms of the domains they cover (Fig. 5). However, this is not the case for query pairs 4 and 5, where positive and negative query formulations tend to retrieve search results from different domains. Comparing the two graphs, we can see that Query Pair 3 in particular seems to retrieve different pages, but within common domains.

It can be seen that participants residing in the US are grouped separately compared to other countries. For query pair 2, participants residing in the US tend to get higher RBO scores compared to the rest (for both full URL and domain). However, query pairs 3 and 4 show a different trend: when full URLs are considered, participants residing in the US tend to obtain different search

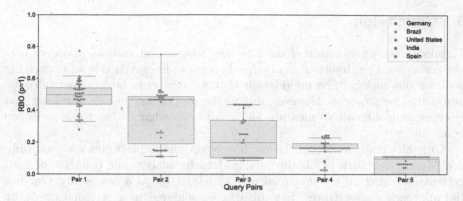

Fig. 4. RBO ($p = 1$) scores between positive and negative query formulations, grouped by pairs, when full URLs of answer items are considered. Colours represent the country of residence as indicated by participants.

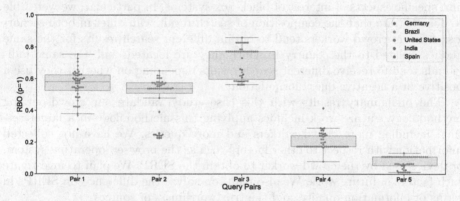

Fig. 5. RBO ($p = 1$) scores between positive and negative query formulations, grouped by pairs, when only domains of answer items are considered. Colours represent the country of residence as indicated by participants.

results with respect to the query formulation. When we look at differences at domain level, different query formulation leads to different search results within the same domain for Pair 3, while for Pair 4 the search results were retrieved from different domains.

We performed a similar analysis using RBO with $p = 0.67$, and observed that a larger gap appears between positive and negative query formulations. This was especially evident for Query Pair 5, where the word 'not' is not used.

Overall, our preliminary analysis indicates that, by analyzing the overlap of search results between SERPs, differences in the composition of search results are seen by people depending on whether positive or negative formulations of queries are used.

6   Conclusion

Thanks to the proliferation of the internet, information and attention are now key resources. Fair, unbiased, and ethical access to information is an underlying goal for our society. The information that we receive is largely controlled by automated technologies. However, due to the proprietary nature of commercial systems, it is difficult to measure and analyze to what extent these goals are being met.

Our pilot study validates the use of crowdsourcing platforms such as Amazon Mechanical Turk to obtain reliable data to analyze the behavior of such systems, focusing on a commercial web search engine as a case study. Our initial approach demonstrates that this can be achieved in a systematic way by developing complementary user representations: we investigated both *between user* variability, and *within user* variability, where the same information needs are instantiated using positive or negative wording. This enabled gaining insight into specific aspects of interest of black-box systems. In particular, we were able to demonstrate that the composition of search results can differ in both scenarios: different crowd workers tend to obtain different search results for the same queries, related to the country in which they are located; and, the same individuals tend to receive different search results depending on whether they use a positive or a negative query formulation.

The preliminary results with this case study validate our crowdsourcing methodology. Future work includes applying this methodology in a larger setting, including more crowd workers and more queries. We have not collected information with respect to other factors such as the browser, operating system, or device used by the crowd worker to obtain the SERP. We plan to investigate such factors in future work. We also plan to analyze the differences in SERPs in terms of information quality, and the trustworthiness of sources.

We believe that approaches such as this – in addition to other more scalable but less controlled methodologies, such as data donation initiatives – will form an essential pillar to support research practices to measure algorithmic bias in black-box systems used to access information, such as search engines, recommender systems, and intelligent assistants.

References

1. Cinelli, M., De Francisci Morales, G., Galeazzi, A., Quattrociocchi, W., Starnini, M.: The echo chamber effect on social media. Proc. Natl. Acad. Sci. **118**(9) (2021). https://doi.org/10.1073/pnas.2023301118
2. Cinelli, M., et al.: The COVID-19 social media infodemic. Sci. Rep. **10**(1), 1–10 (2020). https://doi.org/10.1038/s41598-020-73510-5
3. Difallah, D., Filatova, E., Ipeirotis, P.: Demographics and dynamics of mechanical turk workers. In: Proceedings of the Eleventh ACM International Conference on Web Search and Data Mining, WSDM 2018, pp. 135–143. Association for Computing Machinery, New York (2018). https://doi.org/10.1145/3159652.3159661

4. Friedman, B., Nissenbaum, H.: Bias in computer systems. ACM Trans. Inf. Syst. **14**(3), 330–347 (1996). https://doi.org/10.1145/230538.230561

5. Ge, Y., et al.: Understanding echo chambers in e-commerce recommender systems. In: Proceedings of the 43rd International ACM SIGIR Conference on Research and Development in Information Retrieval, pp. 2261–2270. Association for Computing Machinery, New York (2020). https://doi.org/10.1145/3397271.3401431

6. Ipeirotis, P.G.: Demographics of mechanical turk. Technical report, NYU Working Paper No. CEDER-10-01 (2010). https://ssrn.com/abstract=1585030

7. Jiang, J., Ren, X., Ferrara, E.: Social media polarization and echo chambers in the context of COVID-19: case study. JMIRx Med **2**(3), e29570 (2021). https://doi.org/10.2196/29570. ISSN 2563-6316

8. Jiang, R., Chiappa, S., Lattimore, T., György, A., Kohli, P.: Degenerate feedback loops in recommender systems. In: Proceedings of the 2019 AAAI/ACM Conference on AI, Ethics, and Society, AIES 2019, pp. 383–390. Association for Computing Machinery, New York (2019). https://doi.org/10.1145/3306618.3314288

9. Kitchens, B., Johnson, S.L., Gray, P.: Understanding echo chambers and filter bubbles: the impact of social media on diversification and partisan shifts in news consumption. MIS Q. **44**(4), 1619–1649 (2020). https://doi.org/10.25300/MISQ/2020/16371

10. Loi, M., Spielkamp, M.: Towards accountability in the use of artificial intelligence for public administrations. In: Proceedings of the 2021 AAAI/ACM Conference on AI, Ethics, and Society, AIES 2021, pp. 757–766. Association for Computing Machinery, New York (2021). https://doi.org/10.1145/3461702.3462631

11. Naeem, S.B., Bhatti, R.: The COVID-19 'infodemic': a new front for information professionals. Health Inf. Libr. J. **37**(3), 233–239 (2020). https://doi.org/10.1111/hir.12311

12. Paolacci, G., Chandler, J., Ipeirotis, P.G.: Running experiments on Amazon Mechanical Turk. Judgm. Decis. Making **5**(5), 411–419 (2010). http://journal.sjdm.org/10/10630a/jdm10630a.pdf

13. Saling, L.L., Mallal, D., Scholer, F., Skelton, R., Spina, D.: No one is immune to misinformation: an investigation of misinformation sharing by subscribers to a fact-checking newsletter. PLoS ONE **16**(8), 1–13 (2021). https://doi.org/10.1371/journal.pone.0255702

14. Sandvig, C., Hamilton, K., Karahalios, K., Langbort, C.: Auditing algorithms: research methods for detecting discrimination on internet platforms. Data Discrimination: Converting Crit. Concerns Prod. Inquiry **22**, 4349–4357 (2014). https://social.cs.uiuc.edu/papers/pdfs/ICA2014-Sandvig.pdf

15. Spielkamp, M.: AlgorithmWatch: what role can a watchdog organization play in ensuring algorithmic accountability? In: Cerquitelli, T., Quercia, D., Pasquale, F. (eds.) Transparent Data Mining for Big and Small Data. SBD, vol. 11, pp. 207–215. Springer, Cham (2017). https://doi.org/10.1007/978-3-319-54024-5_9

16. Tommasel, A., Godoy, D., Zubiaga, A.: OHARS: second workshop on online misinformation- and harm-aware recommender systems. In: Fifteenth ACM Conference on Recommender Systems, RecSys 2021, pp. 789–791. Association for Computing Machinery, New York (2021). https://doi.org/10.1145/3460231.3470941

17. Webber, W., Moffat, A., Zobel, J.: A similarity measure for indefinite rankings. ACM Trans. Inf. Syst. **28**(4), 1–38 (2010). https://doi.org/10.1145/1852102.1852106

The Unfairness of Active Users and Popularity Bias in Point-of-Interest Recommendation

Hossein A. Rahmani[1](✉), Yashar Deldjoo[2], Ali Tourani[3],
and Mohammadmehdi Naghiaei[4]

[1] University College London, London, UK
h.rahmani@ucl.ac.uk
[2] Polytechnic University of Bari, Bari, Italy
deldjooy@acm.org
[3] University of Guilan, Rasht, Iran
tourani@msc.guilan.ac.ir
[4] University of Southern California, Los Angeles, USA
naghiaei@usc.edu

Abstract. Point-of-Interest (POI) recommender systems provide personalized recommendations to users and help businesses attract potential customers. Despite their success, recent studies suggest that highly data-driven recommendations could be impacted by data biases, resulting in unfair outcomes for different stakeholders, mainly consumers (users) and providers (items). Most existing fairness-related research works in recommender systems treat user fairness and item fairness issues individually, disregarding that RS work in a two-sided marketplace. This paper studies the interplay between *(i)* the unfairness of active users, *(ii)* the unfairness of popular items, and *(iii)* the accuracy (personalization) of recommendation as three angles of our study triangle.

We group users into advantaged and disadvantaged levels to measure user fairness based on their activity level. For item fairness, we divide items into short-head, mid-tail, and long-tail groups and study the exposure of these item groups into the top-k recommendation list of users. Experimental validation of eight different recommendation models commonly used for POI recommendation (e.g., contextual, CF) on two publicly available POI recommendation datasets, Gowalla and Yelp, indicate that most well-performing models suffer seriously from the unfairness of popularity bias (provider unfairness). Furthermore, our study shows that most recommendation models cannot satisfy both consumer and producer fairness, indicating a trade-off between these variables possibly due to natural biases in data. We choose the POI recommendation as our test scenario; however, the insights should be trivially extendable on other domains.

Keywords: Fairness · Active Users · Popularity Bias · POI Recommendation

L. Boratto et al. (Eds.): BIAS 2022, CCIS 1610, pp. 56–68, 2022.
https://doi.org/10.1007/978-3-031-09316-6_6

1   Introduction

Point-of-Interest (POI) recommendation is an essential service to location-based social networks (LBSNs). Providing personalized POI systems ease the inevitable problem of information overload on users and helps businesses attract potential customers [30, 33]. However, as a highly data-driven system, these systems could be impacted by data or algorithmic bias, providing unfair outcomes and weakening the system's trustworthiness. Consequently, bias and fairness have attracted rapidly growing attention in machine learning and recommender system research communities [7, 9, 25].

Traditional recommender systems (RS) focused on maximizing customer satisfaction by tailoring the content according to individual customers' preferences, thereby disregarding the interest of the producers. Several recent studies [2, 22] have revealed how such customer-centric designs may impair the well-being of the producers. Thus, in recent years, two-sided marketplaces have steadily emerged as a pivotal problem of fairness topics in RS, requiring optimizing supplier preferences and visibility.

Most papers in this field focus on the fairness perspective either on the side of users or items [2, 3, 5, 16, 20]. Contrary to these works, the work at hand aims to look into the interplay between *accuracy*, *producer fairness*, and *consumer fairness* in a multi-sided marketplace ecosystem and the possible trade-off between them. Specifically, we focus on the fairness of state-of-the-art POI recommendation algorithms and investigate the performance of various algorithms on two real-world POI datasets, Gowalla and Yelp, to address the following research questions:

- **RQ1**: To what extent are users or user groups (active vs. inactive) interested in popular POIs? That is identifying natural data bias toward popularity. (cf. Sect. 4).
- **RQ2**: Is there a trade-off among the factors of accuracy, user fairness, and item fairness? (cf. Sect. 5.1).
- **RQ3**: Could we classify algorithms based on their performance on the accuracy, user fairness, and item fairness? Which ones can produce satisfactory results on all three factors, and which one suffers more from bias issues? (cf. Sect. 5.2).

To answer the mentioned questions, we analyze the users' profiles regarding their check-ins behavior and compare several state-of-the-art recommendation algorithms regarding their general popularity bias propagation and the extent to which it affects different groups of users and items. In the following, we review the related works in Sect. 2 and explain the experimental setup in Sect. 3. Then, we conduct experiments and the evaluation results in Sect. 5. We conclude the paper in Sect. 6. Finally, to enable reproducibility of the results, we have made our codes open source.[1]

---

[1] https://github.com/RecSys-lab/FairPOI

2   Related Work

Fairness is becoming one of the most influential topics in recommender systems in recent years [7,22,27]. Burke et al. [6] classified fairness in the recommendation system based on general beneficiaries, consumers (C), providers (P), and both (CP). Deldjoo et al. [9] proposed a flexible framework to evaluate consumer and provider fairness using generalized cross-entropy. Li et al. [22] focused on the fairness in the recommendation systems from the user's perspective in the e-commerce domain, i.e., C-fairness. They created user groups based on their activity level into two groups: advantaged and disadvantaged. They showed that users in the advantaged group (i.e., active users) usually receive higher quality recommendations than disadvantaged groups, while the advantaged users are a small fraction of all users. Then, they proposed a fair re-ranking model by introducing constraints based on the 0-1 integer programming to reduce this gap. Abdollahpouri et al. [3] further researched user-centered evaluation of popularity bias. They proposed a user-centered evaluation method that can effectively tackle popularity bias for different user groups while accounting for users' tolerance towards popularity bias using Jensen divergence. Similarly, we divide the users into four groups based on their activity level and calculate the recommendation accuracy and fairness achieved by state-of-the-art algorithms in the location-based recommender systems among user groups.

Kowald et al. [20] attempted to investigate the user fairness in music recommendation on the Last.fm dataset. The analysis of this paper is in line with the investigation of Abdollahpouri et al. [2] in the domain of movie recommendation. To do this, they split users into three groups and explored the correlation between users' profiles and well-known artists. The result further indicated that the low-mainstream user groups receive a low recommendation quality in all cases. Zhang et al. [38] examined adjusting item popularity bias in recommendation score using the causal intervention and latent factor model by experimenting on three real-world datasets. Similar to the work presented by Abdollahpouri et al. [2], we investigate popularity bias in the POI domain on provider perspectives, i.e., P-fairness, by dividing them into three categories: *short-head*, *mid-tail*, and *long-tail* locations. We then explore the item exposure fairness of these three distinct categories, thus P-Fairness.

Weydemann et al. [35] investigated fairness in the location-based recommender systems by defining various criteria for measuring fairness. Their experiment showed that unfairness in location recommender systems is likely related to location popularity or inclination toward some user groups based on nationality. Lesota et al. [21] investigated item popularity fairness in the music domain using the LFM-2b[2] dataset, i.e., P-fairness, and addressed shortcomings of the statistical analysis in fairness by considering the distribution between user-profiles and recommendation lists. Furthermore, they analyzed whether such algorithmic popularity bias affects users of different genders.

---

[2] http://www.cp.jku.at/datasets/LFM-2b/.

Table 1. Characteristics of the datasets used in the evaluation: $|\mathcal{U}|$ is the number of users, $|\mathcal{P}|$ is the number of POIs, $|\mathcal{C}|$ is the number of check-ins, $|\mathcal{S}|$ the number of social link, $|\mathcal{G}|$ is the number of categories (e.g., restaurant, cafe), $\frac{|\mathcal{C}|}{|\mathcal{U}\times\mathcal{P}|}$ is the density. – shows that on the Gowalla dataset we do not have categorical information of POIs.

Dataset	$|\mathcal{U}|$	$|\mathcal{P}|$	$|\mathcal{C}|$	$|\mathcal{S}|$	$|\mathcal{G}|$	$\frac{|\mathcal{C}|}{|\mathcal{U}|}$	$\frac{|\mathcal{C}|}{|\mathcal{P}|}$	$\frac{|\mathcal{C}|}{|\mathcal{U}\times\mathcal{P}|}$
Yelp	7,135	15,575	299,327	46,778	582	41.95	19.21	0.0026
Gowalla	5,628	30,943	618,621	46,001	–	109.91	19.99	0.0035

Contrary to the works mentioned above that focus on consumers [2,3,22], or provider fairness [1,20,38], our work studies the fairness of recommended items from both perspectives (i.e., CP-Fairness). Mehrotra et al. [26] showed that blindly optimizing for consumer relevance might hurt supplier fairness. Hence, one of the main benefits of this study is to allow us to understand whether there exists a possible trade-off between these factors <accuracy, user fairness, provider fairness> and measure how much we need to sacrifice consumer satisfaction in terms of relevance to have a more fair marketplace.

3 Experimental Setup

3.1 Datasets

In this work, we use two well-known check-in datasets, namely, Gowalla and Yelp provided by [24][3]. The Gowalla dataset was collected from February 2009 to October 2010. Following [4,24,29], we preprocessed the Gowalla dataset by removing cold users, i.e., users who visited locations for less than 15 check-ins. We also excluded POIs of less than 10, which may cause a spam error on the model. The Yelp dataset is provided by the Yelp Dataset Challenge[4] round 7 (access date: Feb 2016) in 10 metropolitan areas across two countries. Also, in this case, we preprocessed the dataset and removed users who had less than 10 visited locations and POIs with less than 10 visits. Table 1 shows the statistics of the final datasets after prepossessing steps.

3.2 Evaluation Metrics

For evaluation, we use NDCG, and two fairness evaluation metrics, namely, Generalized Cross-Entropy (GCE) and Mean Absolute Deviation of ranking performance (MADr) [9]. Both metrics can be used to measure user and item fairness. The difference is that GCE compares the recommendation distribution with a fair one, while the latter compares the absolute deviation between recommendation

---

[3] http://spatialkeyword.sce.ntu.edu.sg/eval-vldb17/.
[4] https://www.yelp.com/dataset/challenge.

models. If the attribute $a \in A$ is discrete or categorical, then the unfairness measure according to GCE is defined as:

$$GCE(m,a) = \frac{1}{\beta \cdot (1-\beta)} \left[\sum_{a_j} p_f^\beta(a_j) \cdot p_m^{(1-\beta)}(a_j) - 1 \right] \qquad (1)$$

in which p_m and p_f stand for recommendation model and target distributions, respectively. Note that the defined unfairness measure indexed by β includes the Hellinger distance for $\beta = 1/2$, the Pearson's χ^2 discrepancy measure for $\beta = 2$, Neymann's χ^2 measure for $\beta = -1$, the Kullback-Leibler divergence in the limit as $\beta \to 1$, and the Burg CE distance as $\beta \to 0$. MAD for ranking (MADr) can be defined formally by:

$$MADr(i,j) = \left| rank^{(i)} - rank^{(j)} \right| \qquad (2)$$

where $rank^{(i)}$ denotes the average ranking performance restricted to those users in group i, and $rank^{(j)}$ captures the same metric score for group j. The reported MADr corresponds to the average MADr between all the pairwise combinations within the groups involved, i.e., $MADr = avg_{i,j}(MADr(R^{(i)}, R^{(j)}))$. Larger values for MADr imply differentiation between groups interpreted as unfairness.

To evaluate the performance of the recommendation methods we partition each dataset into training, validation, and test data. For each user, we use the earliest 70% check-ins as training data, the most recent 20% check-ins as test data, and the remaining 10% as validation data.

4   Popularity Bias in POI Data (RQ1)

In this section, to answer the first research question, we analyze the consumption distribution of POIs across two datasets and the degree of interest that different types of users have towards popular items.

4.1   Consumption Distribution of POIs

In Fig. 1, we show the consumption distribution of POIs across the two datasets chosen for this work, namely, Gowalla and Yelp. In both Figs. 1a and 1e, we observe a long-term distribution of the POI checks-ins, where few items (POIs) are consumed (visited) by many users, while few users only see most POIs. We highlight the popular items in both datasets by segmenting each into three categories (*short-head*, *mid-tail*, and *long-tail*) in such a way that *short-head* items correspond to 50% of check-ins, while *mid-* and *long-tail* items provide the remaining 30% and 20%, respectively. Furthermore, following [24], user groups have been divided into *very inactive*, *slightly inactive*, *slightly active*, and *very active* based on their number of check-ins. Users of Gowalla were mapped to the mentioned classes as "<19", "19–47", "47–94", and ">94", containing 921,

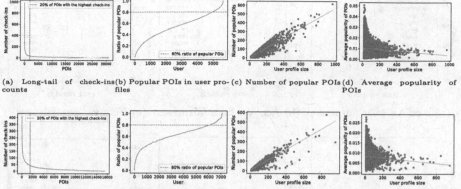

(a) Long-tail of check-ins (b) Popular POIs in user pro- (c) Number of popular POIs (d) Average popularity of
counts   files   POIs

(e) Long-tail of check-ins (f) Popular POIs in user pro- (g) Number of popular POIs (h) Average popularity of
counts   files   POIs

Fig. 1. (a–d) and (e–h) show evaluations on Gowalla and Yelp datasets, respectively. (a), (b), (e), and (h) are long-tail of check-ins, and (c), (d), (g), (h) refer to the correlation of user profile size and the popularity of artists in the user profile.

1992, 1266, and 1449 instances, respectively. The same pattern goes for Yelp with divisions "<51", "51–128", "128–256", and ">256", each with 3099, 2444, 954, and 638 users.

Notably, it can be seen that on Yelp, 9.74% of items have a higher number of check-ins (1,517 items out of 15,575), while the same statistic for Gowalla is 6.19% (1,914 items out of 30,943). Accordingly, it should be noted that the popular items constitute a small portion (less than 10%) of the catalog. In addition, in Figs. 1b and 1f, we plot the popular items in the user profiles for both datasets. We see that for Gowalla 4,910 out of 5,628 users (i.e., around 87% of users) have at least 20% unpopular items in their profiles, while this number for Yelp corresponds to 6,116 out of 7,135 users (i.e., about 86%).

4.2 User Profiles and Popularity Bias

Figures 1c and 1g discuss the correlation between the popularity of items in the user profile and the user profile size on both datasets. We can see that the correlation between the number of popular POIs in the user profile over the profile size is positive, where the values of correlation coefficient R are 0.9319 and 0.9355 for Gowalla and Yelp, respectively. It can be understood that increasing the number of items in a user profile extends the probability of finding popular POIs. In contrast, the correlation between the average popularity of POIs over the user profile sizes is negative ($R = -0.082$ for Gowalla and $R = -0.0785$ for Yelp). Thus, users with fewer items included in their profiles prefer to attend more popular POIs.

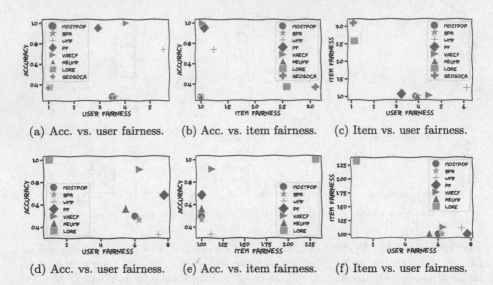

(a) Acc. vs. user fairness.   (b) Acc. vs. item fairness.   (c) Item vs. user fairness.

(d) Acc. vs. user fairness.   (e) Acc. vs. item fairness.   (f) Item vs. user fairness.

Fig. 2. Analysis of trade-off between three factors of accuracy, user fairness and item fairness in recommendation algorithms. The upper row represent the Yelp dataset while the lower row Gowalla. Note that algorithm that stay in the top-right hand corner are the best.

5   Results and Discussion

This section studies active users and popularity bias in state-of-the-art POI recommendation algorithms. To foster the reproducibility of our study, we calculate and evaluate all recommendations with the Python-based open-source recommendation toolkit Cornac[5]. Using Cornac, we formulate our POI recommendations as a top-k recommendation problem, where we recommend a target user a list of POI items, including top-10 POI items with the highest preferences.

We use different types of state-of-the-art algorithms to evaluate and compare, which includes (i) conventional approaches (MostPop, BPR [31], WMF [19], and PF [17]), (ii) neural CF approaches (VAECF [23] and NeuMF [18]), and (iii) contextual-based POI recommendation approaches (i.e., GeoSoCa[6] [36] and LORE [37]).

5.1   Trade-Off on Accuracy, User and Item Fairness (RQ2)

As we observed in Sect. 4, there is a bias in the POI check-ins data from both users' and items' perspectives, i.e., specific POIs are visited frequently while many others are visited by fewer users. On the other hand, some users visits different POIs frequently while most users rarely visit the same POIs. In this section, we analyze whether and how the bias in the data would affect different

---

[5] https://cornac.preferred.ai/.

[6] We evaluate GeoSoCa only on Yelp as we do not have access to the categorical data of the Gowalla dataset.

classes of recommendation models. As can be seen in Fig. 2, we analyzed the relationship between three evaluation objectives, i.e., *accuracy, user fairness*, and *item fairness* with three 2D plots. Hence, each sub-figure (plot) captures two dimensions among three factors. Please note that we use $\frac{1}{MADr}$ to denote fairness (instead of bias), implying that for all dimensions, higher means better. Hence, models that appear on the top-right corner of the plots achieve the best quality of recommendations based on specific evaluation dimensions of each plot (e.g., accuracy vs. user fairness). The following insights can be obtained by analyzing the results generated by different models.

The majority of algorithms do not reside in the top-right corner of the plots, implying the existence of a trade-off between the accuracy and fairness of recommendation models. For instance, although LORE is the best model in terms of accuracy and item fairness (see LORE on the top-right corner in Fig. 2e), it results in poor performance on the user fairness, as for both Fig. 2d and Fig. 2f, LORE resides on the top-left side (i.e., low user fairness). This indicates that LORE sacrifice user fairness to achieve a good level of item fairness and accuracy. We will discuss this in detail in the following sections based on the results in Table 2. On the other hand, from Fig. 2a we can see that WMF and VAECF achieve comparable performance on both accuracy and user fairness, but they suffer seriously from item fairness issues (see Figs. 2a and 2b). These results show that it is hard to achieve a significant accuracy with both user and item fairness, and models usually sacrifice one dimension. For example, in our results, we have seen LORE and WMF achieve the best result on accuracy and items fairness and accuracy and user fairness, respectively. However, neither model could produce satisfactory results on one dimension (LORE on user fairness and WMF on item fairness).

A plausible explanation for this trade-off between different evaluation objectives is data biases. For instance, in Fig. 1 it was shown that (active) users tend to use popular items; thus models such as LORE that achieve significant item fairness recommend the most popular items in their recommendation list. While these models are suitable for active users, they hurt other user groups' experience of recommendations measured in terms of accuracy.

5.2 Popularity Bias in POI Recommendation (RQ3)

A comparison between recommender algorithms can be made by comparing the accuracy measured by NDCG, user fairness, and item fairness values in Table 2. We utilized two metrics in measuring fairness, GCE and MADr. In addition, we computed the area-under-curve (AUC) for the 2D plots shown in Fig. 2. Due to space constraints, we only show results of models computed based on NDCG@10.[7] Note that the largest NDCG corresponds to the most accurate system, while the lower GCE (in an absolute sense) corresponds to the fairest system (for equal distribution GCE = 0). While GCE can tell toward which group the system is providing the highest quality of recommendation or all groups receive

---

[7] The results of other models and metrics are available at https://recsys-lab.github.io/FairPOI/.

Table 2. Accuracy, user fairness, item fairness on Gowalla and Yelp dataset. Note that $Pf_0 = [0.25, 0.25, 0.25, 0.25]$, $Pf_1 = [0.7, 0.1, 0.1, 0.1]$, $Pf_2 = [0.1, 0.7, 0.1, 0.1]$, $Pf_3 = [0.1, 0.1, 0.7, 0.1]$, and $Pf_4 = [0.1, 0.1, 0.1, 0.7]$ characterize the fair distribution as uniform or non-uniform distribution (of resources) among four user groups, i.e., very inactive, slightly inactive, slightly active, very active. Also, $Pf_0 = [0.33, 0.33, 0.33]$, $Pf_1 = [0.7, 0.15, 0.15]$, $Pf_2 = [0.15, 0.7, 0.15]$, and $Pf_3 = [0.15, 0.15, 0.7]$ characterize the fair distribution as uniform or non-uniform distribution (of resources) among item groups, i.e., short-head, mid-tail, and long-tail. AUC represents the area under-curve for any of the evaluation objectives (accuracy, user fairness and item fairness).

Model	Acc	User Fairness						Item Fairness					AUC		
	NDCG	Pf_0	Pf_1	Pf_2	Pf_3	Pf_4	1/MADr	Pf_0	Pf_1	Pf_2	Pf_3	1/MADr	AUC_{au}	AUC_{ai}	AUC_{ui}
						Gowalla									
MostPop	0.0247	-0.0246	-0.6051	-0.6039	-0.6145	-0.2985	6.0141	-1	-0.2143	-2.8333	-2.8333	1.0	1.497	0.248	3.007
BPR	0.0231	-0.0255	-0.6032	-0.6135	-0.6161	-0.2958	6.2659	-1	-0.2143	-2.8333	-2.8333	1.0	1.459	0.232	3.132
WMF	0.0166	-0.0228	-0.3478	-0.4917	-0.6218	-0.6461	7.44	-0.7339	-0.112	-2.2175	-2.2419	1.1108	1.245	0.185	**4.132**
PF	0.034	-0.005	-0.4279	-0.5023	-0.5702	-0.4674	**7.7823**	-0.9928	-0.210	-2.8174	-2.8174	1.0024	2.667	0.343	3.900
VAECF	0.0454	-0.0041	-0.4205	-0.5052	-0.5559	-0.4795	6.3031	-0.7453	-0.108	-2.2532	-2.2664	1.1244	**2.884**	0.514	3.543
NeuMF	0.0279	-0.0226	-0.5952	-0.5943	-0.6107	-0.3057	5.4689	-1	-0.2143	-2.8333	-2.8333	1.0	1.538	0.281	2.734
LORE	**0.0496**	-0.1626	-1.0985	-1.0541	-0.8962	-0.157	1.0	-0.1682	-0.0248	-0.9053	-0.858	**2.3196**	0.5	**1.159**	1.159
						Yelp									
MostPop	0.0097	-0.1514	-1.0666	-1.0083	-0.8917	-0.1512	3.887	-1	-0.2143	-2.8333	-2.8333	1.0	0.488	0.138	1.943
BPR	0.009	-0.1647	-1.1049	-1.0495	-0.9236	-0.145	3.962	-1	-0.2143	-2.8333	-2.8333	1.0	0.497	0.138	1.981
WMF	0.0204	-0.0196	-0.6222	-0.6047	-0.5197	-0.3359	**6.119**	-0.5656	-0.0626	-1.8147	-1.8661	1.245	**2.049**	0.459	**3.810**
PF	0.0327	-0.0294	-0.6497	-0.644	-0.5711	-0.2949	3.241	-0.8386	-0.1436	-2.4688	-2.4746	1.069	1.400	0.509	1.733
VAECF	**0.0334**	-0.0166	-0.5794	-0.5982	-0.5494	-0.3322	4.468	-0.9292	-0.1815	-2.6753	-2.676	1.031	2.027	0.515	2.304
NeuMF	0.0086	-0.1671	-1.1196	-1.058	-0.8992	-0.1646	3.943	-1	-0.2143	-2.8333	-2.8333	1.0	0.495	0.138	1.971
GeoSoCa	0.0197	-0.2782	-1.4354	-1.3774	-1.084	-0.2174	1.101	-0.1009	-0.0574	-0.6934	-0.7062	**3.096**	0.184	**0.571**	1.706
LORE	0.0197	-0.2583	-1.385	-1.3258	-0.9952	-0.2519	1.148	-0.1368	-0.0374	-0.8192	-0.7769	2.580	0.194	0.480	1.481

relatively similar quality (i.e., fair recommendation), MADr can only demonstrate the latter. We compute the AUC according to Fig. 2 for each three relevant factors on both datasets. We use **bold** and underline to show the best and second best results in NDCG, $\frac{1}{MADr}$, and AUCs. Also, we use the blue color to highlight each recommendation model provides the best quality of recommendation to different groups of users, i.e., *very inactive*, *slightly inactive*, *slightly active*, and *very active* in user groups and *short-head*, *mid-tail*, and *long-tail* for item groups. For instance, in the user fairness, if the blue color (minimum value of the GCE) occurs under $pf_0 = [0.25, 0.25, 0.25, 0.25]$, the recommendation model produces a fair recommendation, while if this happens under $pf_1 = [0.7, 0.1, 0.1, 0.1]$ the algorithm is providing better quality to very inactive users. Thus, we can identify the tendency of an algorithm to provide more fair (GCE is minimum under pf_0 and MADr is minimum) or less fair recommendations in favor of/against a particular group of users based on their activity level. By analyzing the results presented in Table 2, the following insights can be identified.

The results on Gowalla and Yelp datasets show different patterns for accuracy and fairness (i.e., users and items). Among all categories of models, the neural approaches (i.e., VAECF and NeuMF) overall achieve the best results among other models on both datasets. For instance, VAECF achieves the best and second-best performance in terms of the accuracy (NDCG) in Yelp and Gowalla datasets respectively. On the other hand, LORE, which is a contextual model, had the best performance on Gowalla, while Yelp's accuracy was not significant. Moreover, VAECF can produce fairest recommendation w.r.t. both user and item fairness. The results on $\frac{1}{MADr}$ on both user and item fairness show that VAECF could perform well in comparison with the best and second-best models. However, the AUCs' results on both Gowalla and Yelp datasets indicate that VAECF is the best and second-best approach on all three relevant factors. These results are proof of the overall performance of VAECF, i.e., while VAECF can achieve significant accuracy, it also can produce an almost fair recommendation based on both consumer and provider sides.

Among the traditional models (i.e., MostPop, BPR, WMF, and PF), the result of BPR is slightly surprising as it very is similar to the MostPop. Our explanation for this observation is that due to the sampling we performed on the dataset for speeding up the experiments as performed in [20], our dataset has been more skewed toward popular items. This can hamper the performance of BPR, which has been shown to be sensitive to popular items [10]. More importantly, although WMF achieves much better results than the MostPop and BPR, in most cases PF has the best performance among the traditional models. This indicate that PF using the Poisson distribution can capture the long-tailed user activity found in most consumption data and model the relation between user and items on implicit feedback (i.e., check-ins) in a better way. This leads to better estimates of users' latent preferences, and therefore superior recommendations, compared to competing methods. However, Yelp tends to produce unfair recommendations for user groups (i.e., GCE minimum under pf_4 under user fairness), while on the Gowalla dataset LORE recommends most popular items that is interesting for active users.

The observation on item fairness shows that all methods have the lowest value of GCE (in absolute sense) under p_{f_1}—i.e., popular items receive higher exposure opportunities. This pattern for the results for item fairness can be verified on both datasets, i.e., Gowalla and Yelp. Thus, we can note a clear unfairness of popularity bias that is introduced in all methods. However, between all models contextual based models (i.e., LORE and GeoSoCa) overall improve item fairness (i.e., maximum $\frac{1}{MADr}$) on both datasets. This indicates that the impact of contextual influence on POI recommendation can provide diversity of items in the recommendation lists.

6   Conclusion and Future Work

It is crucial to avoid potential data or algorithmic bias, respecting the primary task of proposing personalized recommendations in POI. We analyzed the trade-off between accuracy, active users, and popular item exposures fairness where advantaged and disadvantaged user and item groups are determined based on the interactions. Experimental results show that numerous methods failed to balance the item and user fairness due to the natural biases in data. Among 8 POI recommendation models (of different types traditional CF, neural, and contextual), only VAECF produces the best level of accuracy, user fairness, and item fairness. Essentially this shows that VAECF is learning the underlying user-item representation accurately and in the least unbiased way. This result is interesting and confirms the results reported in [8], where between all neural models, only VAECF learns the best underlying representation over the complex non-neural models. Our analysis confirmed this performance also on fairness dimensions. Also, there is variability across algorithms' performances across two datasets. Usually, one aspect, item fairness or user fairness, is compromised to keep the accuracy high. Moreover, we observe that a primary challenge many models face is the unfairness of popularity bias. As for future work, we plan to extend our experiments on more datasets from different domains (e.g., marking in e-commerce [34], media-streaming, e-fashion [13]) and models such as session-based [28], neural [8] and content-based systems [15]. Investigating the different type of bias, such as gender bias, can be a potential direction for future research. Moreover, proposing a single metric that can serve for the evaluation of all these dimensions for a given recommendation algorithm is useful to provide a way to directly compare different recommendation methods considering various types of biases without complicated analysis. We also plan to study approaches that can mitigate two-side fairness while producing accurate recommendations. We also deem the study of multi-sided fairness from a security perceptive an interesting open direction [12,14]. Finally, we plan to examine the impact of data characteristics [11,32] and hyper-parameter tuning on all the above-reported dimensions.

References

1. Abdollahpouri, H., Burke, R., Mobasher, B.: Managing popularity bias in recommender systems with personalized re-ranking. In: The Thirty-Second International Flairs Conference (2019)
2. Abdollahpouri, H., Mansoury, M., Burke, R., Mobasher, B.: The unfairness of popularity bias in recommendation. arXiv preprint arXiv:1907.13286 (2019)
3. Abdollahpouri, H., Mansoury, M., Burke, R., Mobasher, B., Malthouse, E.: User-centered evaluation of popularity bias in recommender systems. In: Proceedings of the 29th ACM Conference on User Modeling, Adaptation and Personalization, pp. 119–129 (2021)
4. Baral, R., Li, T.: Exploiting the roles of aspects in personalized poi recommender systems. Data Min. Knowl. Disc. **32**(2), 320–343 (2018)
5. Boratto, L., Fenu, G., Marras, M., Medda, G.: Consumer fairness in recommender systems: Contextualizing definitions and mitigations. arXiv preprint arXiv:2201.08614 (2022)
6. Burke, R.: Multisided fairness for recommendation. arXiv preprint arXiv:1707.00093 (2017)
7. Chen, J., Dong, H., Wang, X., Feng, F., Wang, M., He, X.: Bias and debias in recommender system: a survey and future directions. arXiv preprint arXiv:2010.03240 (2020)
8. Dacrema, M.F., Cremonesi, P., Jannach, D.: Are we really making much progress? A worrying analysis of recent neural recommendation approaches. In: Proceedings of the 13th ACM Conference on Recommender Systems, pp. 101–109 (2019)

9. Deldjoo, Y., Anelli, V.W., Zamani, H., Bellogin, A., Di Noia, T.: A flexible framework for evaluating user and item fairness in recommender systems. User Model. User-Adapted Interact. **31**, 1–55 (2021)
10. Deldjoo, Y., Bellogin, A., Di Noia, T.: Explaining recommender systems fairness and accuracy through the lens of data characteristics. Inf. Process. Manag. **58**(5), 102662 (2021)
11. Deldjoo, Y., Di Noia, T., Di Sciascio, E., Merra, F.A.: How dataset characteristics affect the robustness of collaborative recommendation models. In: Proceedings of the 43rd International ACM SIGIR Conference on Research and Development in Information Retrieval, pp. 951–960 (2020)
12. Deldjoo, Y., Di Noia, T., Merra, F.A.: Adversarial machine learning in recommender systems (AML-RecSys). In: Proceedings of the 13th International Conference on Web Search and Data Mining, pp. 869–872 (2020)
13. Deldjoo, Y., et al.: A review of modern fashion recommender systems. arXiv preprint arXiv:2202.02757 (2022)
14. Deldjoo, Y., Noia, T.D., Merra, F.A.: A survey on adversarial recommender systems: from attack/defense strategies to generative adversarial networks. ACM Comput. Surv. (CSUR) **54**(2), 1–38 (2021)
15. Deldjoo, Y., Schedl, M., Cremonesi, P., Pasi, G.: Content-based multimedia recommendation systems: definition and application domains. In: Proceedings of the 9th Italian Information Retrieval Workshop (2018)
16. Gómez, E., Boratto, L., Salamó, M.: Provider fairness across continents in collaborative recommender systems. Inf. Process. Manag. **59**(1), 102719 (2022)
17. Gopalan, P., Hofman, J.M., Blei, D.M.: Scalable recommendation with hierarchical poisson factorization. In: Proceedings of the Thirty-First Conference on Uncertainty in Artificial Intelligence, pp. 326–335 (2015)
18. He, X., Liao, L., Zhang, H., Nie, L., Hu, X., Chua, T.S.: Neural collaborative filtering. In: Proceedings of the 26th International Conference on World Wide Web, Perth, Australia, pp. 173–182. ACM (2017)
19. Hu, Y., Koren, Y., Volinsky, C.: Collaborative filtering for implicit feedback datasets. In: 2008 Eighth IEEE International Conference on Data Mining, pp. 263–272. IEEE (2008)
20. Kowald, D., Schedl, M., Lex, E.: The unfairness of popularity bias in music recommendation: a reproducibility study. In: Jose, J.M., et al. (eds.) ECIR 2020. LNCS, vol. 12036, pp. 35–42. Springer, Cham (2020). https://doi.org/10.1007/978-3-030-45442-5_5
21. Lesota, O., et al.: Analyzing item popularity bias of music recommender systems: are different genders equally affected? In: Fifteenth ACM Conference on Recommender Systems, pp. 601–606 (2021)
22. Li, Y., Chen, H., Fu, Z., Ge, Y., Zhang, Y.: User-oriented fairness in recommendation. In: Proceedings of the Web Conference 2021, pp. 624–632 (2021)
23. Liang, D., Krishnan, R.G., Hoffman, M.D., Jebara, T.: Variational autoencoders for collaborative filtering. In: Proceedings of the 2018 World Wide Web Conference, pp. 689–698 (2018)
24. Liu, Y., Pham, T.A.N., Cong, G., Yuan, Q.: An experimental evaluation of point-of-interest recommendation in location-based social networks. Proc. VLDB Endow. **10**(10), 1010–1021 (2017)
25. Mehrabi, N., Morstatter, F., Saxena, N., Lerman, K., Galstyan, A.: A survey on bias and fairness in machine learning. ACM Comput. Surv. (CSUR) **54**(6), 1–35 (2021)

26. Mehrotra, R., McInerney, J., Bouchard, H., Lalmas, M., Diaz, F.: Towards a fair marketplace: Counterfactual evaluation of the trade-off between relevance, fairness & satisfaction in recommendation systems. In: Proceedings of the 27th ACM International Conference on Information and Knowledge Management, pp. 2243–2251 (2018)

27. Olteanu, A., et al.: FACTS-IR: fairness, accountability, confidentiality, transparency, and safety in information retrieval. In: ACM SIGIR Forum, vol. 53, pp. 20–43. ACM, New York (2021)

28. Quadrana, M., Karatzoglou, A., Hidasi, B., Cremonesi, P.: Personalizing session-based recommendations with hierarchical recurrent neural networks. In: Proceedings of the Eleventh ACM Conference on Recommender Systems, pp. 130–137 (2017)

29. Rahmani, H.A., Aliannejadi, M., Ahmadian, S., Baratchi, M., Afsharchi, M., Crestani, F.: LGLMF: local geographical based logistic matrix factorization model for POI recommendation. In: Wang, F.L., et al. (eds.) AIRS 2019. LNCS, vol. 12004, pp. 66–78. Springer, Cham (2020). https://doi.org/10.1007/978-3-030-42835-8_7

30. Rahmani, H.A., Aliannejadi, M., Baratchi, M., Crestani, F.: Joint geographical and temporal modeling based on matrix factorization for point-of-interest recommendation. In: Jose, J.M., et al. (eds.) ECIR 2020. LNCS, vol. 12035, pp. 205–219. Springer, Cham (2020). https://doi.org/10.1007/978-3-030-45439-5_14

31. Rendle, S., Freudenthaler, C., Gantner, Z., Schmidt-Thieme, L.: BPR: Bayesian personalized ranking from implicit feedback. In: Proceedings of the Twenty-Fifth Conference on Uncertainty in Artificial Intelligence, pp. 452–461 (2009)

32. Sachdeva, N., Wu, C.J., McAuley, J.: On sampling collaborative filtering datasets. arXiv preprint arXiv:2201.04768 (2022)

33. Sánchez, P., Bellogín, A.: Point-of-interest recommender systems: a survey from an experimental perspective. arXiv preprint arXiv:2106.10069 (2021)

34. Wan, M., Ni, J., Misra, R., McAuley, J.: Addressing marketing bias in product recommendations. In: Proceedings of the 13th International Conference on Web Search and Data Mining, pp. 618–626 (2020)

35. Weydemann, L., Sacharidis, D., Werthner, H.: Defining and measuring fairness in location recommendations. In: Proceedings of the 3rd ACM SIGSPATIAL International Workshop on Location-Based Recommendations, Geosocial Networks and Geoadvertising, pp. 1–8 (2019)

36. Zhang, J.D., Chow, C.Y.: Geosoca: exploiting geographical, social and categorical correlations for point-of-interest recommendations. In: Proceedings of the 38th International ACM SIGIR Conference on Research and Development in Information Retrieval, Santiago, Chile, pp. 443–452. ACM (2015)

37. Zhang, J.D., Chow, C.Y., Li, Y.: Lore: exploiting sequential influence for location recommendations. In: Proceedings of the 22nd ACM SIGSPATIAL International Conference on Advances in Geographic Information Systems, Dallas Texas, US, pp. 103–112. ACM (2014)

38. Zhang, Y., et al.: Causal intervention for leveraging popularity bias in recommendation. arXiv preprint arXiv:2105.06067 (2021)

The Unfairness of Popularity Bias in Book Recommendation

Mohammadmehdi Naghiaei[1] , Hossein A. Rahmani[2]([✉]) ,
and Mahdi Dehghan[3]

[1] University of Southern California, Los Angeles, USA
naghiaei@usc.edu
[2] University College London, London, UK
h.rahmani@ucl.ac.uk
[3] Shahid Beheshti University, Tajrish, Iran

Abstract. Recent studies have shown that recommendation systems commonly suffer from popularity bias. Popularity bias refers to the problem that popular items (i.e., frequently rated items) are recommended frequently while less popular items are recommended rarely or not at all. Researchers adopted two approaches to examining popularity bias: (i) from the users' perspective, by analyzing how far a recommendation system deviates from user's expectations in receiving popular items, and (ii) by analyzing the amount of exposure that long-tail items receive, measured by overall catalog coverage and novelty. In this paper, we examine the first point of view in the book domain, although the findings may be applied to other domains as well. To this end, we analyze the well-known *Book-Crossing* dataset and define three user groups based on their tendency towards popular items (i.e., Niche, Diverse, Bestseller-focused). Further, we evaluate the performance of nine state-of-the-art recommendation algorithms and two baselines (i.e., Random, MostPop) from both the accuracy (e.g., NDCG, Precision, Recall) and popularity bias perspectives. Our results indicate that most state-of-the-art recommendation algorithms suffer from popularity bias in the book domain, and fail to meet users' expectations with Niche and Diverse tastes despite having a larger profile size. Conversely, Bestseller-focused users are more likely to receive high-quality recommendations, both in terms of fairness and personalization. Furthermore, our study shows a tradeoff between personalization and unfairness of popularity bias in recommendation algorithms for users belonging to the Diverse and Bestseller groups, that is, algorithms with high capability of personalization suffer from the unfairness of popularity bias. Finally, across the models, our results show that WMF and VAECF can provide a higher quality recommendation when considering both accuracy and fairness perspectives.

Keywords: Algorithmic fairness · Recommender systems · Popularity bias · Item popularity · Book recommendation · Reproducibility

ⓒ The Author(s), under exclusive license to Springer Nature Switzerland AG 2022
L. Boratto et al. (Eds.): BIAS 2022, CCIS 1610, pp. 69–81, 2022.
https://doi.org/10.1007/978-3-031-09316-6_7

1   Introduction

Recommender systems have been utilized in various information spaces such as entertainment, education, and online dating. They aim to support users in finding desired information that is typically hard and time-consuming to find without such systems. Recommendation algorithms proposed in the literature can be categorized into multiple groups according to the context of recommendation and how they learn user preference.

Collaborative Filtering (CF) is one of the most widely-investigated classes of algorithms used for recommendation. These algorithms generate recommendations based on explicit or implicit interactions between users and items in the system [19,24] without benefiting from the content information, as opposed to content-based recommendation techniques. Hence, one limitation of CF algorithms is the problem of popularity bias which causes the popular (i.e., short-head) items to be over-emphasized in the recommendation list. In contrast, the majority of less popular (i.e., long-tail) items do not get enough visibility in the recommendation lists. Tackling popularity bias can make the recommender system more applicable in the real world for various reasons [7,8]. A recommender system suffering from popularity bias would result in the market being dominated by a few well-known brands and deprive the discovery of new and unpopular items, which could ignore the interest of users with niche tastes.

Popularity bias has been largely investigated from the item-centered perspective, that is, how frequently popular items appear in recommendation lists. The item-centered perspective study ignores users' interest in popular or less popular items, which causes a limitation as the popularity bias does not affect users equally [3]. Recently, Abdollahpouri et al. [2] have conducted a research study to look at the popularity bias from a different perspective: the users'. To shed light on this topic, suppose a user rated 40 long-tail (less-popular) items and 60 popular items. Therefore, we expect the recommendation algorithm to end up with the same ratio of popular items in the recommended list presented to this user. Despite our expectations, most recommendation algorithms generate a recommendation list including close to 100 popular items. Furthermore, Abdollahpouri et al. [2] evaluate how popularity bias leads to unfair treatment of different user groups according to their interests in popular movies. Their experiments demonstrate that the state-of-the-art recommendation algorithms can not comprehensively understand users who tend to be interested in unpopular items [1].

Popularity biases are known to arise from the underlying characteristics of the data, such as the number of interactions per item or user, sparsity, and an unbalanced distribution of interactions among items. As a result, in this work, we aim to reproduce the research study of Abdollahpouri et al. [2] and conduct it in a different domain and dataset. In particular, we select the book domain and Book-Crossing dataset due to a variety of reasons. First, the Book-Crossing data characteristic differs significantly from the previous study on the MovieLens 1M

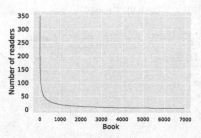 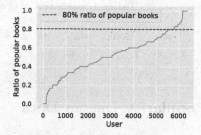

(a) The long-tail of item popularity   (b) The ratio of popular items in users' profiles

Fig. 1. Reading distribution of books.

dataset in that it reports (256.46, 165.59) interactions per item and users respectively, as opposed to (12.79, 13.92) in Book-Crossing dataset. Table 1 summarizes the main data characteristic of Book-Crossing dataset. Additionally, there are several aspects of book recommendations that make them different, challenging, and somehow more important than recommendations entertainment industry, such as movie and music recommendations [5,9]. For instance, although book-reading must become more prevalent in society, the investigation proves the opposite i.e., the practice of reading for pleasure or education is declining, particularly among the young [5]. Also, since a reader spends much time reading books, it is crucial that the content matches their known preferences and expectations. The experience of finding a match that is suitable can be rewarding for readers, but an inappropriate recommendation could result in losing interest, further contributing to the downward trend. It is, therefore, crucial to examine the existence of popularity bias from a user-centered perspective in book recommendations and, for reasons of comparability, we would like to answer the same two research questions as in the study of Abdollahpouri et al. [2]:

- **RQ1**: How much are different individuals or groups of users interested in popular books?
- **RQ2**: How does the popularity bias in recommendation algorithms impact users with different tendencies toward popular books?

In the following, we explore the Book-Crossing dataset characteristics and investigate **RQ1** in Sect. 2. Then, we examine **RQ2** in Sect. 3. We discuss the findings of our study and conclude the paper in Sects. 4 and 5, respectively. Finally, to enable reproducibility of the experiment, we have made our codes open source.[1]

---

[1] https://github.com/rahmanidashti/FairBook.

Table 1. Statistics of the Book-Crossing dataset.

#Users	#Books	#Interactions	$\frac{\#Interactions}{\#Users}$	$\frac{\#Interactions}{\#Books}$	Sparsity
6,358	6,921	88,552	13.92	12.79	99.80%

2 Popularity Bias in Data

In this paper, we utilize the well-known *Book-Crossing*[2] dataset that contains 1,149,780 anonymous explicit and implicit ratings of approximately 340,556 books made by 105,283 users in a 4-week crawl (August - September 2004) [25]. From the dataset, we first removed all the implicit ratings, then we removed users who had fewer than 5 ratings so that the retained users were those who were likely to have rated enough long-tail items. The limit of 5 ratings was also used to remove distant long-tail items. Once short-profile users and distant long-tail items are removed, the Book-Crossing dataset consists of 6,358 users who rated 6,921 books, totaling 88,552 in ratings. In the following, we will address the first research question. Table 1 shows the characteristics of the Book-Crossing datasets.

2.1 Reading Distribution of Books

Figure 1 illustrates the distribution of readings in Book-Crossing dataset. Figure 1a indicates that reading counts of books follow a long-tail distribution as expected. That means a small proportion of books are read by many users, whereas a significant proportion (i.e., the long-tail) is read by only a small number of readers. Additionally, we illustrate in Fig. 1b the ratio of popular books to all books read by users. Same as [2], we sort books based on the number of readers and consider them as popular if they are within the top-20% of the sorted list. By this definition, we observe that around 5,256 out of 6,358 users (i.e., around 83% of users) have read at least 20% of unpopular books in their profile.

2.2 User Profile Size and Popularity Bias in Book Data

In Fig. 2 we investigate whether a correlation exists between the size of the user profile and the presence of popular books in the profile. Specifically, in Fig. 2a, we depict the number of popular books in a user's profile over the size of the profile. As could be expected, there is a positive correlation since the more items in a user profile, the greater probability there are popular items in the profile. On the other hand, when plotting the average popularity of books in a user profile over the profile size in Fig. 2b, we observe a negative correlation, which indicates that users having a smaller profile size tend to read books with higher average popularity. Same as [2], we define the popularity of a book as the ratio of users who have read that book.

---

[2] http://www2.informatik.uni-freiburg.de/~cziegler/BX/.

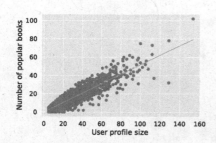
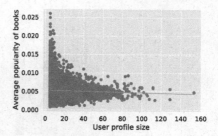
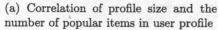

(a) Correlation of profile size and the number of popular items in user profile

(b) Correlation of profile size and the average popularity of items in user profile

Fig. 2. Correlation of user profile size and the popularity of books in the user profile. While there is a positive correlation between profile size and number of popular books, there is a negative correlation between profile size and the average book popularity.

As stated before, in this work, we investigate the popularity bias from the users' perspective, same as [2]. To this end, we categorized all users into three groups according to their profile's ratio of popular items (i.e., book). This ratio indicates how interested they are in popular items.

– **Niche users**: After sorting users based on the ratio of popular items in their profiles, we refer to the bottom 20% of the sorted list as Niche users.
– **Bestseller-focused users**: We consider the top 20% users of the sorted list as Bestseller-focused users interested in popular books.
– **Diverse users**: The rest of the users fall within this category. Users in this category have varied interests in popular and unpopular books.

Figure 3 indicates the average profile size of different user groups. As expected, Diverse users have the largest profile size, followed by Niche users. The Bestseller-focused group has the smallest average profile size. Based on our analysis in Sect. 2.2, diverse users have larger average profile size; therefore, we can expect them to read more popular books than niche users. Furthermore, the small profile size of Bestseller-focused users implies that they are focused on reading solely popular books. Finally, we expect that recommendation algorithms influenced by popularity bias will provide Bestseller-focused users with the best recommendation quality (i.e., accuracy), followed by Diverse users. Furthermore, Niche users are likely to receive the lowest recommendation quality, as they have the lowest ratio of popular items in their profile. We will explore these expectations in the next section.

Hence, in this section, we find that majority of users (i.e., around five-seventh) have read at least 20% of unpopular books. Furthermore, we find that users with a small profile size tend to read more popular books than users having a larger profile size. To sum up, we investigated **RQ1** in this section and our findings are in agreement with what Abdollahpouri et al. have reported in [2].

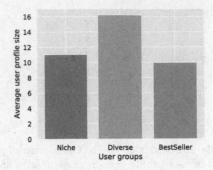

Fig. 3. The average profile size in different user groups

3   Popularity Bias in Book Recommendation

In this section, we study popularity bias in state-of-the-art book recommendation algorithms. In order to foster the reproducibility of this study, we implement and evaluate all recommendation algorithms using Cornac[3], which is a Python-based open source recommendation framework [21,22]. Therefore, we formulate the book recommendation using Cornac as a rating prediction problem, where we predict the preference of a target user u for a target book b. Then, we recommend the top-10 books with the highest predicted preferences.

For ease of comparison, we use the same evaluation setup used in [2] to evaluate the performance of the recommendation algorithms. To this end, we set aside 80% of the Book-Crossing dataset as training set and the remaining 20% as the test set. We further extended the prior study of [2] by incorporating a more comprehensive range of state-of-the-art algorithms, including (i) baseline approaches, (ii) K-Nearest Neighbour (KNN) approaches, (iii) Matrix Factorization (MF) approaches, and (iv) Neural Network (NN) approaches. Specifically, we evaluate two baselines approaches, i.e., Random and MostPop. We include the UserKNN [6], which is a KNN-based method. We also evaluate five MF-based approaches, including MF [13], PMF [18], NMF [15], WMF [12], and PF [10]. We also consider BPR [20] as one of the well-know ranking-based algorithms. Eventually, we include two state-of-the-art NN-based approaches, i.e., NeuMF [11] and VAECF [16]. We adopt the recommendation algorithm with the default hyperparameter settings suggested in their original paper.

3.1   Recommendation of Popular Books

As shown in our analysis in Sect. 2, there is an imbalanced distribution in the book rating data, i.e., certain books are rated very frequently while the majority of items are rated by only a few users. In this section, we investigate to what

---

[3] https://cornac.preferred.ai/.

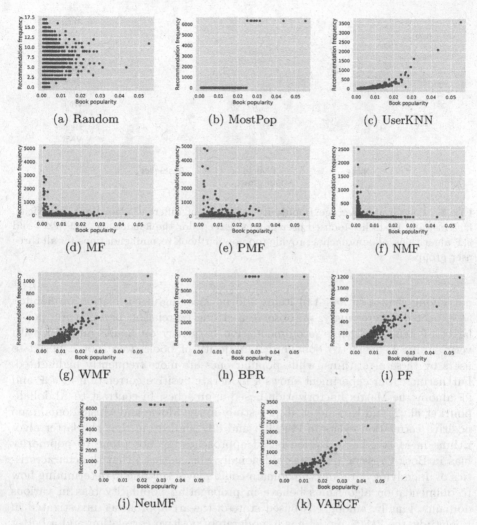

Fig. 4. The correlation between the popularity score of items and the number of times they are being recommended using different algorithms

extent different recommendation algorithms propagate this bias into their recommendations. First, we examine algorithms' overall performance without taking into account how they perform for different users or groups of users based on their tendency towards popular items. In Fig. 4, we illustrate the correlation of book popularity and how often the eight algorithms recommend these books. Among baseline algorithms, we are seeing a strong positive correlation on MostPop showing algorithm tendency to recommend popular items frequently

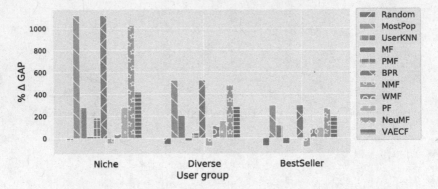

Fig. 5. The Group Average Popularity (ΔGAP) of different algorithms for Niche, Diverse, and Bestseller-focused user groups. Except for the Random, MF, NMF, PMF, and WMF algorithms, all approaches provide too popular book recommendations for all three user groups.

not giving chance to long-tail items and no meaningful correlation on Random as expected. Interestingly, we observe a strong correlation between the popularity of items and their recommendation frequency on NeuMF and BPR with very similar behavior to MostPop. A majority of books were not exposed to users by these algorithms, while popular ones are more frequently highlighted. Furthermore, our experiment shows a moderate positive correlation in WMF and PF among the Matrix Factorization-based approaches. In contrast to Abdollahpouri et al. [2] and Kowald et al. [14] study in the Movie and Music domain, no positive correlation exists in PMF, MF, and NMF, indicating that the latter algorithms in Matrix Factorization-based approaches are not prone to popularity bias in Book-Crossing dataset. Additionally, this suggests that the characteristics of underlying data and the domain could play a key role in determining how recommendation algorithms behave in propagating popularity bias in various domains. Finally, among NN-based state-of-the-art approaches investigated in this study, the VAECF model has a moderately positive correlation and a better performance than the NeuMF model.

3.2 Popularity Bias for Different User Groups

In this section, we investigate the effect of popularity bias on different user groups (i.e., Niche, Diverse, and Bestseller-focused) in book recommendations. To this end, we use *delta Group Average Popularity* (ΔGAP) metric proposed by Abdollahpouri et al. [2] to evaluate the unfairness of popularity bias. We further use *MAE, Precision, Recall,* and *NDCG* to evaluate the performance of recommender algorithms. For each recommendation algorithm and user group, ΔGAP measures the difference between the average popularity of the

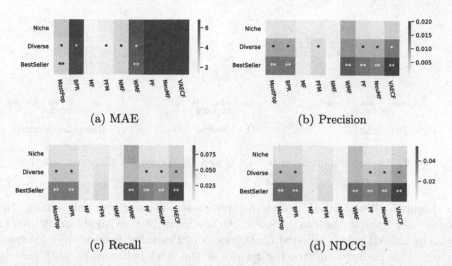

(a) MAE

(b) Precision

(c) Recall

(d) NDCG

Fig. 6. The performance of models for the three user groups in terms of MAE (the lower, the better) and Precision, Recall, and NDCG (the higher, the better). The best results are always given for the **Bestseller-focused** user group (statistically significant according to a t-test with $p < 0.005$ as indicated by **). Across the algorithms, the best results are provided by **VAECF** (indicated by dark blue colour). (Color figure online)

recommended books and the average expected popularity shown in the user's profiles history as follows:

$$\Delta GAP = \frac{GAP(g)_r - GAP(g)_p}{GAP(g)_p} \quad (1)$$

where g is a certain user group (i.e., Niche, Diverse, or Bestseller-focused), $GAP(g)_r$ and $GAP(g)_p$ represent the GAP value for recommendation lists and user profiles, respectively, and it is defined as follows:

$$GAP(g) = \frac{\sum_{u \in g} \frac{\sum_{i \in p_u} \phi(i)}{|p_u|}}{|g|} \quad (2)$$

where $\phi(i)$ is the popularity of item i, which is the number of times it is rated divided by the total number of users, and p_u is the list of items in the profile of user u. The value of $\Delta GAP = 0$ indicates a fair recommendation meaning that the average popularity of recommended books matches the average popularity of the user profile.

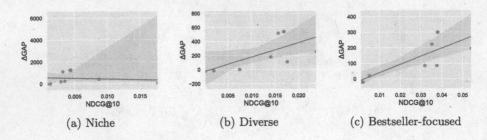

Fig. 7. The correlation between NDCG and ΔGAP for the three user groups.

Figure 5 shows ΔGAP values for recommendation algorithms among the three user groups. As can be seen, Niches users receive significantly higher average ΔGAP values followed by Diverse and Bestseller-focused users, respectively. This finding confirms the results of the Abdollahpouri et al. [2] study and suggests that the popularity bias affects Niche users the most, that is, despite being interested in unpopular items, they receive recommendations of popular items. Interestingly, although the Bestseller-focused group receives the most favorable recommendations, the average ΔGAP is 126.55, revealing how algorithms can propagate the popularity bias even further than the Bestseller-focused user groups' interest in popular items. Figure 5 further illustrates that algorithms investigated in this study show similar behavior in terms of popularity bias among different user groups. Moreover, in line with our analysis in Sect. 3.1, Random, MF, and NMF models provide the fairest recommendations, while MostPop, BPR, and NeuMF suffer from the propagation of popularity bias across all user groups.

Then, to address **RQ2**, we analyze the results of MAE (the lower, the better), Precision, Recall, and NDCG (the higher, the better) of the recommendation algorithms on three users groups. Moreover, we determine the statistically significant differences using the two-tailed paired t-test at a 95% confidence interval ($p < 0.05$). As we see in Fig. 6, the Niche group receives significantly worse recommendations than two other groups (i.e., Diverse and Bestseller-focused), while the Bestseller-focused group gets the best performance. According to this result, algorithms are not capable of detecting the difference in taste between users, even though the average size of user profiles for Niche users is larger than that of the Bestseller-focused group (i.e., more training data), further emphasizing the unfairness of popularity bias. Across the algorithms, we see that WMF and VAECF algorithms provide the highest accuracy in all user groups. Notably, the WMF algorithm displayed the best performance in Niche group when considering both accuracy and fairness.

3.3   Unfairness of Popularity Bias vs. Personalization

The main objective of this part is to explore the potential correlation or trade-off between unfairness of popularity bias and personalization measured by NDCG, between groups of users who have differing preferences for popular items. To this purpose, Fig. 7 shows the correlation plot between NDCG@10 and ΔGAP for three user groups defined in Sect. 2.2 where each point represents the performance of a state-of-the-art recommendation algorithm. Interestingly, we observe an uphill (positive) correlation between NDCG and ΔGAP in the Bestseller-focused and Diverse user groups with the p-value and Pearson's coefficient of (0.01, 0.79) and (0.05, 0.66), respectively. In contrast, we find no meaningful correlation (i.e., p-value of 0.69) between accuracy and unfairness of popularity bias among users with Niche tastes. These results indicate that algorithms with a high accuracy score fall short on popularity bias fairness from the perspective of users with Diverse and Bestseller-focused tastes, prompting further studies on how to incorporate users' taste and expectations in recommendation without sacrificing the overall accuracy.

4 Discussion

In this section, we present a summary of the answers we found to the research questions in Sect. 1.

- **Answer to RQ1**: In line with the previous study of Abdollahpouri et al. [2], our experiments demonstrate that different users have a considerably different tendency towards popular items. Moreover, we discovered that around 83% of users have read at least 20% of unpopular books in their profile and expect to receive some of these items in recommendations. Our result further reveals that users with larger profile sizes who contribute most to the system have diverse tastes and interact with a substantial amount of unpopular items.
- **Answer to RQ2**: Our results for various state-of-the-art recommendation algorithms demonstrate that most algorithms are unfair to users who have a niche or diverse taste in books in terms of popularity, i.e., these users receive recommendations that have lower accuracy and mainly consist of popular books. In addition, the study shows popularity bias negatively affects all user groups, even those focusing on bestsellers, but the magnitude of this effect varies greatly depending on the user group.

5 Conclusion and Future Work

In this paper, we reproduced the study of Abdollahpouri et al. [2] on the unfairness of popularity bias from the user's perspective in the Movie domain, which we have applied to the book domain. Similar to the original paper, we divided all users into three groups (i.e., Niche, Diverse and Bestseller-focused) based on their level of interest in popular items. Our results on various state-of-the-art recommendation algorithms reveal that the most widely adopted algorithms fail to capture users' interest in unpopular items and recommend mostly popular items. Notably, the quality of recommendations received by users with a Diverse or Niche taste is significantly lower than that of users with Bestsellers taste, despite having a large profile size. Moreover, our experiments led to new observations and possible directions for future research. First, we noticed that algorithms could differ significantly in their ability to capture users' tastes based on the domain. For instance, the NMF algorithm suffers from the unfairness of popularity bias in the music domain [14] while offering an entirely fair recommendation in Book-Crossing dataset. A future research direction that would be interesting is identifying the underlying reason for the variance, in particular, which feature of the data (e.g., sparsity, average user interaction) plays the primary role in propagating the popularity bias. Additionally, our results suggest that an underlying tradeoff exists between personalization and fairness of popularity bias in Diverse and Bestseller-focused groups, that is, algorithms with high personalization abilities tend to experience fairness issues. Thus, further research could be worthwhile into implementing a recommendation algorithm that can find the optimal tradeoff between personalization and the unfairness of popularity biases to enhance the system's overall effectiveness. Finally, it would be interesting to investigate popularity bias on other domains and algorithms such as session-based [23], content-based [17], or reinforcement learning-based recommendation [4] methods, as well as incorporating further evaluation metrics such as novelty and coverage.

Reproducibility. To enable reproducibility of the results, we provide our dataset, source codes with all used parameter settings, and more experimental results and analysis on our webpage: https://rahmanidashti.github.io/FairBook/.

References

1. Abdollahpouri, H., Burke, R., Mobasher, B.: Managing popularity bias in recommender systems with personalized re-ranking. In: The Thirty-Second International Flairs Conference (2019)
2. Abdollahpouri, H., Mansoury, M., Burke, R., Mobasher, B.: The unfairness of popularity bias in recommendation. arXiv preprint arXiv:1907.13286 (2019)
3. Abdollahpouri, H., Mansoury, M., Burke, R., Mobasher, B., Malthouse, E.: User-centered evaluation of popularity bias in recommender systems. In: Proceedings of the 29th ACM Conference on User Modeling, Adaptation and Personalization, pp. 119–129 (2021)
4. Afsar, M.M., Crump, T., Far, B.: Reinforcement learning based recommender systems: a survey. arXiv preprint arXiv:2101.06286 (2021)
5. Alharthi, H., Inkpen, D., Szpakowicz, S.: A survey of book recommender systems. J. Intell. Inf. Syst. **51**(1), 139–160 (2017). https://doi.org/10.1007/s10844-017-0489-9
6. Breese, J.S., Heckerman, D., Kadie, C.: Empirical analysis of predictive algorithms for collaborative filtering. arXiv preprint arXiv:1301.7363 (2013)
7. Celma, Ò., Cano, P.: From hits to niches? Or how popular artists can bias music recommendation and discovery. In: Proceedings of the 2nd KDD Workshop on Large-Scale Recommender Systems and the Netflix Prize Competition, pp. 1–8 (2008)
8. Ciampaglia, G.L., Nematzadeh, A., Menczer, F., Flammini, A.: How algorithmic popularity bias hinders or promotes quality. Sci. Rep. **8**(1), 1–7 (2018)

9. Deldjoo, Y., Bellogin, A., Di Noia, T.: Explaining recommender systems fairness and accuracy through the lens of data characteristics. Inf. Process. Manag. **58**(5), 102662 (2021)
10. Gopalan, P., Hofman, J.M., Blei, D.M.: Scalable recommendation with hierarchical poisson factorization. In: Proceedings of the Thirty-First Conference on Uncertainty in Artificial Intelligence, pp. 326–335 (2015)
11. He, X., Liao, L., Zhang, H., Nie, L., Hu, X., Chua, T.S.: Neural collaborative filtering. In: Proceedings of the 26th International Conference on World Wide Web, Perth, Australia, pp. 173–182. ACM (2017)
12. Hu, Y., Koren, Y., Volinsky, C.: Collaborative filtering for implicit feedback datasets. In: 2008 Eighth IEEE International Conference on Data Mining, pp. 263–272. IEEE (2008)
13. Koren, Y., Bell, R., Volinsky, C.: Matrix factorization techniques for recommender systems. Computer **42**(8), 30–37 (2009)
14. Kowald, D., Schedl, M., Lex, E.: The unfairness of popularity bias in music recommendation: a reproducibility study. In: Jose, J.M., et al. (eds.) ECIR 2020. LNCS, vol. 12036, pp. 35–42. Springer, Cham (2020). https://doi.org/10.1007/978-3-030-45442-5_5
15. Lee, D.D., Seung, H.S.: Algorithms for non-negative matrix factorization. In: Proceedings of the 13th International Conference on Neural Information Processing Systems, NIPS 2000, pp. 535–541. MIT Press, Cambridge (2000)
16. Liang, D., Krishnan, R.G., Hoffman, M.D., Jebara, T.: Variational autoencoders for collaborative filtering. In: Proceedings of the 2018 World Wide Web Conference, pp. 689–698 (2018)
17. Lops, P., Gemmis, M.D., Semeraro, G.: Content-based recommender systems: state of the art and trends. In: Recommender Systems Handbook, pp. 73–105 (2011)
18. Mnih, A., Salakhutdinov, R.R.: Probabilistic matrix factorization. In: Advances in Neural Information Processing Systems, pp. 1257–1264 (2008)
19. Rahmani, H.A., Aliannejadi, M., Baratchi, M., Crestani, F.: Joint geographical and temporal modeling based on matrix factorization for point-of-interest recommendation. In: Jose, J.M., et al. (eds.) ECIR 2020. LNCS, vol. 12035, pp. 205–219. Springer, Cham (2020). https://doi.org/10.1007/978-3-030-45439-5_14
20. Rendle, S., Freudenthaler, C., Gantner, Z., Schmidt-Thieme, L.: BPR: Bayesian personalized ranking from implicit feedback. In: Proceedings of the Twenty-Fifth Conference on Uncertainty in Artificial Intelligence, pp. 452–461 (2009)
21. Salah, A., Truong, Q.T., Lauw, H.W.: Cornac: a comparative framework for multimodal recommender systems. J. Mach. Learn. Res. **21**(95), 1–5 (2020)
22. Truong, Q.T., Salah, A., Tran, T.B., Guo, J., Lauw, H.W.: Exploring cross-modality utilization in recommender systems. IEEE Internet Comput. **25**(4), 50–57 (2021)
23. Wang, S., Cao, L., Wang, Y., Sheng, Q.Z., Orgun, M.A., Lian, D.: A survey on session-based recommender systems. ACM Comput. Surv. (CSUR) **54**(7), 1–38 (2021)
24. Zhang, S., Yao, L., Sun, A., Tay, Y.: Deep learning based recommender system: a survey and new perspectives. ACM Comput. Surv. (CSUR) **52**(1), 1–38 (2019)
25. Ziegler, C.N., McNee, S.M., Konstan, J.A., Lausen, G.: Improving recommendation lists through topic diversification. In: Proceedings of the 14th International Conference on World Wide Web, pp. 22–32 (2005)

Mitigating Popularity Bias in Recommendation: Potential and Limits of Calibration Approaches

Anastasiia Klimashevskaia[1]([✉]), Mehdi Elahi[1], Dietmar Jannach[2],
Christoph Trattner[1], and Lars Skjærven[3]

[1] University of Bergen, Bergen, Norway
`{anastasiia.klimashevskaia,mehdi.elahi,christoph.trattner}@uib.no`
[2] University of Klagenfurt, Klagenfurt, Austria
`dietmar.jannach@aau.at`
[3] TV 2, Bergen, Norway
`lars.skjerven@tv2.no`

Abstract. While recommender systems are highly successful at helping users find relevant information online, they may also exhibit a certain undesired bias of mostly promoting only already popular items. Various approaches of quantifying and mitigating such biases were put forward in the literature. Most recently, *calibration* methods were proposed that aim to match the popularity of the recommended items with popularity preferences of individual users. In this paper, we show that while such methods are efficient in avoiding the recommendation of too popular items for some users, other techniques may be more effective in reducing the popularity bias on the platform level. Overall, our work highlights that in practice choices regarding metrics and algorithms have to be made with caution to ensure the desired effects.

Keywords: Recommender Systems · Bias · Multi-Metric Evaluation

1 Introduction and Background

The value of recommender systems, e.g., on e-commerce or media streaming sites—both for consumers and providers—is undisputed [12]. Yet, such systems may sometimes lead to the undesired effect that they mainly promote already popular items [9,10]. A strong *popularity bias* of underlying algorithms may lead to limited exposure of long-tail items through the recommendations and, ultimately, to limited discovery effects and missed sales or engagement opportunities [22].

Various algorithmic approaches were proposed in the literature to deal with such a bias [1,4,5]. Usually, this mitigation process involves handling a trade-off between predicted item relevance (accuracy) and item popularity. Other strategies are possible as well, including re-ranking of an accuracy-optimized list, introducing popularity aspects in the loss function or when sampling data during learning [6,13,21]. An important question in this context is how the popularity

L. Boratto et al. (Eds.): BIAS 2022, CCIS 1610, pp. 82–90, 2022.
https://doi.org/10.1007/978-3-031-09316-6_8

bias of an algorithm is quantified, i.e., which metrics are used. One commonly applied approach is to generate top-n recommendation lists for each user, and to then determine average popularity of the items in these lists [13].

Such an approach allows us to quantify the popularity bias on a *platform level*, i.e., across all users. Boratto et al. [3], for instance, studied different algorithms in the course recommendation domain, analyzing how certain techniques can amplify or mitigate biases within the system. Later, Kowald et al. [15] performed similar studies within the music domain.

In recent years, alternative approaches have been receiving more attention, which deal with biases on an *individual level*. The idea of such *calibration* approaches [14,19] is to create recommendation lists which match the individual user's past preference profile in terms of the distribution of certain item properties, e.g. item type, genre or popularity. Practically, the goal is therefore often to minimize the distance between two distributions, quantified, e.g., through the Kullback-Leibler divergence. In a recent work [2], Abdollahpouri et al. proposed and investigated the effectiveness of a particular user-specific approach named Calibrated Popularity (CP) for the mitigation of popularity biases.

Their proposed re-ranking technique aims to minimize the distance between two probability distributions, named UPD (User Popularity Deviation), as done earlier in [14,17,19]. As a main outcome of their experiments, the authors found that their method is not only effective in considering individual user tendencies, as expected by design, but may also help to improve existing metrics on the platform level.

The work in this paper is based on the needs of an industrial partner, the Norwegian broadcaster TV 2, who observed a significant popularity bias in their current recommendations [8]. One specific goal of the partner is thus to investigate the effectiveness of current popularity bias mitigation strategies. In this work, we present the results of such an analysis based both on a proprietary dataset from TV 2 and on a publicly available movie ratings dataset MovieLens. Going beyond existing works, we consider a selection of six "beyond-accuracy" metrics in our experiments to obtain a more fine-grained picture of the effects of three bias mitigation strategies. Moreover, like in [2], we consider mitigation re-ranking strategies of different types, including the recent CP approach.

In our analysis we could reproduce the findings from [2] regarding the effectiveness of CP with respect to the UPD criterion also for our additional dataset. However, it turns out that other methods are more effective when it comes to reducing the popularity bias on the *platform* level. From the perspective of a practitioner, the choice of the mitigation strategy should therefore be informed by the relative importance of the intended effects, i.e., if it is more important to match past consumer preference distributions or to increase the exposure of long-tail items. While the ultimate effects of the explored mitigation strategies on relevant Key Performance Indicators of TV 2 can only be determined through a field test, the offline analyses in this paper may serve as a basis for informing the choice of algorithms to be included in ongoing and future A/B tests at TV 2.

2   Research Methodology

To investigate the effectiveness of different bias mitigation strategies with respect to accuracy and popularity-related metrics, we ran extensive computational experiments. We describe the details of our experimental design in terms of considered algorithms, metrics, and datasets next.

2.1   Baseline Algorithms and Re-ranking Algorithms

Baseline Methods. In our study, we focus on re-ranking (post-processing) strategies for popularity bias mitigation, which take an accuracy-optimized list as a starting point. To generate this starting point, we use the ALS (Alternating Least Squares) method [20] for two main reasons. First, a version of this method is used by the industry partner as one of the techniques in their production systems. Second, ALS was also used as a baseline in [2]. We have systematically tuned the hyper-parameters of ALS for both datasets individually using grid search.

Besides ALS, we consider a simple and non-personalized popularity-based method for comparison in our study. This method, which we refer to as *Pop*, gives us an upper-bound in terms of some of the considered metrics.

Bias Mitigation Methods. In accordance with the objectives of the industry partner, we focus only on re-ranking (post-processing) methods in this study, leaving out the model-based ones. We have reused or re-implemented the following algorithms that were considered in [2]:

- **Calibrated Popularity [CP]**: This is the main method proposed in [2]. This calibration-based algorithm[1] personalizes the recommendations in terms of popularity of the recommended items, considering the previous preference history of every user separately. The algorithm differentiates between head, middle and (long) tail items.
- **Personalized Long Tail Promotion [XQ]**: This approach, originally proposed in [1], is based on the xQuAD algorithm [18] from IR. XQ aims to balance the proportion of head and tail items in recommendation lists by leveraging the user propensity towards popular items. Only two categories of items are distinguished in the method: head and tail items.
- **FA*IR [FS]**: This method, proposed in [24], gives "protected items" from the candidate list more exposure. In this particular case the protected group is represented by the tail items.

Definition of Item Popularity Groups. A common practice in the literature—and for the considered methods—is to split the items into different groups according to their level of popularity. Besides distinguishing between head and tail items, some works further split the tail items into the sub-groups, i.e., *middle* and

---

[1] Similar ideas were proposed earlier in [14] and [17], and later independently popularized under the term *calibration* in [19].

distant tail items [2]. In this work, we follow this latter approach, which allows us to focus on specific subgroups of items when conducting our analyses. For that, we first sort all items in descending order of their popularity, where we use the number of interactions per item in the data as a popularity indicator. Then we compute the sum of the corresponding (normalized) item popularity scores as *total_pop*. To create the set of *head* items, we add items from the top of the popularity sorted list until the sum of popularity scores in *head* reaches 20% of *total_pop*. Then, items from the end of the popularity-sorted list are added to the *tail* set until the set of tail items reaches 20% of *total_pop*. The remaining items then form the *middle* set of items.

2.2   Metrics

In the research literature, different metrics for quantifying popularity biases have been proposed. Since one goal of our study is to investigate the effects of bias mitigation strategies in a comprehensive way, we consider the following set of metrics:

- **User Popularity Deviation (UPD).** This metric was introduced in [2] as the average popularity deviation across different user groups G:

$$UPD = \frac{\sum_{g \in G} UPD(g)}{|G|}$$

with

$$UPD(g) = \frac{\sum_{u \in g} JSD(P(u), Q(u))}{|g|}$$

calculated for every user group defined in the algorithm. $JSD(P(u), Q(u))$ is the Jensen-Shannon divergence [16], which measures the distance between two probability distributions, wigh $P(u)$ being the popularity distribution of items in the user u profile and $Q(u)$ the popularity distribution in the recommendation list for the user u. See also [2] for more details and illustrative examples.

UPD indicates how well the re-ranking algorithm adjusts the recommendation to the user interest history, matching the distribution of head and tail items. UPD is the optimization goal of the CP method. Like earlier works, who used the Earth Mover's Distance [17] or the Kullback-Leibler divergence, UPD measures the difference between distributions, and lower values therefore mean a better personalization. Increasing UPD, however, does not necessarily lead to a much *lower* popularity on the platform level. Lovers of "blockbuster" movies, for example, would by design still receive many highly-popular movies as recommendations.

- **Average Recommendation Popularity (ARP).** This commonly used metric simply returns the average popularity of the items in the top-n recommendation lists produced by an algorithm for all users. This metric was defined in [23] as follows:

$$ARP = \frac{1}{|U|} \sum_{u \in U} \frac{\sum_{i \in L_u} \phi(i)}{|L_u|}$$

where $\phi(i)$ is the popularity of an item i, i.e., the number of ratings or interactions that are observed for it in the training set, and $L(u)$ is the list of items recommended to user u. This averaging metric should however be interpreted with care, since recommending only a few very unpopular items to everyone can lead to relatively low ARP values.

- **Average Percentage of Long Tail Items (APLT), Average Coverage of Long Tail items (ACLT).** In [1], these metrics are defined as follows:

$$APLT = \frac{1}{|U_t|} \sum_{u \in U_t} \frac{|\{i, i \in (L_u \cap \Gamma)\}|}{|L_u|}$$

$$ACLT = \frac{1}{|U_t|} \sum_{u \in U} \sum_{i \in L_u} 1(i \in \Gamma)$$

where Γ is the set of tail items. These metrics quantify the effect of the reranking with respect to long tail items. The first metric measures the average percentage of tail items in user recommendation lists, while the second one indicates the exposure of the tail items in the entire recommendation.

- **Aggregate Diversity and Gini Index.** In addition to UPD, Abdollahpouri et al. [2] report Aggregate Diversity and the Gini Index of the UPD-optimized recommendations, defining them as follows:

$$AggDiv = \frac{\cup_{u \in U} L_u}{|I|}$$

$$Gini(L) = 1 - \frac{1}{|I| - 1} \sum_{k=1}^{|I|} (2k - |I| - 1) p(i_k|L)$$

where L is the combined list of all the recommendations for all the users in U, and where $p(i|L)$ is the occurrence ratio of item i in L.

Aggregate Diversity informs about how many different items appear in recommendation lists of users, which is thus a form of *Item Coverage*. The Gini Index, in contrast quantifies how uneven the distribution of recommended items is. Higher values mean higher concentration.

Note that Item Coverage and the Gini index are not necessarily tied to popularity aspects. To obtain high Item Coverage, it is sufficient that many items appear at least once in a recommendation list. In terms of the Gini index, an algorithm that only recommends the most unpopular items to everyone would lead to high concentration, but not to a popularity bias. Realistically, however, we expect a higher concentration of short-head items for typical collaborative filtering algorithms. Usually, popularity metrics and measures like the Gini index are also often highly correlated with *novelty* metrics, as these are commonly based on popularity considerations, see [7].

Generally, we iterate that these metrics do not necessarily correlate, i.e., higher aggregate diversity may not necessarily mean a lower level of platform-wide popularity bias, as expressed, for example through the ARP measure. In terms of accuracy measures, we report *Precision* as done in [2] as well, which is also the target of our hyper-parameter optimization process.

2.3 Datasets

We have evaluated the different bias mitigation strategies on two datasets. First, we used a proprietary dataset provided by our industry partner TV 2. Second, like [2], we used a MovieLens dataset [11] to ensure reproducibility on publicly available data.[2] The dataset provided by TV 2 originally consisted of logged movie interaction data on the streaming of the provider. The recorded interactions, e.g., viewing times, were transformed into implicit feedback signals and a user-item interaction matrix by our industry partner. Given this dataset, we performed the same pre-processing steps as described in [2] including, for example, data filtering. The resulting dataset contains about 518K interactions by 9408 users on 1795 items. Since some of the examined algorithms, in particular CP, are computationally demanding, we have resorted to randomly sampling 1000 users for re-ranking and metric calculations. As done in [2] as well, we organized the datasets into an 80% training split and use the remaining 20% for testing.

3 Results

Table 1 shows the results of our evaluation. In terms of *accuracy*, we observe that all re-ranking methods, as expected, led to a small to modest decrease in Precision (about 2.0% to 4% for TV 2 and about 2.5% to 11% for MovieLens).

In terms of *UPD*, the CP method performs much better than the other techniques. Again, this is expected as CP directly aims to optimize for this *user-individual* metric. Looking at *platform-wide* metrics (ARP, APLT, ACLT), however, it turns out XQ leads to the strongest effects in popularity-bias reduction. Compared to the baseline (ALS), the average popularity of the recommended items (ARP), for example, goes down by at least 30%. The effects of the CP method on the ARP (and on the other platform-wide metrics) are, in contrast, much smaller, e.g., about 10% on the TV 2 dataset.[3]

Thus, when the goal is to mitigate platform-wide popularity effects, methods like XQ appear to be a better choice than user-centered calibration effects. In the reported experiments, XQ leads to a slightly stronger accuracy decrease than CP.

---

[2] Differently from [2], we used the MovieLens dataset with about 100k ratings by 943 users on 1612 items of in our experiments.

[3] Interestingly, in [2], CP was favorable over XQ also on the ARP measure. We could not reproduce this finding for both datasets. Unfortunately, the authors of [2] could not reproduce the code of the CP method. The observed discrepancy might therefore be both related to dataset characteristics and differences in the implementation.

Table 1. Evaluation results. Arrows indicate whether lower or higher values are better.

Dataset	Algorithm	Accuracy	Calibration	Long Tail Exposure			Equal Exposure	
		Prec ↑	UPD ↓	ARP ↓	APLT ↑	ACLT ↑	Agg-Div ↑	Gini ↓
TV 2	Pop	0.301	0.644	0.301	0.000	0.000	0.006	0.994
	Base (ALS)	**0.875**	0.286	0.143	0.639	0.292	0.321	0.874
	XQ	0.818	0.358	**0.100**	**0.956**	**0.364**	0.343	0.850
	FS	0.857	0.249	0.126	0.772	0.299	0.328	0.856
	CP	0.837	**0.123**	0.130	0.672	0.314	**0.392**	**0.844**
ML	Pop	0.381	0.629	0.381	0.000	0.000	0.007	0.993
	Base (ALS)	**0.738**	0.261	0.243	0.634	0.391	0.425	0.851
	XQ	0.656	0.378	**0.167**	**0.989**	**0.442**	0.412	0.848
	FS	0.697	0.237	0.202	0.839	0.397	0.432	0.835
	CP	0.720	**0.101**	0.223	0.676	0.408	**0.477**	**0.821**

Depending on the application, XQ can however also be further tuned to focus more on accuracy. Such a tuning was however not the focus of our work.

Looking at the results for the remaining metrics, we find that all the re-ranking methods have at least a slight positive impact on Gini Index, with CP having the strongest effect. For Aggregate Diversity (Agg-Div) the values are mixed and depend on the dataset. Again, CP has the strongest effect across the methods. Remember, however, that Agg-Div and the Gini Index cannot inform us directly if popularity bias issues are successfully reduced.

4 Summary and Future Work

Our work highlights that calibrated recommendations—while being effective for matching the recommendations with past user tendencies—may not be the best possible choice when the goal is to mitigate platform-wide popularity bias effects. Thus, in practice, the choice of the bias mitigation algorithm and the popularity metrics have to be done with care and be dependent on the desired effects. If, for example, the general goal of the platform is to give the tail items more exposure, then the provider may consider XQ method, which performs best in terms of long tail exposure metrics in our study. However, this method should tuned with care, because in our experiments it led to the largest drop in accuracy compared to the other methods. If, on the other hand, the most important feature for the provider is to adjust the popularity distribution of the recommended items to the user's preference, then CP and similar approaches [14, 19] are preferable. Yet, such approaches may not necessarily lead to a strong reduction of platform-wide popularity biases. In an extreme case, where all users are blockbuster lovers, mainly the popular items would receive attention after calibration. Finally, if a provider is uncertain which of the aspects are more important to address, some middle-ground approach, e.g., a hybrid of the evaluated methods, may be adopted to balance the goals of reducing popularity biases at the platform level while considering individual past user popularity tendencies.

Overall, while the experiments reported in this paper lead to some interesting insights, some limitations remain, which we plan to address in our future work. First, we have so far only made experiments in one particular domain, that of movie recommendations. Second, also due to the requirements of the industry partners, only post-processing techniques—as opposed to *model-based* techniques—were investigated so far. Third, it could be intriguing as well to investigate different approaches to head-tail split of the items in the catalogue and how that might affect the outcome of the debiasing techniques application.

In our future work, we will therefore explore different domains and algorithms and furthermore design approaches that are able balance all three mentioned aspects: accuracy, individual-level and platform-wide effects. Moreover, we plan to evaluate the described methods in A/B tests with our industry partner.

Acknowledgement. This work was supported by industry partners and the Research Council of Norway with funding to MediaFutures: Research Centre for Responsible Media Technology and Innovation, through The Centres for Research-based Innovation scheme, project number 309339.

References

1. Abdollahpouri, H., Burke, R., Mobasher, B.: Managing popularity bias in recommender systems with personalized re-ranking. In: FLAIRS 2019, pp. 413–418 (2019)
2. Abdollahpouri, H., Mansoury, M., Burke, R., Mobasher, B., Malthouse, E.: User-centered evaluation of popularity bias in recommender systems. In: ACM UMAP 2021, pp. 119–129 (2021)
3. Boratto, L., Fenu, G., Marras, M.: The effect of algorithmic bias on recommender systems for massive open online courses. In: European Conference on Information Retrieval, pp. 457–472 (2019)
4. Boratto, L., Fenu, G., Marras, M.: Combining mitigation treatments against biases in personalized rankings: use case on item popularity. In: IIR 2021 (2021)
5. Boratto, L., Fenu, G., Marras, M.: Connecting user and item perspectives in popularity debiasing for collaborative recommendation. IP&M **58**(1), 102387 (2021)
6. Borges, R., Stefanidis, K.: On mitigating popularity bias in recommendations via variational autoencoders. In: ACM/SIGAPP SAC 2021, pp. 1383–1389 (2021)
7. Castells, P., Hurley, N.J., Vargas, S.: Novelty and diversity in recommender systems. In: Ricci, F., Rokach, L., Shapira, B. (eds.) Recommender Systems Handbook, pp. 881–918. Springer, New York (2015)
8. Elahi, M., Jannach, D., Skjærven, L., et al.: Towards responsible media recommendation. AI and Ethics (2021)
9. Elahi, M., Kholgh, D.K., Kiarostami, M.S., Saghari, S., Rad, S.P., Tkalcic, M.: Investigating the impact of recommender systems on user-based and item-based popularity bias. Inf. Process. Manage. **58**, 102655 (2021)

10. Fleder, D., Hosanagar, K.: Blockbuster culture's next rise or fall: the impact of recommender systems on sales diversity. Manage. Sci. **55**, 697–712, 102655 (2009)
11. Harper, F.M., Konstan, J.A.: The MovieLens datasets: history and context. ACM TIIS **5**(4), 1–19, 102655 (2015)
12. Jannach, D., Jugovac, M.: Measuring the business value of recommender systems. ACM Trans. Manage. Inf. Syst. **10**(4) (2019)
13. Jannach, D., Lerche, L., Kamehkhosh, I., Jugovac, M.: What recommenders recommend: an analysis of recommendation biases and possible countermeasures. User Model. User-Adap. Inter. **25**(5), 427–491 (2015). https://doi.org/10.1007/s11257-015-9165-3
14. Jugovac, M., Jannach, D., Lerche, L.: Efficient optimization of multiple recommendation quality factors according to individual user tendencies. Expert Syst. Appl. **81**, 321–331 (2017)
15. Kowald, D., Schedl, M., Lex, E.: The unfairness of popularity bias in music recommendation: a reproducibility study. In: European Conference on Information Retrieval, pp. 35–42 (2020)
16. Lin, J.: Divergence measures based on the Shannon entropy. IEEE Trans. Inf. Theory **37**(1), 145–151 (1991)
17. Oh, J., Park, S., Yu, H., Song, M., Park, S.T.: Novel recommendation based on personal popularity tendency. In: ICDM 2011, pp. 507–516 (2011)
18. Santos, R.L., Macdonald, C., Ounis, I.: Exploiting query reformulations for web search result diversification. In: WWW 2010, pp. 881–890 (2010)
19. Steck, H.: Calibrated recommendations. In: ACM RecSys 2018, pp. 154–162 (2018)
20. Takács, G., Tikk, D.: Alternating least squares for personalized ranking. In: ACM RecSys 2012, pp. 83–90 (2012)
21. Trattner, C., Elsweiler, D.: Investigating the healthiness of internet-sourced recipes: implications for meal planning and recommender systems. In: WWW 2017, pp. 489–498 (2017)
22. Trattner, C., et al.: Responsible media technology and AI: challenges and research directions. AI and Ethics, pp. 1–10 (2021)
23. Yin, H., Cui, B., Li, J., Yao, J., Chen, C.: Challenging the long tail recommendation. Proc. VLDB Endow. **5**(9), 896–907 (2012)
24. Zehlike, M., Bonchi, F., Castillo, C., Hajian, S., Megahed, M., Baeza-Yates, R.: FA*IR: a Fair Top-k ranking algorithm. In: CIKM 2017, pp. 1569–1578 (2017)

Analysis of Biases in Calibrated Recommendations

Carlos Rojas[1], David Contreras[1(✉)] ⓘ, and Maria Salamó[2,3] ⓘ

[1] Universidad Arturo Prat, Avenida Arturo Prat, 2120, Iquique, Chile
{carlrojasc,david.contreras}@unap.cl
[2] Dept. de Matemàtiques i Informàtica, Universitat de Barcelona,
Gran Via de les Corts Catalanes, 585, Barcelona, Spain
[3] Institute of Complex Systems (UBICS), Universitat de Barcelona, Barcelona, Spain
maria.salamo@ub.edu

Abstract. While recommender systems have mainly focused on the effectiveness of their results, beyond-accuracy perspectives have been recently explored. One of the most prominent is *algorithmic bias*, which analyzes if existing imbalances in the input data are exacerbated in the produced recommendations. On the other hand, *calibrated recommendations* ensure that the recommendations reflect the distribution of the original preferences of each user (e.g., in terms of item genres). In this paper, we connect these two perspectives, to analyze how the original calibration method deals with the bias in the state-of-the-art recommendation models. Our analysis on real-world data shows that the calibration effectiveness is impacted by how a recommendation model handles bias.

Keywords: Recommender Systems · Calibration · Algorithmic bias

1 Introduction

Recommender Systems help users search a large amount of digital contents and services, thus allowing users to identify the items that are likely to be more attractive and useful [20]. Imbalances in the input data can lead to biases in the results of different recommendation models [5,10]. Concretely, the problem is that in most cases, the recommendations produced by a model differ from the users play history, when considering attributes from the data. These attributes are dependent on the data set and, for example in MovieLens data set, the attribute might be the categories of items (i.e., movie genres). Thus, if a user liked 30% of Romance movies and 70% of Action movies, it is safe to assume that the user would prefer recommendations that follow this ratio of genres.

In recent years, there has been a growing use of calibration techniques for reducing prediction errors in machine learning models [4]. An algorithm is called calibrated if the predicted proportions of the various classes agree with the actual proportions of data points in the available data [25]. Their use is fundamental for high risk applications and sensitive domains, such as medical diagnosis prediction

L. Boratto et al. (Eds.): BIAS 2022, CCIS 1610, pp. 91–103, 2022.
https://doi.org/10.1007/978-3-031-09316-6_9

and criminal justice. Unfortunately, predictive errors in machine learning models could lead to bias and discrimination in these models [3, 7, 8, 22, 23].

It is well known that many recommender systems are based on machine learning models, such as latent factor models, neighborhoods-based models, artificial neural networks, and visual models, among others. Keeping this in mind, a calibration technique can be used to bring the recommendations closer to the user's interaction history (thus producing that are likely to be more effective) and considering the eventual biases that the genre distribution may produce in the input data to the recommendation. The recent work by Steck [25] has motivated the importance of calibration as an additional objective besides recommendation accuracy. The proposed calibration algorithm, tested on a Weighted Regularized Matrix Factorization algorithm, is effective in generating calibrated recommendations that reflect the various interests of each individual user.

Considering that different recommendation models handle data imbalances in different way, thus producing more or less biased results, it becomes natural to ask ourselves *if the original calibration method can be transferred to other recommendation models*. Concretely, if the bias produced by a model is strong (e.g., by recommending only items of certain categories), it might be challenging to produce recommendations that reflect the original distribution of the users' preferences. Hence, in this paper, we analyze to what extent a calibration introduced via post-processing method can be effective when applied to the output of different recommendation models. We believe that an in-depth reflection is needed, to understand the pros and cons of calibrated recommendations by paying attention to the evaluation of varying types of recommendation models. In particular, we focus on the following research questions:

- **RQ1.** How does a calibration algorithm deal with the bias associated with the recommended items' distribution, when considering several recommendation models?
- **RQ2.** Can the calibration algorithm impact the effectiveness of different recommendation models?

To address these research questions, in this paper, we analyze the behavior of the calibration algorithm [25] with several recommendation models, with the aim to detect how calibration is affected by the biases in the recommendation models and assess how calibration affects the accuracy of different recommendations model (i.e., based on neighborhoods and latent factor models).

The rest of the paper is organized as follows: in Sect. 2 we review related work on bias and calibration. We continue in Sect. 3 describing the data set, recommendations models, and calibration metrics used in the experiments. In Sect. 4, we discuss the analysis of the results. Finally, in Sect. 5 we provide concluding remarks and future work.

2   Related Work

This section covers related studies on bias and calibration in recommender systems (RS). Section 2.1 describes studies of bias in recommender systems. Next, in Sect. 2.2 we continue with research focused on the calibration concept.

2.1   Biases in Recommender Systems

Recommendation biases may be present in many of today's content applications, such as Web Search Engines, Youtube, Netflix among others [17,18]. Biases in RS are receiving more and more attention. For instance, the recent survey of Chen *et al.* [12] provides a taxonomy of recommendation biases in both recommendation data and recommendation results, and describe in depth seven types of biases (selection bias, exposure bias, conformity bias, position bias, inductive bias, popularity bias and unfairness). The popularity bias is a typical example of biases in RS, where popular items may be over-recommended while long-tail ones are nearly invisible. Bias in sensitive attributes may produce unfair recommendations, as denoted by Boratto *et al.* [6,8], Gómez *et al.* [13–16], and Abdollahpouri *et al.* [1]. Boratto and Marras also gave tutorials on recent advances on the assessment and mitigation of data and algorithmic bias in RS [9–11].

2.2   Calibration

Nowadays, most of the RS are based on machine learning algorithms, such as the popularity collaborative filtering recommenders [19]. In fact, calibration techniques allow to improve the probability estimation or the error distribution of machine learning models. Bella *et al.* [4] present the most common calibration techniques and calibration metrics in machine learning models. A more specific study of calibration metrics in Deep Learning algorithms is presented in [21]. Zadrozny and Elkan [26] present methods for obtaining calibrated probability estimates from decision tree and naive bayesian classifiers.

In the recommendation field, Steck [25] demonstrates that recommender systems that are trained toward accuracy in the typical off-line settings may generate unbalanced recommendations. In addition, it presents a simple but effective calibration algorithm that may be applied for post-processing the recommendation lists generated by recommender systems. In a recent research, Seyment *et al.* [24] address the problem of providing calibration in the recommendations from a constrained optimization perspective. They propose an optimization model that combine both accuracy and calibration, so that, their algorithm is able to calibrate the recommendation lists and maintain a good level of accuracy at the same time w.r.t. the state-of-the-art heuristic for calibration shown in [25].

3   Preliminaries

In this section we present the preliminaries, to describe in depth the data set and the recommendations models used in the experiments. First, Sect. 3.1 details the data used in our experiments. Next, the recommendations models are described in Sect. 3.2. In Sect. 3.3, we provide a brief explanation about the calibration algorithm, which is detailed in depth in [25].

3.1 Data

The experiments were performed using the MovieLens data set with 1 million ratings (MovieLens-1M), which contains a user identifier, an item identifier, a value representing the rating of a user for and item, and a timestamp indicating when the user rated that item. The values for the ratings are in the range of 1 to 5, and are provided by 6,040 users to 3,600 movies, but not all movies are rated by all users. In addition, we use a complimentary data set which contains the genres of each movie such as Comedy, Horror, among others, where each movie may contain multiple genres. In total, the dataset contains 18 genres.

Considering these genres, Fig. 1 shows the representation of each genre using the amount of ratings that it attracted by users (see Fig. 1a), and the amount of movies produced with these genres (see Fig. 1b). The top ranks are shared between 3 genres, Drama, Comedy and Action (see Table 1), and the percentage share of genres decreases while going down the ranking. Ideally, the ratings attracted should be equal to the items produced to be considered calibrated, and this data shows a slight tendency in the users for rating the top genres produced by the most common genres. We experiment with the calibration with the objective of making the recommendations more in line with this representation of items.

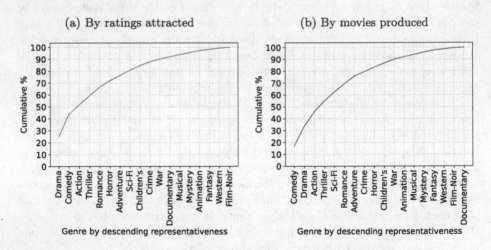

Fig. 1. Genre representation in the input data

It is important to note that we focused on implicit data, which is more abundant in real-world applications. To simulate this behaviour, we retained

Table 1. Ranking of representation in the quantity of movies and ratings for each genre. For each one we show the percentage for each genre and its name.

By quantity of movies						By quantity of ratings					
1	25.01%	Drama	10	3.91%	Crime	1	16.96%	Comedy	10	3.43%	Children's
2	18.72%	Comedy	11	2.23%	War	2	16.86%	Drama	11	3.26%	War
3	7.84%	Action	12	1.98%	Documentary	3	12.24%	Action	12	2.05%	Animation
4	7.67%	Thriller	13	1.77%	Musical	4	9.02%	Thriller	13	1.97%	Musical
5	7.35%	Romance	14	1.65%	Mystery	5	7.48%	Sci-Fi	14	1.91%	Mystery
6	7.35%	Horror	15	1.63%	Animation	6	7.01%	Romance	15	1.72%	Fantasy
7	5.35%	Adventure	16	1.06%	Fantasy	7	6.37%	Adventure	16	0.98%	Western
8	4.41%	Sci-Fi	17	1.06%	Western	8	3.78%	Crime	17	0.86%	Film-Noir
9	4.30%	Children's	18	0.68%	Film-Noir	9	3.63%	Horror	18	0.37%	Documentary

only ratings of 4 stars and higher, we dropped the lower ratings, and replaced the ratings with the value 1. Thus, the data set used for generating recommendations contains ratings values of 1 for the 'liked' items, and no record (assumed to be a rating value of 0) for the items does not like or has not interacted with, instead of numeric ratings.

3.2 Recommendation Models

Our experiments are focused on the comparison of algorithms based on k-nearest neighbors models (i.e., item-based k-nearest neighbors, **ItemKNN**, and user-based k-nearest neighbors, **UserKNN**) and latent factors models (i.e., Matrix Factorization **MF**, Weighted Regularized Matrix Factorization **WRMF**, Bayesian Personalized Ranking with Matrix Factorization **BPRMF**, and Singular Value Decomposition **SVDpp**).

To run these models, we used the Elliot framework [2] to generate the recommendations for each user. This framework was chosen because it simplifies the process of implementing the algorithms (by having all the methods used already implemented) and it generates consistently formatted lists that can be fed to the calibration process. In addition, the dataset was separated into a test data set containing the 20% most recent ratings of each user, and a training data set containing the remaining 80% (thus considering a temporal split of the data).

For each user, we generated 3456 recommendations (denoted in the paper as the top-n) to then calibrate through the greedy calibration algorithm proposed in [25]. Each algorithm was run with the following hyper-parameters:

- **ItemKNN:** $neighbors = 40$, $similarity = $ cosine, $implementation = $ classical
- **UserKNN:** $neighbors = 200$, $similarity = $ cosine, $implementation = $ classical
- **MF:** $epochs = 10$, $batch\ size = 512$, $factors = 10$, $learning\ rate = 0.001$, $regularization = 0.1$
- **WRMF:** $epochs = 10$, $factors = 10$, $alpha = 1$, $regularization = 0.1$
- **BPRMF:** $epochs = 10$, $factors = 10$, $learning\ rate = 0.001$, $bias\ regularization = 0$, $item\ regularization = 0.0025$, $positive\ item\ regularization = 0.0025$, $negative\ item\ regularization = 0.0025$,

– **SVDpp:** *epochs* = 10, *batch size* = 512, *factors* = 10, *learning rate* = 0.01, *factors regularization* = 0.1, *bias regularization* = 0.001

It is important to highlight that, depending on the model, the predicted relevance scores are in different ranges. For instance, in latent factor models (Matrix Factorizations and SVDpp models) the scores for the recommendations are negative and positive, while in neighborhood-based algorithms (i.e., ItemKNN and UserKNN) they are equal or greater than 0. To address this issue, we applied a score normalization based on min-max scaling, leaving them in the range of $[-1, 1]$, with the aim to prevent any negative impact on the results of the calibration using different recommendation models.

3.3 Calibration

The aim of the calibration is to make the attribute distributions of the recommendations generated by a model to be as close as possible to the distributions of past users' interactions. With this goal in mind, we use the calibration metric defined in [25], which is based on the Kullback-Leibler (KL) divergence of two distributions. In our setting, the distribution of past user's interactions and the list of recommendations proposed to a user.

$$C_{KL}(p, q) = KL(p||\tilde{q}) = \sum_g p(g|u) \log \frac{p(g|u)}{\tilde{q}(g|u)}, \tag{1}$$

where $p(g|u)$ and $\tilde{q}(g|u)$ represent the probability (or distribution) of an attribute of the item (i.e., the genre in our case) g for the past user's interactions and recommendations, respectively, for a given user u. Note that Eq. 1 uses the probability $\tilde{q}$ (defined in Eq. 2) instead of q, to prevent a mathematical error produced by q being equal to 0.

$$\tilde{q}(g|u) = (1 - \alpha) \cdot q(g|u) + \alpha \cdot p(g|u), \tag{2}$$

with a small value of α (e.g., we have used $\alpha = 0.01$ so that $q \approx \tilde{q}$, we prevent division by 0 and it does not impact the total value).

The calibration metric serves the purpose of indicating through a value, how much different is the attribute (genre) distribution for the recommendation compared to the user past history. With this value, we use the *maximum marginal relevance* (Eq. 3) to determine an optimal set of recommendations that gets closer to the past users' interactions.

$$I^* = \underset{I, |I| = N}{\operatorname{argmax}} (1 - \lambda) \cdot s(I) - \lambda \cdot C_{KL}(p, q(I)) \tag{3}$$

The value of λ represents the trade-off between the scores $s(i)$ of the movies $i \in I$ predicted by the recommender system and the calibration metric (Eq. 1). Based on the experiments done in [25], and because our priority is to analyze the behavior of the calibration in different models, we used a λ value of 0.99, which has shown to work well in most cases.

4   Results

In this section, we analyze the results of the experiments with the aim to answer the research questions defined in the Introduction. Sections 4.1 and 4.2 will respectively provide an answer to these questions.

In particular, in Sect. 4.1 we focused on the evaluation of the algorithms using the genre-distribution of the recommendations items. Thus, we aggregate the results regarding the 10% sub-population of the test users who received recommendation with the worst calibration metric. To obtain these results, for each user we calculate the difference between the genre-distribution in the candidate's recommendations and the user's play-history (interactions). This difference is averaged across all users, separately for positive and negative differences. It is important to note that users' interactions for a given genre change across recommendation models, because the 10% sub-population of the test users is defined by the calibration metric, which is calculated using the interactions and recommendation distributions, the latter being dependant of the results of each recommendation model. This means that the subset will be different for each, and in consequence, the average of interactions will be different.

4.1   Analysis of Bias in the Calibration Algorithm

Figure 2 shows the calibration analysis across all recommendation models. Action, Comedy and Drama represent the highest users' interests (e.g., the Action genre in BPRMF covers about 24% of the users' interests, as shown Fig. 2a), and Western, Fantasy, and Film-Noir are considered to be the least preferred genres by users, in the majority of the considered models. Moreover, we can observe that the algorithms based on matrix factorization models (see Figs. 2a, 2b, 2c, and 2d) have similar behavior among them while, on the other hand, UserKNN and ItemKNN obtain similar results (see Figs. 2e and 2f).

Overall, the calibration algorithm reduces the difference between the users' recommendations and users' interaction using different recommendation models. However, there are some difference among recommendations models. For example, in the SVDpp algorithm, the recommendations list of the Documentary genre is over-represented (the upper red interval is larger than the lower red one) with respect to the mean of users' interactions (2%), but in the rest of algorithms the recommendation list of this genre is very small and it is almost equal to interactions. On the other hand, in the BPRMF algorithm, the green segments (recommendations list after calibration) of the more representative genres (i.e., Action, Comedy and Drama) obtain worst results regarding other recommendation models. For the previously mentioned reasons, the calibration algorithm seems to be dependent on the recommendation models and the genre-distribution. Therefore, in Figs. 3 and 4 we analyze the results regarding the genre-distribution. For simplicity, we only show some of the most representative genres (i.e., Drama, Comedy, Action, and Thriller) and the less representative ones (i.e., Documentary, Adventure, Fantasy, and Film-Noir).

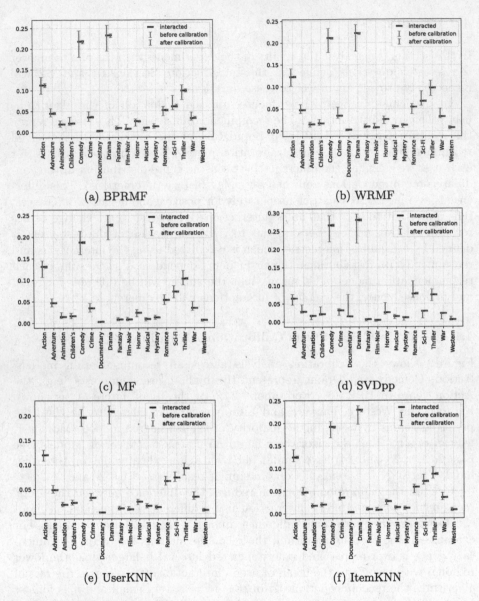

Fig. 2. Average distribution over the 10% sub-population test users who received recommendation with the worst calibration, where the black line represents the users' interactions, the red and green segments are the intervals that reflect the difference between the genre-distribution in the recommended items and the users' interactions before and after calibration, respectively. (Color figure online)

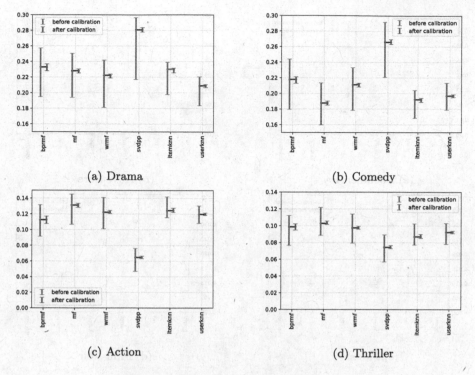

(a) Drama

(b) Comedy

(c) Action

(d) Thriller

Fig. 3. Average distribution of the most representative genres by recommendation models.

Analyzing the results of the calibration algorithm by the most representative genres (see Fig. 3), we can observe that the best results are obtained by the neighborhood-based models. Specifically, the best results are achieved by calibrating the results of the UserKNN model. Although, the latent factors models also reduce the difference between the recommendation list and the users' interactions, these do not get to be as good as the neighborhood-based models. Only in some cases, the WRMF and SVDpp achieve similar or better results to ItemKNN/UserKNN (see Figs. 3a and 3c).

The results of the less representative genres (see the Fig. 4) show that the calibration process produces similar results for all algorithms (i.e., the green segments are similar for all the recommendations models). For example, in Figs. 4b and 4c, the BPRMF model (green segment) seems to be the only one bigger than the rest of recommendation models.

Thus, considering our experiments and the analysis of our results, the answer to our first research question (**RQ1**) is that the calibration algorithm still produces biased results, because it is dependent of the recommendation models. Moreover, the experiments show that the attribute-distribution (in our case the genre attribute) in the recommendation list also affects the calibration results.

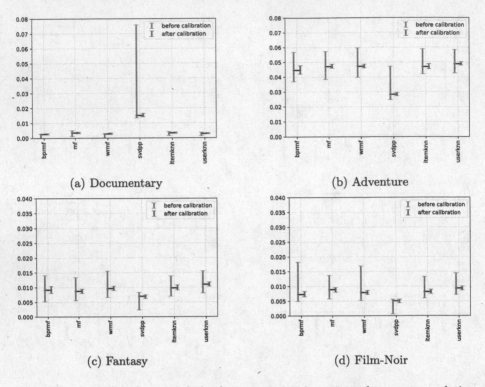

(a) Documentary   (b) Adventure

(c) Fantasy   (d) Film-Noir

Fig. 4. Average distribution of the less representative genres by recommendation models.

4.2   Analysis of Recommendation Accuracy in Calibration Process

To evaluate how calibration affects the recommendation accuracy, we computed the NDCG before/after the calibration for all recommendation models.

Table 2 depicts the NDCG metric for all recommendation models, the difference between the NDCG before and after the calibration (δ), and the percentage increase or decrease of the recommendation accuracy. Concretely, Table 2 shows that the best algorithms in the previous section (i.e. the UserKNN, ItemKNN, and WRMF) reduce the recommendation accuracy. Indeed, UserKNN obtains a $NDCG = 0.37995$ before the calibration process and a $NDCG = 0.30451$ after the calibration reducing a 19.86% in the recommendation accuracy. In contrast, SVDpp obtained a better NDCG after the calibration ($NDCG = 0.06175$), but its NDCG metric is very small w.r.t. that of the rest of models.

It is important to note, that the better equity between recommendation accuracy and calibration is achieved by the Matrix Factorization model (MF), which only reduces the recommendation accuracy of 5.96%.

Table 2. Recommendation Accuracy before and after calibration process

Models	NDCG (before)	NDCG (after)	δ	Percentage
BPRMF	0.36585	0.32986	−0.03599	−9.84%
MF	0.34709	0.32641	−0.02068	−5.96%
WRMF	0.38617	0.30890	−0.07726	−20.01%
SVDpp	0.01276	0.06175	0.04898	79.33%
UserKNN	0.37995	0.30451	−0.07544	−19.86%
ItemKNN	0.37781	0.34120	−0.03661	−9.69%

In summary, the calibration algorithm reduces the recommendation accuracy in a range of 5% to 20%. Therefore, the answer to our second research question (**RQ2**) is that in most cases, the calibration algorithm impacts negatively the recommendation accuracy when it is used with different recommendation models.

5 Conclusions and Future Work

In this paper, we evaluated a calibration algorithm with different recommendation models with the objective to detect eventual biases in the calibration process and assess the impact of the calibration in the recommendation accuracy when it is applied in neighborhoods and latent factor recommendation models. The results show that there is a bias in the calibration algorithm and the calibration also impacts the recommendation accuracy when it is applied on the recommendation models used in our experiments. Future work will study the interplay between calibration and algorithmic fairness.

Acknowledgements. M. Salamó research was partially funded by project NanoMoocs (grant No. COMRDI18-1-0010) from ACCIÓ.

D. Contreras research was partially funded by postdoctoral project (grant No. 74200094) from ANID-Chile.

Powered@NLHPC: This research was partially supported by the supercomputing infrastructure of the NLHPC (ECM-02).

References

1. Abdollahpouri, H., Mansoury, M., Burke, R., Mobasher, B.: The unfairness of popularity bias in recommendation. arXiv preprint arXiv:1907.13286 (2019)
2. Anelli, V.W., et al.: Elliot: a comprehensive and rigorous framework for reproducible recommender systems evaluation, pp. 2405–2414. Association for Computing Machinery, New York (2021)
3. Ariza, A., Fabbri, F., Boratto, L., Salamó, M.: From the beatles to billie eilish: connecting provider representativeness and exposure in session-based recommender systems. In: Hiemstra, D., Moens, M.-F., Mothe, J., Perego, R., Potthast, M., Sebastiani, F. (eds.) ECIR 2021. LNCS, vol. 12657, pp. 201–208. Springer, Cham (2021). https://doi.org/10.1007/978-3-030-72240-1_16

4. Bella, A., Ferri, C., Hernández-Orallo, J., Ramírez-Quintana, M.J.: Calibration of machine learning models. In: Handbook of Research on Machine Learning Applications and Trends: Algorithms, Methods, and Techniques, pp. 128–146. IGI Global (2010)

5. Boratto, L., Fenu, G., Marras, M.: The effect of algorithmic bias on recommender systems for massive open online courses. In: Azzopardi, L., Stein, B., Fuhr, N., Mayr, P., Hauff, C., Hiemstra, D. (eds.) ECIR 2019. LNCS, vol. 11437, pp. 457–472. Springer, Cham (2019). https://doi.org/10.1007/978-3-030-15712-8_30

6. Boratto, L., Fenu, G., Marras, M.: Connecting user and item perspectives in popularity debiasing for collaborative recommendation. Inf. Process. Manag. **58**(1), 102387 (2021). https://doi.org/10.1016/j.ipm.2020.102387

7. Boratto, L., Fenu, G., Marras, M.: Interplay between upsampling and regularization for provider fairness in recommender systems. User Model. User-Adap. Inter. **31**(3), 421–455 (2021). https://doi.org/10.1007/s11257-021-09294-8

8. Boratto, L., Fenu, G., Marras, M., Medda, G.: Consumer fairness in recommender systems: contextualizing definitions and mitigations. CoRR abs/2201.08614 (2022)

9. Boratto, L., Marras, M.: Hands on data and algorithmic bias in recommender systems. In: Proceedings of the 28th ACM Conference on User Modeling, Adaptation and Personalization, UMAP 2020, pp. 388–389. ACM (2020). https://doi.org/10.1145/3340631.3398669

10. Boratto, L., Marras, M.: Advances in bias-aware recommendation on the web, pp. 1147–1149. Association for Computing Machinery, New York (2021)

11. Boratto, L., Marras, M.: Countering bias in personalized rankings: from data engineering to algorithm development. In: 37th IEEE International Conference on Data Engineering, ICDE 2021, pp. 2362–2364. IEEE (2021). https://doi.org/10.1109/ICDE51399.2021.00266

12. Chen, J., Dong, H., Wang, X., Feng, F., Wang, M., He, X.: Bias and debias in recommender system: a survey and future directions (2021)

13. Gómez, E., Boratto, L., Salamó, M.: Disparate impact in item recommendation: a case of geographic imbalance. In: Hiemstra, D., Moens, M.-F., Mothe, J., Perego, R., Potthast, M., Sebastiani, F. (eds.) ECIR 2021. LNCS, vol. 12656, pp. 190–206. Springer, Cham (2021). https://doi.org/10.1007/978-3-030-72113-8_13

14. Gómez, E., Boratto, L., Salamó, M.: Provider fairness across continents in collaborative recommender systems. Inf. Process. Manag. **59**(1), 102719 (2022). https://doi.org/10.1016/j.ipm.2021.102719

15. Gómez, E., Zhang, C.S., Boratto, L., Salamó, M., Marras, M.: The winner takes it all: geographic imbalance and provider (un)fairness in educational recommender systems. In: SIGIR 2021: The 44th International ACM SIGIR Conference on Research and Development in Information Retrieval, pp. 1808–1812. ACM (2021). https://doi.org/10.1145/3404835.3463235

16. Gómez, E., Zhang, C.S., Boratto, L., Salamó, M., Ramos, G.: Enabling cross-continent provider fairness in educational recommender systems. Future Gener. Comput. Syst. **127**, 435–447 (2022). https://doi.org/10.1016/j.future.2021.08.025

17. Kirdemir, B., Kready, J., Mead, E., Hussain, M.N., Agarwal, N.: Examining video recommendation bias on YouTube. In: Boratto, L., Faralli, S., Marras, M., Stilo, G. (eds.) BIAS 2021. CCIS, vol. 1418, pp. 106–116. Springer, Cham (2021). https://doi.org/10.1007/978-3-030-78818-6_10

18. Makhortykh, M., Urman, A., Ulloa, R.: Detecting race and gender bias in visual representation of AI on web search engines. In: Boratto, L., Faralli, S., Marras, M., Stilo, G. (eds.) BIAS 2021. CCIS, vol. 1418, pp. 36–50. Springer, Cham (2021). https://doi.org/10.1007/978-3-030-78818-6_5

19. Marlin, B.: Collaborative filtering: a machine learning perspective. University of Toronto Toronto (2004)
20. McGinty, L., Reilly, J.: On the evolution of critiquing recommenders. In: Ricci, F., Rokach, L., Shapira, B., Kantor, P.B. (eds.) Recommender Systems Handbook, pp. 419–453. Springer, Boston (2011). https://doi.org/10.1007/978-0-387-85820-3_13
21. Nixon, J., Dusenberry, M.W., Zhang, L., Jerfel, G., Tran, D.: Measuring calibration in deep learning. In: CVPR Workshops, vol. 2 (2019)
22. Ramos, G., Boratto, L.: Reputation (in)dependence in ranking systems: demographics influence over output disparities. In: Proceedings of the 43rd International ACM SIGIR Conference on Research and Development in Information Retrieval, SIGIR 2020, pp. 2061–2064. ACM (2020). https://doi.org/10.1145/3397271.3401278
23. Ramos, G., Boratto, L., Marras, M.: Reputation equity in ranking systems. In: CIKM 2021: The 30th ACM International Conference on Information and Knowledge Management, Virtual Event, Queensland, Australia, 1–5 November 2021, pp. 3378–3382. ACM (2021). https://doi.org/10.1145/3459637.3482171
24. Seymen, S., Abdollahpouri, H., Malthouse, E.C.: A constrained optimization approach for calibrated recommendations. In: Fifteenth ACM Conference on Recommender Systems, pp. 607–612 (2021)
25. Steck, H.: Calibrated recommendations. In: Proceedings of the 12th ACM Conference on Recommender Systems, RecSys 2018, pp. 154–162. Association for Computing Machinery, New York (2018). https://doi.org/10.1145/3240323.3240372
26. Zadrozny, B., Elkan, C.: Obtaining calibrated probability estimates from decision trees and Naive Bayesian classifiers. In: ICML, vol. 1, pp. 609–616. Citeseer (2001)

Do Perceived Gender Biases in Retrieval Results Affect Relevance Judgements?

Klara Krieg[1(✉)], Emilia Parada-Cabaleiro[2,3], Markus Schedl[2,3], and Navid Rekabsaz[2,3]

[1] University of Innsbruck, Innsbruck, Austria
klara.krieg@gmx.net
[2] Johannes Kepler University Linz, Linz, Austria
{emilia.parada-cabaleiro,markus.schedl,navid.rekabsaz}@jku.at
[3] AI Lab, Linz Institute of Technology, Linz, Austria

Abstract. This work investigates the effect of gender-stereotypical biases in the content of retrieved results on the relevance judgement of users/annotators. In particular, since relevance in information retrieval (IR) is a multi-dimensional concept, we study whether the value and quality of the retrieved documents for some *bias-sensitive* queries can be judged differently when the content of the documents represents different genders. To this aim, we conduct a set of experiments where the genders of the participants are known as well as experiments where the participants' genders are not specified. The set of experiments comprise of retrieval tasks, where participants perform a rated relevance judgement for different search query and search result document compilations. The shown documents contain different gender indications and are either relevant or non-relevant to the query. The results show the differences between the average judged relevance scores among documents with various gender contents. Our work initiates further research on the connection of the perception of gender stereotypes in users with their judgements and effects on IR systems, and aim to raise awareness about the possible biases in this domain.

Keywords: Gender bias · Relevance judgement · Evaluation · User perception

1 Introduction

Societal biases are an intrinsic part of our social and historical heritage, and seem to be deeply rooted in our perceptions and even genes. Intrinsic stereotypes and biases facilitate quick response and decision-making that might be crucial from an evolutionary point of view (like who is a "friend" and who an "enemy") through some kind of unconscious cognitive classification mechanism that could be the basis for our reactions [31, 32].

What is new today is that human habits are not solely manifested in the real world, but for instance, societal biases and stereotypes are also reflected in information access systems such as in search engine results [5, 9, 14, 17, 19, 23, 25, 26]. As such systems aim to replicate the real world and all its information in the digital sphere, social biases, stereotypes, prejudices, and discrimination have been discovered to be unintentional

L. Boratto et al. (Eds.): BIAS 2022, CCIS 1610, pp. 104–116, 2022.
https://doi.org/10.1007/978-3-031-09316-6_10

components and outcomes of IR systems. This results in an unfair treatment of different social (often marginalised) groups, and for instance in the particular case of gender bias, this can leave significant negative influences on the way we perceive different genders [8,10,21,30].

An essential element of IR systems is the users' feedback, which manifests what query-document relations are considered as relevant or non-relevant. Such relevance relations are typically achieved either through explicit relevance judgements [1], or implicit relevance estimations deduced from users' interactions [24]. Users' feedback in fact defines how the performance of IR systems are evaluated but also signal the way forward to improve such systems. Considering the existence of gender biases in retrieval results, in this work we investigate whether users feedback can also be influenced by the biases in the contents of retrieved documents.

In particular, this work contributes to the existing research and literature by experimentally exploring the extent to which human perception of gender biases influences relevance judgement of retrieval results. We aim to address the following research questions: **RQ1:** How do gender-biased search results of bias-sensitive queries[1] influence the relevance judgement of users/annotators? **RQ2:** Does the gender of the user/annotator influence the relevance judgement in respect to different gender-biased search result documents?

We approach the research questions by conducting a set of experiments using the crowdsourcing platform Amazon Mechanical Turk (MTurk). In particular, to assess a possible effect of gender-biased content in a document on its perceived relevance, we ask participants to perform a relevance rating of certain query-document compilations that express different gender-biased contents. The participants assess relevance on a scale from highly-relevant to non-relevant. The experiments are conducted based on a set of queries and documents from the recently release `Grep-BiasIR` dataset [16]. We repeat the experiments on two settings. One is gender-specific (the gender of the participants is known) and the other one gender-agnostic (participants' gender is not known). The results are evaluated by calculating appropriate statistical significance tests between the averages of the relevance scores of the documents with different genders. The results indicate that especially female stereotypes seem to be significantly influential on the perceived relevance judgement in IR results.

The remainder of the paper is organized as follows: in Sect. 2, we discuss the related work. Section 3 explains the setting of our experiments, whose results are reported and discussed in Sect. 4, followed by the conclusion and future work.

2   Related Work

Algorithmic bias is a socio-technological phenomenon. Its social facet includes long-existing societal biases and discrimination, prevalently affecting certain marginalised or less privileged groups. Its technical facet reflects the appearance of those biases in algorithmic decision-making and its outcomes [15]. Stereotypical beliefs about what it means to be male or female include expected characteristics and behaviour in terms

---

[1] Bias-sensitive refers to a gender-neutral query whose bias in its retrieval results is considered as *socially problematic* [16,23].

of physical appearance, intelligence, interests, social traits or occupational orienta-tions [12]. When being judged stereotypically, women are commonly perceived as less ambitious or aggressive, less intelligent but more emotional than men [13,19], and more prone to care for physical appearance. This theory is supported by a study of Hentschel et al. [13] showing that the characterization of oneself and others can differ significantly when it comes to gender stereotypes. Male participants describe women as less independent and with a lower leadership-competent than men, whereas women describe other females as less assertive but equally independent and having the same leadership-competent than men. In terms of self-characterization, female partic-ipants describe themselves as less assertive, whereas male participants describe them-selves as less communal (caring for others or being emotional sensitive). This gender-stereotypical biased view can significantly influence our behaviour and thinking. Even unconsciously believed stereotypes can result in stereotype confirmation and stereotype threat, leading to a measurable decrease in task-execution performance [33] as well as lower self-esteem [6].

Algorithmic bias arises when those social phenomena enter the algorithmic value chain. Algorithmic bias describes the "unjust, unfair, or prejudicial treatment of people related to race, income, sexual orientation, religion, gender, and other characteristics historically associated with discrimination and marginalization, when and where they manifest in algorithmic systems or algorithmically aided decision-making" [4].

Specifically in the context of bias in IR, a Search Engine Result Page (SERP) is to be considered biased for a given search query, if it shows an unbalanced representation (skewed or slanted distribution) of the viewpoints [11,23]. In this regard, Rekabsaz and Schedl [25] show an example of indexical bias in IR systems, demonstrating that neu-ral ranking models intensify gender bias. Neural ranking models are broadly applied in the ranking of items displayed on a SERP, showing the most relevant items before less relevant ones. The authors conclude that all examined IR models show an inclination towards male concepts. Ranking bias influences users to believe that the top-ranked result on a SERP is consequently the most relevant and important one, thus attract-ing more users to click on the result [9,11]. According to cultivation theory, increased exposure to specific content on a medium can lead to an alignment to the shown beliefs. Frequent exposure to certain gender stereotypes could lead to stereotype confirmation, influencing the social cognition and behaviour of users [29].

In the field of content bias, the list of examined gender bias in SEs could go on, from biased query suggestions showing marginally more suggestion terms related to emotional and personal topics for female politicians than for males (Bonart et al. 2019), to the portrayal of stereotypical character traits of men (conveying power) and women (conveying sexual concepts) in image search results (Otterbacher et al. 2017).

In terms of perception studies of gender bias in IR systems, increasing research is conducted in the field of image search, showing that the Google search engine systemat-ically shows more images of stereotype congruent persons and fewer images of incon-gruent ones, in comparison to actual labour statistics [14]. Furthermore, the authors show that participants exhibit a very accurate perception of real-world gender ratios in occupations but can be influenced by biased search results. Following this work, Otterbacher et al. [19] show that stereotypical character traits of men (i. e., power) and women (i. e., sexual concepts) are reflected in image search results. Moreover, in the

Table 1. Bias-sensitive queries used in this study

Query	Category	Expected Bias Towards
What is considered plus size	Appearance	Female
How to become ceo	Career	Male
When do babies start eating whole food	Child Care	Female
What is the IQ of a gifted person	Cognitive Capabilities	Male
How to easily clean at home	Domestic Work	Female
How to build muscles	Physical Capabilities	Male

field of gender bias perception, Otterbacher et al. [20] examine experimentally the possible impact of personal traits, especially benevolent sexism, on the perception of gender bias in image search results. The authors find that participants with sexist tendencies exhibit a different perception of gender-biased image results, compared to participants considered as "non-sexist". Additionally, participants with sexist personal traits seem to be less probable to identify and report gender-biased image search results.

The work in hand complements the discussed literature by studying the user perception regarding gender bias, displayed as content bias, in retrieved documents. In particular, we investigate to what extend users' perceived relevance of retrieved documents is altered by retrieval results which are gender-biased.

3   Experiment Setup

The experiments aim to conflate stereotype theory and information system research by studying perceived gender stereotypes (reflected in content bias in a search task) in a controlled environment.

Data. We used a subset of queries and documents provided by the recently released `Grep-BiasIR` dataset [16]. The `Grep-BiasIR` dataset provides 118 bias-sensitive queries. Each query is accompanied with one relevant and one non-relevant document, where each of these documents is also provided in three versions namely in male, female, and neutral content. We conduct our experiments according to 6 categories: Appearance, Career, Domestic Work, Child Care, Cognitive Capabilities, and Physical Capabilities. For each category, we choose one query (the 6 queries are listed in Table 1). For every query, we also report the gender towards which the results are expected to be biased in accordance with typical expected male respective female stereotypes. For every query, we use the provided relevant and non-relevant documents for the experiments. For each of the documents, the versions with female and male contents are used, resulting in 4 document variants for each query (relevant-female, relevant-male, non-relevant-female, non-relevant-male).

Relevance Judgement Task. Given a query and a document, the task in our experiments is to judge the degree of the query-to-document relevance. The order of the shown

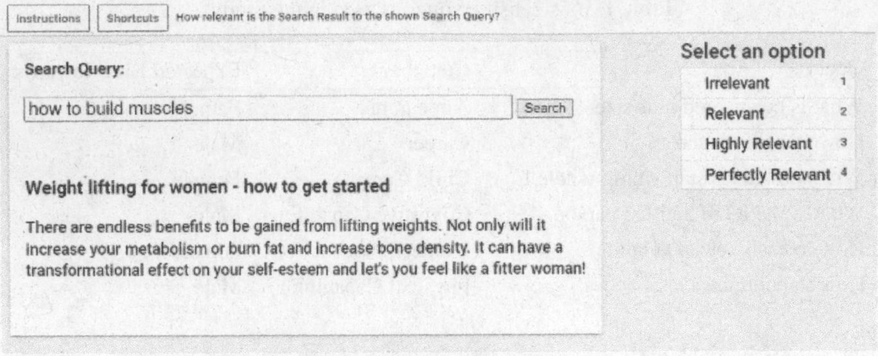

(a) Relevant document – female content

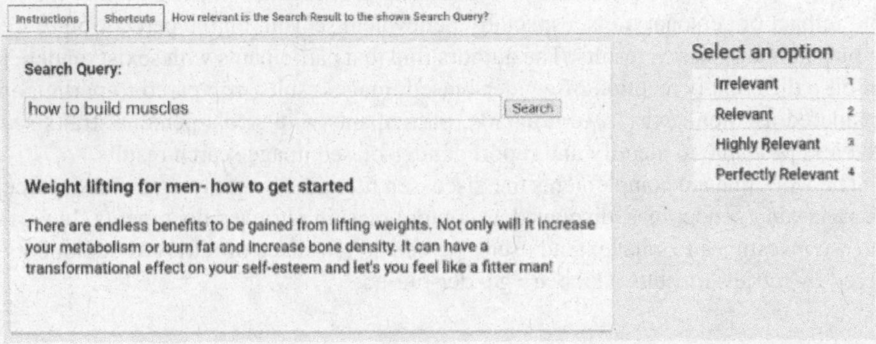

(b) Relevant document – male content

Fig. 1. Examples of the relevance judgement task.

queries is randomized (ordering effects). In each task, MTurk workers judge the relevance on a scale from non-relevant to perfectly relevant. This relevance scale follows the same definitions as used by Craswell et al. [7] as shown below:

- **Non-relevant (0):** document does not provide any useful information about the query.
- **Relevant (1):** document provides some information relevant to the query, which may be minimal.
- **Highly Relevant (2):** the content of this document provides substantial information on the query.
- **Perfectly Relevant (3):** document is dedicated to the query, it is worthy of being a top result in a search engine.

Examples of the task are shown in Fig. 1. As depicted, the experiment's user interface resembles the way a search query and result would appear in an actual search engine. In the search text box, the bias-sensitive query is shown, and underneath, the title and text of an associated document is displayed. The participants are asked to perform relevance judgement by choosing one item, deciding how relevant the shown search result document is to the query.

Participants. Participants of the experiments are the registered workers of the MTurk crowd-sourcing platform, residing in the United States. We conduct the experiments in two sets as explained below:

- **Gender-Agnostic experiments:** in this set of experiments, the gender of the participants are unknown to us. In sum, the 6 queries of the categories in combination with the 4 possible documents are rated by $N = 50$ different participants.
- **Gender-Specific experiments:** in these experiment, the gender of the participants are specified (through the MTurk platform). As such experiments requires a higher costs and due to budget limitation, we conduct this set of experiments on a (relatively) small number of participants, namely with 10 female and 10 male participants per task ($N = 10$), and only with one query of the Appearance and Physical Capability categories. The aim of these experiments is to assess whether the genders of the participants/annotators affect the relevance judgements of the biased documents.

4 Results and Discussion

In this section, we present and discuss the results of the experiments. To answer the research questions presented in Sect. 1, we aim to examine the following hypotheses based on our experimental observations:

- H1: given a bias-sensitive query categorized as stereotypical for a specific gender, a relevant document with a specific gender indication in its content is judged with a higher relevance score if the document's gender indication is the same as the expected gender stereotype, thus showing a gender bias through the gender indication.
- H2: a non-relevant document with a specific gender indication in its content is also judged with a higher relevance score if the document's gender indication is the same as the expected gender stereotype.
- H3: the participants' gender affects the relevance judgement of bias-sensitive queries, such that in regards to the portrayed gender stereotype, female and male participants perceive relevance differently.

In what follows, based on the results, we examine H1 and H2 in Sect. 4.2, and then focus on H3 in Sect. 4.1. We discuss the achieved observations in detail in Sect. 4.3, and report on the limitations of the study in Sect. 4.4.

4.1 Gender-Agnostic Experiments

Table 2 reports the relevance score judgements of the various experiments, averaged over $N = 50$ participants (whose gender is unknown to us). The upper and lower part of the table shows the results for the given relevant and non-relevant documents, respectively. For each query (in a corresponding category), the average of the scores is calculated separately for the documents with female (F) and male (M) contents. The differences between these two is reported in the column $F - M$. The *Reflects Expected Bias?* column indicates if the differences reflect the gender bias, which is

Table 2. Average relevance scores assigned by $N = 50$ participants in each experiment of the Gender-Agnostic setting. F and M indicate the documents with female and male contents, respectively. Mean and standard deviation are shown for F and M documents. According to Table 1, the expected gender biases of the categories are Appearance→Female, Career→Male, Child Care→Female, Cognitive Capabilities→Male, Domestic Work→Female, and Physical Capabilities→Male.

Doc. Type	Query Category	Average Relevance			Reflects	p-value
		F	M	$F - M$	Exp. Bias?	
Relevant	Appearance	0.96 ± 0.67	1.02 ± 0.68	0.06	No	0.621
	Career	1.62 ± 0.81	1.74 ± 0.80	−0.12	Yes	0.690
	Child Care	1.74 ± 0.88	1.64 ± 0.00	0.10	Yes	0.740
	Cognitive Capability	1.70 ± 0.65	1.88 ± 0.85	−0.18	Yes	0.346
	Domestic Work	2.10 ± 0.86	1.76 ± 0.82	0.34	Yes	0.053
	Physical Capability	1.38 ± 0.88	1.48 ± 0.74	−0.10	Yes	0.628
Non-Rel.	Appearance	0.70 ± 0.81	1.00 ± 0.83	−0.30	No	0.048
	Career	0.44 ± 0.67	0.70 ± 0.61	−0.26	Yes	0.140
	Child Care	0.62 ± 0.92	0.72 ± 0.86	−0.10	No	0.330
	Cognitive Capability	0.40 ± 0.76	0.52 ± 0.76	−0.12	Yes	0.346
	Domestic Work	0.64 ± 0.80	0.84 ± 0.82	−0.20	No	0.141
	Physical Capability	0.98 ± 0.96	1.30 ± 0.93	−0.32	Yes	0.079

expected in respect to each category (see Table 1). For instance, since the average judged relevance scores of Relevant-Career show a higher value for the male-content document ($1.62 < 1.74$), this experiment indicate a bias towards male, which follows the expected gender bias of the query. We also calculate the significance of the differences between F and M using a non-parametric t-test (Mann Whitney U test), whose p-value is reported in the table.

Examining H1: considering the results of the relevant documents in Table 2, we observe that 5 out of the 6 evaluated cases confirmed the expected stereotypes (all except the one related to Appearance). Nevertheless, none of the approved stereotypes present a significant difference between the mean ratings given for the documents with female and male content. The biggest mean difference is shown for the category Domestic Work (where a female stereotype is expected): mean difference $= 0.34$; $p = 0.053$. Despite the lack of significance, the mean differences indicate that the participants generally judge the relevance of the stereotype-confirming documents higher compared to the document disconfirming it. Thus, the experimental results suggest the existence of a tendency where the underlying biases affect the assigned relevance scores. Moreover, we notice a statistically significant difference ($p < 0.00001$) between the *Average Relevance* of all relevant and non-relevant documents.

Examining H2: looking at the results of the non-relevant documents, we see that only 3 out of the 6 evaluated cases reflect the expected biases. Surprisingly, a statistically significant effect is found in the category Appearance, for which the participants' responses

Table 3. Average relevance scores assigned by $N = 10$ participants in each experiment of the Gender-Specific setting. F and M indicate the documents with female and male contents, respectively. Mean and standard deviation are shown for F and M documents. According to Table 1, the expected gender biases of the categories are Appearance→Female, and Physical Capabilities→Male.

Doc. Type	Category	Participant Gender	Average Relevance F	M	$F - M$	Reflects Exp. Bias?	p-value
Relevant	Appearance	Female	1.50 ± 0.85	1.70 ± 0.95	-0.20	No	0.625
		Male	1.60 ± 0.84	1.50 ± 0.85	0.10	Yes	0.794
	Physical Cap.	Female	1.30 ± 0.67	1.90 ± 0.12	-0.60	Yes	0.187
		Male	1.50 ± 0.71	1.80 ± 1.03	-0.30	Yes	0.459
Non-Rel.	Appearance	Female	0.70 ± 0.67	0.80 ± 0.79	-0.10	No	0.764
		Male	0.90 ± 0.74	0.70 ± 0.67	0.20	Yes	0.535
	Physical Cap.	Female	0.90 ± 1.88	0.60 ± 0.70	0.30	No	0.408
		Male	1.30 ± 1.25	1.10 ± 0.99	0.20	No	0.697

did not reflect the expected stereotype ($p = 0.048$). Based on these results, and contrary to our expectations, a generally lower perceived relevance is shown for stereotype-confirming content in the non-relevant documents.

4.2   Gender-Specific Experiments

We now aim to examine whether the gender of the participants affects their judgements (H3), and additionally, whether future research should factor in participants' genders when conducting such relevance judgement experiments. To this end, we conduct a two-way Analysis of variance (ANOVA) test aimed to examine if there exist effects of the query stereotype (independent variable 1 – IV1) or participants' genders (independent variable 2 – IV2) on relevance scores (dependent variable – DV), along with the determination of a possible interaction effect between both independent variables. As mentioned in Sect. 3, we conduct the gender-specific experiments on two queries (from the Appearance and Physical Capability categories), each with $N = 10$ participants. In this regard, we notice a statistically significant difference (p < 0.00001) between the *Average Relevance* of all relevant and non-relevant documents.

For each category, two independent two-way ANOVA tests (one for relevant and another for non-relevant documents) were performed. The results for Appearance indicate that interaction effect between IV1 and IV2 is not statistically significant, neither for relevant ($p = 0.772$) nor for non-relevant documents ($p = 0.76$). The experiments on Physical Capability show similar results, such that no statistically significant interaction between IV1 and IV2 is observed ($p = 0.336$ and $p = 0.697$ for relevant and non-relevant documents, respectively). For the sake of completeness, the detailed average results of the experiments, separated over the participants' genders are reported in Table 3.

Examining H3: the results of the ANOVA test do not show any statistically significant interaction between the effects of participant gender and stereotypes on the relevance judgements. These results provide a practical benefit, particularly when considering the commonly existing extra costs and constraints for specifying the gender of participants. Nevertheless, our results should be taken cautiously due to the small sample considered in our study.

4.3 Discussion

Due to the number of queries and the population size, we are generally not able to arrive at any reliable conclusions and can solely notice a possible tendency regarding the relevance judgement of participants to be influenced by the expected gender stereotype of a document. Thus, the research questions are addressed as follows: For answering RQ1, we consider hypotheses H1, and H2. In the statistical evaluation of the results, it is shown that participants perceive search results in the stereotypical female category Domestic Work as more relevant, when a female stereotype is expressed in the result document. In association with the query *how to easily clean at home*, the document expressing a female bias mentions a *Housewife*, whereas the male-biased document contains the word *Houseman*. An explanation of these results can be the stereotypical female expectation to perform care work, which seems to contribute to the different relevance judgements. According to Caroline Criado-Perez [22], 75% of globally done unpaid work is carried out by women – creating an unpaid-work imbalance between the genders, which is still an existing problem in today's modern society. Even though political efforts have been made to change this gender gap globally, it is still the reality that "working women" is not understood as tautology per se [22]. Taking into consideration that unpaid housework (predominantly consisting of cleaning activities) comprises the main workload of unpaid care work, it is not surprising that the experiment reveals the shown results. Thus, when users search for information in terms of cleaning at home, they do not seem to be negatively surprised or unsatisfied when confronted with a female-biased search result. On the contrary, a male-biased document seems to be perceived as less relevant, supporting the stated thesis of the understanding of stereotypical male and female activities and work in this area.

Regarding H2, the results of the experiment contradict our expectations. For the category Appearance, where a female stereotype is expected, the relevance judgement shows that non-relevant documents with male gender indication are rated higher in relevance than their female-indicating pendants. We should also highlight that a possible explanation of these results could be due to the formulation of the document content. For the query *what is considered plus size*, the non-relevant documents have titles such as *Percentage of men classified as underweight* and *Percentage of women classified as underweight*. Both documents include the sentence *Even if it does not seem so: a lot of men [women] struggle with their weight being too low but is it a gut feeling or is he [she] really underweight - let's find out!*. The combination of both title and text could imply semantically that it is astonishing and unexpected if the addressed person is underweight. Therefore, the reason for the shown results could be that participants perceive the stereotype-disconfirming (in the case of the male content) as more relevant due to the emphasis on the unexpectedness of men being underweight. In accordance, studies find that females are stereotypically perceived to be more susceptible to struggle with their weight and appearance, being more critical of their bodies [27]. Thus, in this context, it seems to be of more relevance to users to find information about men, surprisingly being underweight in contrast to women.

Considering the results of the categories Career, Child Care, Cognitive Capability and Physical Capability, no significant effect between the relevance judgement and stereotype expectation is found. One interpretation of this result is that participants do not perceive gender-biased search results differently in their relevance and are not influenced by their gender stereotype expectation. We should however also take into account other reasons for those findings such as the overall setup of the experiment in combination with the formulation of document title and text, explained in detail in Sect. 4.4.

Lastly, RQ2 is assessed in the gender-specific experiment. In particular, H3 examines whether the genders of participants influence the perception of gender-biased retrieval results. Based on the experiments, no statistical significance between the participant's gender, the expected stereotype, and the relevance judgement is observed. In conclusion, participant gender appears to have no influence on the decision of the perceived stereotype confirmation or disconfirmation. Nevertheless, this result should be taken cautiously due to the small sample used in our study. Indeed, it contradicts some of the observations done in the studies of the presented literature. For instance, Hentschel et al. [13] show that gender stereotype perception differs in the evaluation of selves and others between males and females. Also, none of the genders seems to show an affinity to perceive stereotypical content predominantly different. A backlash effect, as observed in gender stereotype portrayal in image search results [19], or the perception of the social status of men [18] is not observed in our experiments.

4.4 Limitations of the Experiments

To begin with, any study conducted on Amazon Mechanical Turk must be critically reflected in view of associated ethical implications. The participants in our set of experiments received 0.1$ per assignment. One task published on the platform comprised three to six different assignments, i.e. three to six different relevance judgements. The average completion time per judgement was averagely around 300 s. In the scope of this work, the decision to utilize Amazon Mechanical Turk for the experiment conduction is based mainly on time and budget restrictions. For further experiments, the realisation of experiments beyond such platforms is recommended, e.g. in a laboratory setting with university students.

One of the main limitations of our study lays in the examined population that participated in the experiment. Just as in every laboratory environment, the presented results can only be considered as a reflection of reality to a certain extend. In terms of statistical power, the 50 participants per task of the gender-agnostic experiment and 10 participants per task of the gender-specific experiment do not represent large sample size, which may have affected the statistical conclusions based on the study's outcome. To extend the external validity, the experiment design could be adapted so that a real search engine environment and search task is simulated. This could be achieved by displaying a search result document after clicking the search button for a certain query so that a more realistic interaction is experienced.

Another limitation of the results lays in the choice of including only binary gender, namely male and female. This decision is mainly due to the limitations of the crowd-sourcing framework. For studies based thereupon, the inclusion of non-binary gender in the query-document compilations as well as in the participant selection is highly recommended. Today, self-identification beyond male or female is already strongly anchored in our real world - but rarely included in the overall IR systems research domain. The effects that this inclusion could have on the field of gender bias perception studies could open up a completely new perspective inside the whole research area and create deep insights into the role of gender-related concepts in information systems.

5   Conclusion and Future Work

Gender biases and stereotypes play a central role in the way how we perceive ourselves and others, and are found to be existent and particularly persistent in the IR systems we interact with. This paper aims to approach the question of whether expressed gender bias in the content of retrieval results influences the perceived user judgement of its relevance. By showing one-sided search results that reflect different gender stereotypes, an effort is made to bring together recent theories from sociology (i. e., gender stereotype perception) and the information system research (i. e., gender bias perception in IR systems), done through the lens of a set of human studies. As shown, participants are influenced by biased retrieval results in their relevance judgement, especially in female-related categories. These findings raise concerns in regard to the negative effects of gender bias in IR systems, and calls for more algorithmic accountability and transparency, especially for commonly used IR systems.

In this work, we focused on the relevance rating of one search result per query, absent of further context (such as source url or date) or the choice between different ranked documents that might influence the relevance perceived by users in real-world situations. We also do not address differences in the perception of stereotypical biased content in participants from distinct cultures or age groups, as our current study was limited to a group of MTurk workers. Possible effects of participants' gender attitudes and beliefs, as introduced by Behm-Morawitz and Mastro [2], on their relevance judgement of differently gender-biased content may be assessed in further experiments. Future work might also try to extend the developed experimental setup to include other SE-related concepts found to contain biases, such as automated query suggestions [3]. Here, our Grep-BiasIR dataset [16] opens the possibility to conduct further related experiments. Till then, as one of the first studies to explore effects of perceived gender biases in retrieval results on relevance judgements, this study presents an initial empirical contribution.

As a final remark, within what sometimes seems like a Chicken-Egg-Problem, questioning if humans produce biased systems or if biased systems produce or reinforce biases in humans, the protagonists of different disciplines (legal, commercial and federal) are required to act. Beyond that, a general improvement of diversity in the technology sector – free of gender, race or other social categories – could contribute to overall bias mitigation, beginning in every individual's mind and ending in each technological creation [28].

Acknowledgements. This work received financial support by the Austrian Science Fund (FWF): P33526 and DFH-23; and by the State of Upper Austria and the Federal Ministry of Education, Science, and Research, through grant LIT-2020-9-SEE-113 and LIT-2021-YOU-215. We thank Robert Bosch GmbH for providing financial support for the conference registration and travel costs of the first author.

References

1. Bajaj, P., et al.: MS MARCO: a human generated machine reading comprehension dataset. arXiv:1611.09268 [cs], October 2018
2. Behm-Morawitz, E., Mastro, D.: The effects of the sexualization of female video game characters on gender stereotyping and female self-concept. Sex Roles **61**(11–12), 808–823 (2009). https://doi.org/10.1007/s11199-009-9683-8
3. Bonart, M., Samokhina, A., Heisenberg, G., Schaer, P.: An investigation of biases in web search engine query suggestions. Online Inf. Rev. **44**(2), 365–381 (2019)
4. Chang, K.W., Prabhakaran, V., Ordonez, V.: Bias and fairness in natural language processing. In: Proceedings of the 2019 Conference on Empirical Methods in Natural Language Processing and the 9th International Joint Conference on Natural Language Processing (EMNLP-IJCNLP): Tutorial Abstracts (2019)
5. Chen, L., Ma, R., Hannák, A., Wilson, C.: Investigating the impact of gender on rank in resume search engines. In: Proceedings of the 2018 CHI Conference on Human Factors in Computing Systems, pp. 1–14 (2018)
6. Cohen, G.L., Garcia, J.: "i am us": negative stereotypes as collective threats. J. Pers. Soc. Psychol. **89**(4), 566 (2005)
7. Craswell, N., Mitra, B., Yilmaz, E., Campos, D., Voorhees, E.M.: Overview of the TREC 2019 deep learning track. arXiv preprint arXiv:2003.07820 (2020)
8. Danks, D., London, A.J.: Algorithmic bias in autonomous systems. In: Proceedings of the 26th International Joint Conference on Artificial Intelligence, pp. 4691–4697 (2017)
9. Fabris, A., Purpura, A., Silvello, G., Susto, G.A.: Gender stereotype reinforcement: measuring the gender bias conveyed by ranking algorithms. Inf. Process. Manag. **57**(6), 102377 (2020)
10. Gerhart, S.: Do web search engines suppress controversy? First Monday **9**(1) (2004). https://doi.org/10.5210/fm.v9i1.1111
11. Gezici, G., Lipani, A., Saygin, Y., Yilmaz, E.: Evaluation metrics for measuring bias in search engine results. Inf. Retrieval J. **24**(2), 85–113 (2021). https://doi.org/10.1007/s10791-020-09386-w
12. Glick, P., Fiske, S.T.: Sexism and other "isms": independence, status, and the ambivalent content of stereotypes. In: Sexism and Stereotypes in Modern Society: The Gender Science of Janet Taylor Spence, pp. 193–221. American Psychological Association (1999). https://doi.org/10.1037/10277-008
13. Hentschel, T., Heilman, M.E., Peus, C.V.: The multiple dimensions of gender stereotypes: a current look at men's and women's characterizations of others and themselves. Front. Psychol. **10**, 11 (2019)
14. Kay, M., Matuszek, C., Munson, S.A.: Unequal representation and gender stereotypes in image search results for occupations. In: Proceedings of the 33rd Annual ACM Conference on Human Factors in Computing Systems, pp. 3819–3828 (2015)
15. Kordzadeh, N., Ghasemaghaei, M.: Algorithmic bias: review, synthesis, and future research directions. Eur. J. Inf. Syst. **31**(3), 388–409 (2021)

16. Krieg, K., Parada-Cabaleiro, E., Medicus, G., Lesota, O., Schedl, M., Rekabsaz, N.: Grep-BiasIR: a dataset for investigating gender representation-bias in information retrieval results. arXiv:2201.07754 [cs] (2022)

17. Melchiorre, A.B., Rekabsaz, N., Parada-Cabaleiro, E., Brandl, S., Lesota, O., Schedl, M.: Investigating gender fairness of recommendation algorithms in the music domain. Inf. Process. Manag. (2021). https://doi.org/10.1016/j.ipm.2021.102666

18. Moss-Racusin, C.A., Phelan, J.E., Rudman, L.A.: When men break the gender rules: status incongruity and backlash against modest men. Psychol. Men Masculinity 11(2), 140 (2010)

19. Otterbacher, J., Bates, J., Clough, P.: Competent men and warm women: gender stereotypes and backlash in image search results. In: Proceedings of the 2017 CHI Conference on Human Factors in Computing Systems, pp. 6620–6631 (2017)

20. Otterbacher, J., Checco, A., Demartini, G., Clough, P.: Investigating user perception of gender bias in image search: the role of sexism. In: The 41st International ACM SIGIR Conference on Research & Development in Information Retrieval, pp. 933–936 (2018)

21. Pan, B., Hembrooke, H., Joachims, T., Lorigo, L., Gay, G., Granka, L.: In Google we trust: users' decisions on rank, position, and relevance. J. Comput. Mediated Commun. 12(3), 801–823 (2007)

22. Perez, C.C.: Invisible Women: Exposing Data Bias in a World Designed for Men. Random House (2019)

23. Rekabsaz, N., Kopeinik, S., Schedl, M.: Societal biases in retrieved contents: measurement framework and adversarial mitigation of BERT rankers. In: Proceedings of the 44th International ACM SIGIR Conference on Research and Development in Information Retrieval, pp. 306–316 (2021)

24. Rekabsaz, N., Lesota, O., Schedl, M., Brassey, J., Eickhoff, C.: TripClick: the log files of a large health web search engine. In: Proceedings of the 44th International ACM SIGIR Conference on Research and Development in Information Retrieval, pp. 2507–2513. Association for Computing Machinery, New York, July 2021

25. Rekabsaz, N., Schedl, M.: Do neural ranking models intensify gender bias? In: Proceedings of the 43rd International ACM SIGIR Conference on Research and Development in Information Retrieval, pp. 2065–2068 (2020)

26. Rekabsaz, N., West, R., Henderson, J., Hanbury, A.: Measuring societal biases from text corpora with smoothed first-order co-occurrence. In: Proceedings of the Fifteenth International AAAI Conference on Web and Social Media, ICWSM 2021, Held Virtually, 7–10 June 2021, pp. 549–560. AAAI Press (2021)

27. Sattler, K.M., Deane, F.P., Tapsell, L., Kelly, P.J.: Gender differences in the relationship of weight-based stigmatisation with motivation to exercise and physical activity in overweight individuals. Health Psychol. Open 5(1) (2018)

28. Shah, H.: Algorithmic accountability. Philos. Trans. Roy. Soc. A Math. Phys. Eng. Sci. 376(2128), 20170362 (2018)

29. Sherman, J.W.: Development and mental representation of stereotypes. J. Pers. Soc. Psychol. 70(6), 1126 (1996)

30. Silva, S., Kenney, M.: Algorithms, platforms, and ethnic bias. Commun. ACM 62(11), 37–39 (2019)

31. Simpson, J.A., Kenrick, D.T.: Evolutionary Social Psychology. Psychology Press (2014)

32. Stangor, C., Jhangiani, R., Tarry, H., et al.: Principles of Social Psychology. BCcampus (2014)

33. Steele, C.M., Aronson, J.: Stereotype threat and the intellectual test performance of African Americans. J. Pers. Soc. Psychol. 69(5), 797 (1995)

Enhancing Fairness in Classification Tasks with Multiple Variables: A Data- and Model-Agnostic Approach

Giordano d'Aloisio$^{(\boxtimes)}$ ⓘ, Giovanni Stilo ⓘ, Antinisca Di Marco ⓘ,
and Andrea D'Angelo ⓘ

Department of Engineering and Information Sciences and Mathematics,
University of L'Aquila, L'Aquila, Italy
`giordano.daloisio@graduate.univaq.it`,
`{giovanni.stilo,antinisca.dimarco}@univaq.it`,
`andrea.dangelo6@student.univaq.it`

Abstract. Nowadays assuring that *search* and *recommendation* systems are fair and do not apply discrimination among any kind of population has become of paramount importance. Those systems typically rely on machine learning algorithms that solve the classification task. Although the problem of fairness has been widely addressed in binary classification, unfortunately, the fairness of multi-class classification problem needs to be further investigated lacking well-established solutions. For the aforementioned reasons, in this paper, we present the *Debiaser for Multiple Variables*, a novel approach able to enhance fairness in both binary and multi-class classification problems. The proposed method is compared, under several conditions, with the well-established baseline. We evaluate our method on a heterogeneous data set and prove how it overcomes the established algorithms in the multi-classification setting, while maintaining good performances in binary classification. Finally, we present some limitations and future improvements.

Keywords: Machine learning · Bias and fairness · Multi-class classification · Preprocessing algorithm

1 Introduction

Bias impacts human beings as individuals or groups characterized by a set of legally-protected sensitive attributes (e.g., their race, gender, or religion). If not managed, the inequalities reinforced by search and recommendation algorithms can lead to *severe societal consequences*, such as discrimination and unfairness [14]. Both *search* and *recommendation* algorithms provide a user with ranked results that fit and match their needs and interests. Both tasks often convey and strengthen bias in terms of *imbalances* and *inequalities*, primarily if they rely on or encompass machine learning algorithms as those which solve classification problems. For this reason, assuring that search and recommendation

L. Boratto et al. (Eds.): BIAS 2022, CCIS 1610, pp. 117–129, 2022.
https://doi.org/10.1007/978-3-031-09316-6_11

systems are fair and do not apply discrimination among any kind of population has become of paramount importance, mainly because they are pervasive in several domains (e.g., justice [26], health care [30], education [4], etc.).

Over the years, different methods have been proposed to mitigate bias at several levels of data processing. However, we notice that the multi-class classification problem is still not effectively addressed, even if it is widely adopted and constitutes a building block for personalization and search systems in several domains [16,21,29].

For this reason, in this paper, we present the *Debiaser for Multiple Variables (DEMV)*. This novel approach is a generalization of the *Sampling* algorithm proposed by Kamiran et al. in [17]. DEMV is model and data-agnostic, allowing its introduction in already existing systems without particular effort and without introducing structural changes. The DEMV enhances fairness both in binary and multi-class classification problems, handling any number of sensitive variables and with any classifier. We exhaustively show, with different datasets, that our method outperforms the state-of-the-art methods in the multi-class classification while achieving comparable performances in the binary one.

This paper is structured as follows: in Sect. 2, we recall some background knowledge used in our work and describe some bias mitigation methods in the context of multi-class classification problem; in Sect. 3, we describe in detail the proposed approach; Sect. 4 is dedicated to the experimental analysis that has been conducted both in binary and multi-classification problems; finally, Sect. 5 describes some points of improvement of our approach and concludes the paper.

2   Background Knowledge and Related Work

In the last ten years, the study of bias and fairness in machine learning acquired considerable relevance in literature. Many definitions and metrics have been proposed to address different kinds of bias and fairness [23]. In this section, we recall the definition of fairness we use in this paper and then, we describe the related work in the context of bias mitigation in multi-class classification problem.

2.1   Fairness Definition

Demographic (Statistical) Parity (DP) [11,20] is one of the most used definitions of *group fairness* [23], which assumes the independence among the predicted positive label y_p and the sensitive variables $S_1, \ldots, S_n$.

Formally, let $\hat{Y}$ be the predicted value and S be a generic binary sensitive variable where $S = 1$ and $S = 0$ identify the privileged and unprivileged groups, respectively. A predictor is *fair* under DP if:

$$P(\hat{Y} = y_p | S = 1) = P(\hat{Y} = y_p | S = 0) \tag{1}$$

A different formulation for the DP is the *Disparate Impact* [12], which considers the ratio among the two probabilities:

$$0.8 \leq \frac{P(\hat{Y} = y_p | S = 1)}{P(\hat{Y} = y_p | S = 0)} \leq 1.2 \tag{2}$$

In this case, following the *80% rule* [12], the value must be between 0.8 and 1.2 in order to have *fairness*. DP falls into the *We Are Equal (WAE)* metrics family, which holds that all groups have similar abilities concerning the task (i.e., have the same probability of being classified in a certain way) [13].

2.2 Related Works

Over the years, many methods have been proposed to mitigate bias at different levels of data processing [7, 23]. In particular, we distinguish among **pre-processing** methods, which modify the data to remove the underlying bias; **in-processing** methods, which change the learning algorithm to remove discrimination during the model training process; **post-processing** methods, which re-calibrate an already trained model using a holdout set not used during the training phase. In general, the sooner a technique can be applied, the better because it can be chained with other bias mitigation methods in the later processing phases [1, 31].

Among *pre-processing* methods, one widely adopted is the *Sampling* algorithm proposed by Kamiran et al. in [17]. Its method rebalances both privileged and unprivileged users in the case of binary classification with a single sensitive variable.

Formally, let be S the sensitive variable with $\{w, b\} \in S$ representing the privileged and unprivileged groups, respectively, and let be Y the target label with $\{+, -\} \in Y$ defining the positive and negative outcomes. The sampling algorithm first splits the original dataset into four groups:

- Deprived group with Positive label (DP): all instances with $S = b \wedge Y = +$;
- Deprived group with Negative label (DN): all instances with $S = b \wedge Y = -$;
- Favored group with Positive label (FP): all instances with $S = w \wedge Y = +$;
- Favored group with Negative label (FN): all instances with $S = w \wedge Y = -$.

Then, the algorithm balances the groups iteratively until their *observed* sizes are equal to their *expected* ones.

We like to note that very few methods are able to mitigate the bias in the multi-class classification problems. Among those are the two *post-processing* methods proposed by Krishnaswamy et al. [19]. They start from the definition of a set of deterministic classifiers H and a class of groups G made by elements in the form $g : N \rightarrow \{1, -1\}$, where $g(i) = 1$ iff item i is in group g, -1 otherwise. For each group g, they identify the best classifier h_g^* as the one assuring the highest accuracy for that group. Then, they define fairness as a constraint among the accuracy of each possible classifier and the optimal one for each group g. The core difference between the two proposed approaches lays in the definition of G. The first one, named *Proportional Fairness (PF)*, considers each possible subset of the dataset, so there is no limitation on G. The second method, *BeFair (Best-effort Fair)*, considers instead each linearly separable group (i.e., if $g \in G$, then g and $N \backslash g$ are linearly separable). To solve the unfairness of the input classifier, both methods optimize a MinMax function.

An *in-processing* method that solves unfairness in multiple classification settings is the one presented by Agarwal et al. [2]. The algorithm addresses two definitions of fairness at once: *Demographic Parity* and *Equalized Odds* [15]. The authors formulate such definitions as linear constraints and then build an Exponentiated Gradient reduction algorithm that yields a randomized classifier with the lowest error subject to the desired fairness constraints. Also, in this case, the method follows a MinMax approach in which the players try to minimize the given constraint and maximize the classifier's score. Although the authors study their algorithm mainly in binary classification problems, they also show how it can be applied to regression and multi-classification problems.

Note that most of the methods in the literature are primarily designed for binary classification problems, and the minority of them apply during the *pre-processing* phase. On the contrary, our proposed method is able to work in the pre-processing stage. Since it can be used at the beginning of the processing phase, it can be possibly chained with other algorithms in later steps. Moreover, it natively supports multi-class classification and multiple sensitive variables in an affordable yet successful way, as is shown in the experimental Sect. 4.

3   Debiaser for Multiple Variables (DEMV)

In this section, we describe in detail *Debiaser for Multiple Variables (DEMV)*, a bias mitigation method for multiple sensitive variables in the classification context.

The main idea behind the proposed method is that all the possible combinations of the sensitive variables values and of the label's values for the definition of the sampling groups must be considered. We approach the problem by recursively identifying all the possible groups given by combining all the values of the sensible variables with the belonging label (class). For each group, we compute its expected and observed sizes, defined respectively as:

$$W_{exp} = \frac{|\{X \in D | S = s\}|}{|D|} * \frac{|\{X \in D | L = l\}|}{|D|} \tag{3}$$

$$W_{obs} = \frac{|\{X \in D | S = s \wedge L = l\}|}{|D|} \tag{4}$$

where $S = s$ is a generic condition on the value of the sensitive variables[1] and $L = l$ is a condition on the label's value. If $W_{exp} \backslash W_{obs} = 1$ implies that the group is fully balanced. Otherwise, if the ratio is less than one, the group size is larger

---

[1] The variables can be binary, discrete or categorical ones.

than expected, so we have to delete a random element from the considered group. Instead, if the ratio is greater than one, the group is smaller than expected, so we have to duplicate an item from the group by random sampling. For each group, we recursively repeat this operation until $W_{exp}\backslash W_{obs}$ converge to one.

The group-balancing operation is implemented by the SAMPLE function, whose pseudo-code is depicted in listing Algorithm 1. This function takes as input the group g and the expected (W_{exp}) and observed size (W_{obs}). The core of this algorithm is a while loop that checks if the value of $W_{exp}\backslash W_{obs}$ is different from 1. If so, the algorithm selects a random index in the range of $(0, length(g) - 1)$ and duplicates the corresponding item if $W_{exp}\backslash W_{obs} > 1$ or removes it if $W_{exp}\backslash W_{obs} < 1$. Finally, the algorithm returns the sampled group when the while condition becomes true.

Algorithm 1: Pseudo-code of SAMPLE

Input: (Group g, Expected size W_{exp}, Observed size W_{obs})
Output: Balanced group g

1 **while** $W_{exp}\backslash W_{obs}\ != 1$ **do**
2      $i =$ random value $\in \{0, \ldots, length(g) - 1\}$
3   **if** $W_{exp}\backslash W_{obs} > 1$ **then**
4        $\lfloor$ duplicate item at position i in g
5   **else if** $W_{exp}\backslash W_{obs} < 1$ **then**
6        $\lfloor$ remove item at position i from g
7   recompute W_{obs}
8 **return** g

The SAMPLE algorithm is invoked inside DEMV whose pseudo-code is showed in listing Algorithm 2. The main *DEMV* function takes as input the dataset D, the categorical sensitive variables $S_1, \ldots, S_n$, the label L and other parameters useful for the recursion: a counter i initially set to 0, an array G initially empty and a boolean *condition* initially set to *true*. Lines from 2 to 9 define the base condition of the function. They check if the counter i is equal to the number of sensitive variables. If so, the algorithm iterates the possible values of the label and creates the corresponding group g. Then, it computes the expected and observed sizes and it balances the group using the SAMPLE function (listing Algorithm 1). Finally, the approach adds the balanced group g_b to the array G (used to collect all the sampled groups) and returns it. Lines from 10 to 14 identify the recursive part of the function. In particular, if the value of i is not equal to the number of sensitive variables, the algorithm increments the value of i by one and appends to G the result of a series of recursive calls. These recursive invocations differ from each other only in the condition passed as input. In fact, the algorithm iterates for all the possible values of the sensitive variable S_i and, for each value s, it does a recursive call adding the condition of $S_i == s$ to the previous ones through an $\wedge$ connector. Finally, lines from 15 to

19 define the returning conditions of the function. In particular, the maximum
number of samples obtainable from the combination of n sensitive variables plus
the label is given by the product of all the sensitive variables' and label's values,
that is:

$$\prod_{1,\ldots,n}^{i} |S_i| * |L|$$

If the length of G is equal to this value, then the function has considered and
balanced all the groups and it returns the final sampled dataset D_S. Otherwise,
the function being in the middle of the recursive tree, returns G which will be
again merged with the result of other recursive functions. DEMV algorithm can
also be applied to binary classification problems; in that case, the number of
sampling groups will be equal to:

$$\prod_{1,\ldots,n}^{i} |S_i| * 2$$

Algorithm 2: Pseudo-code of DEMV

Input: (Dataset D, Sensitive variables $S_1, S_2, \ldots, S_n$, Label L, $i = 0$, $G = []$,
condition=$true$)

Output: Sampled dataset D_S

1   $n = length(\{S_1, S_2, \ldots, S_n\})$
2   **if** $i == n$ **then**
3   **foreach** $l \in L$ **do**
4       $g = \{X \in D|\ \text{condition} \wedge L == l\}$
5       $W_{exp} = \dfrac{|\{X \in D|\text{condition}\}|}{|D|} * \dfrac{|\{X \in D|L == l\}|}{|D|}$
6       $W_{obs} = \dfrac{|g|}{|D|}$
7       $g_b = SAMPLE(g, W_{exp}, W_{obs})$
8   add g_b to G
9   **return** G
10 **else**
11     $i = i + 1$
12   **foreach** $s \in S_i$ **do**
13       $G' = DEMV(D, S_1, \ldots, S_n, i, G, \text{condition} = condition \wedge S_i == s)$
14   add G' to G
15   **if** $length(G) == \prod_{1\ldots n}^{i} |S_i| * |L|$ **then**
16   D_S = merge all $g \in G$
17   **return** D_S
18   **else**
19   **return** G

The implementation of *DEMV* is available at the Territori Aperti RI.

4   Experimental Analysis

This section describes the experiments we conducted to evaluate the proposed method. We analyzed *DEMV* under heterogeneous conditions where a set of binary and multi-class datasets were employed. Our method was compared with *Exponentiated Gradient* [2] (whose adopted implementation is available on the Fairlearn library [5]). Following the documentation available online, we used as for the *Exponentiated Gradient (EG)*: the *Demographic Parity* for binary classifications and *Zero-one Loss* [10] for multi-class problems.

We used a Logistic Regression classifier and conducted *10-fold* cross-validation [27]. We decided to apply DEMV and EG only on the training set.

For all the experiments, we computed the following metrics on the testing set: *Statistical Parity (SP)* [11,20], *Disparate Impact (DI)* [12], *Zero-one Loss (Z.O. Loss)* [10], and *Accuracy (Acc.)* [28]. In addition, since DEMV has a stochastic behavior, for each training set, we ran DEMV and computed the corresponding metrics 30 times so that we can investigate how the removal or duplication of different samples can influence the *accuracy* and the *fairness* of our method. Since DI tends to show a reverse-bias situation more than SP and the other selected metrics, to highlight the maximum fairness point under DI better, we use the formulation proposed by Radovanovic et al. in [24]:

$$DI = min \left(\frac{p(\hat{y} = 1|s = 1)}{p(\hat{y} = 1|s = 0)}, \frac{p(\hat{y} = 1|s = 0)}{p(\hat{y} = 1|s = 1)} \right) \tag{5}$$

This metric computes the minimum among two formulations of DI wherein one the unprivileged group $(s = 0)$ is at the numerator, and the other is at the denominator. The metric value is hence between 0 and 1, where 1 means complete fairness.

4.1   Employed Datasets

The experiments have been conducted by employing eight well-known datasets (3 for the binary classification and 5 for the multi-class task), coming from the Bias and Fairness literature:

- **Adult Income (ADULT)** [18]: a binary dataset that comprises 30,940 items by 102 features (one-hot encoded). The goal is to predict if a person has an income higher than 50k a year. This information is represented by the `income` variable. The protected attributes are `sex`, and `race` and the unprivileged group is *black women* (items with `sex` and `race` equal to zero). The positive label is *"high income"*.
- **ProPublica Recidivism (COMPAS)** [3]: This binary dataset is made of 6,167 samples by 399 attributes. The sensitive variables are `sex` and `race`. The goal is to predict if a person will recidivate in the next two years. The favorable label, in this case, is *no*, and the privileged group is *Caucasian women* (items with `sex` and `race` equal to one).

- **German Credit (GERMAN)** [25]: This binary dataset classifies people described by a set of attributes as good or bad credit risks (`credit` variable). The dataset consists of 1,000 instances by 59 features (one-hot encoded). The sensitive variables are `sex`, and `age` and the unprivileged group is *women with less than 25 years*. The positive label is *low credit risk*.
- **Contraceptive Method Choice (CMC)** [22]: This multi-class dataset comprises 1,473 instances and ten columns about women's contraceptive method choice (*not-use*, *short-use*, and *long-use*). The sensitive variables are `religion` and `work`. The unprivileged group is *Islamic women who do not work* (both values equal one), and the positive label is *long-term use*.
- **Communities and Crime (CRIME)** [26]: This multi-class dataset is made of 1,994 instances by 100 attributes and contains information about the per-capita violent crimes in a community (variable `ViolentCrimesPerPop`). Since the label is continuous, we transformed it by grouping the values in 6 classes using equidistant quantiles. Following [6] the sensitive attribute is the percentage of the black population, but we also considered the ratio of the Hispanic population to have two sensitive variables. The unprivileged group is communities with a *high percentage of both black and Hispanic people* (both variables equal to 1), and the positive label is 100 (class of *low rate of crimes*).
- **Law School Admission (LAW)** [4]: This multi-class dataset comprises 20,694 samples by 14 attributes and contains information about the bar passage data of Law School students. We grouped the continuous label (GPA) in 3 groups using equidistant quantiles. The sensitive variables are `race` and `gender` and the unprivileged group are *black women* (both variables equal to one), and the positive label is 2 (class of high scores).
- **The Trump Effect in Europe (TRUMP)** [9]: This multi-class dataset is the result of a survey about political preference in Europe after Trump's presidential election. It is made of 7,951 features and 204 attributes. The label is `political view` and the sensitive variables are `gender` and `religion`. The unprivileged group is *non-catholic women* (both variables equal to 0), and the positive label is equal to 3.
- **Wine Quality (WINE)** [8]: This multi-class dataset comprises 6,438 instances and 13 attributes about wine quality. The sensitive attributes are the wine's color (`type` variable) and the alcohol percentage lower or higher than 10 (`alcohol` variable). The unprivileged group is *white wine with alcohol percentage* ≤ 10, and the positive label is 6 (high quality).

Table 1 summarizes the key datasets' information.

4.2 Experimental Results

In this section, we present the results in binary and multi-class classification. For both experiments, we report charts showing the mean and the standard deviation for each of the metrics described in Sect. 4 (y-axis) at each DEMV iteration (x-axis). At iteration zero, the graphics report the metrics of the original biased dataset, while at the end of the curves they show the metrics computed, on the

Table 1. Datasets information

	Adult	Compas	German	CMC	Crime	Law	Trump	Wine
Scope	Social	Justice	Social	Social	Justice	Education	Social	Food
Instances	30,940	6,167	1,000	1473	1,994	20,427	7,951	6,438
Features	102	399	59	10	100	14	204	13
Type	binary	binary	binary	multi	multi	multi	multi	multi
Sensitive variables	sex race	sex race	sex age	work religion	black hisp	gender race	religion gender	type alcohol
Percentage of sensitive group	5.02%	54.71%	10.50%	64.83%	23.62%	8.42%	30.71%	11.40%

whole, balanced dataset. On the right part of the plots are reported using bigger points, the same metrics obtained by the EG algorithm.

Binary Classification. The results for binary classification are shown in Fig. 1 where the performance of DEMV at each iteration (x-axis) is shown.

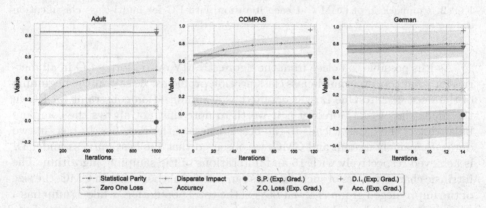

Fig. 1. Comparison of DEMV at each sampling iteration with EG for binary classification datasets.

The EG method can find the best trade-off between fairness and accuracy in the binary classification case. Instead, our approach has more difficulty improving fairness, especially when the bias is very high (see Adult dataset). However, our method can keep a high accuracy level when the dataset is fully balanced. In all the analyses, we can see that the complete balancing of the dataset leads to the best fairness of the classifier.

Multi-class Classification. Similarly, the results for multi-class classification are shown in Fig. 2 where the performance of DEMV is shown at each iteration (x-axis).

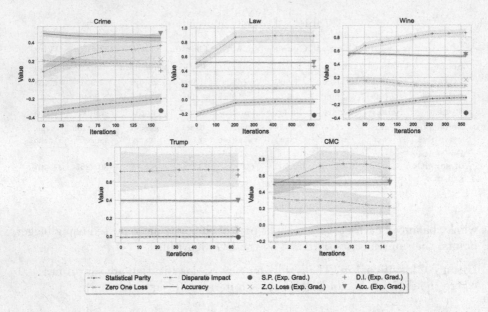

Fig. 2. Comparison of DEMV at each iteration with EG for multi-class classification datasets.

As it is possible to notice from the figure, DEMV outperforms EG in all metrics for what concerns multi-class classification problems. As said at the beginning of the Sect. 4, Zero-One Loss is adopted as a minimization constraint for EG in the multi-class task. Moreover is it worth to note that not always the complete balancing of the dataset leads to the best fairness of the classifier. In fact, in two datasets, namely Trump and CMC, we observed that the best fairness under DI is achieved respectively with 15 and 9 iterations of the sampling algorithm. The intrinsic characteristics of such datasets can justify this behavior: in CMC, the size of the unprivileged group is about 65% of the total population, while Trump has a very shallow bias. In such situations, we observed that it is not convenient to fully balance the datasets' groups. Finally, we observe that DI has a higher variance than SP, especially in datasets with a shallow bias like Trump.

Discussion. From the above analyses, we can draw the following considerations about DEMV. Our method can constantly improve the fairness of the classifier both in binary and multi-class classification, with respect to the initial biased classifier, keeping the accuracy almost unchanged (up to 0.05 points in case of CRIME). Moreover, DEMV algorithm has the advantage of being data and model agnostic, meaning that it can be applied to any dataset with any number of sensitive variables and any number of label's values, and it can be used with any classifier.

Concerning binary classification, DEMV little improves fairness, especially when the bias is very high; while other existing methods may perform better in these cases. For multi-classification setting, instead, our method outperforms the baseline, improving the fairness significantly (up to 0.4 points for DI in the case of the Law dataset). In addition, we observed that, in some particular circumstances (like CMC and Trump), achieving a complete balance of the sensitive groups does not lead to the best possible fairness. In such situations, a partial sampling of the groups is preferable.

5   Conclusion and Future Work

In this paper, we extended the work of [17] to present the *Debiaser for Multiple Variables*, a novel approach to enhance fairness in multi-class classification problems with any number of sensitive variables. We exhaustively compared it with the baseline method described in [2] performing both binary and multi-class classification.

We can summarise the following take away outcomes:

- DEMV is a novel approach, primarily defined for the under explored multi-class classification;
- DEMV is a better strategy to adopt than EG in the multi-class task;
- performing a complete balancing is not always the optimal solution for all the datasets; .
- we used DEMV also in binary classification, observing an improvement for all metrics. However, as expected, other specifically designed methods perform better in such cases.

In the future, we like to investigate further which are the characteristics of the dataset that lead to optimal performance before a complete balance within the groups. Furthermore, we want to determine the impact of adopting a higher or lower number of sensible variables and if the method remains consistent both in terms of *accuracy* and *fairness*. Given the independence among the predicted positive label, DP may not be the best metric to use in case of multi-class classification, hence we will explore other metrics for evaluation. Finally, we will widely evaluate our approach with respect to other existing multi-class bias mitigation methods, also considering a more extensive set of datasets covering different domains and having distinct, not overlapping characteristics.

Acknowledgments. This work is partially supported by Territori Aperti a project funded by Fondo Territori Lavoro e Conoscenza CGIL CISL UIL, by SoBigData-PlusPlus H2020-INFRAIA-2019-1 EU project, contract number 871042 and by "FAIR-EDU: Promote FAIRness in EDUcation institutions" a project founded by the University of L'Aquila.

References

1. AI Fairness 360 - Resources. https://aif360.mybluemix.net/resources#guidance
2. Agarwal, A., Beygelzimer, A., Dudík, M., Langford, J., Wallach, H.: A reductions approach to fair classification. arXiv:1803.02453 [cs], July 2018. arXiv: 1803.02453

3. Angwin, J., Larson, J., Mattu, S., Kirchner, L.: Machine Bias. ProPublica, pp. 139–159, 23 May 2016
4. Austin, K.A., Christopher, C.M., Dickerson, D.: Will I pass the bar exam: Will I pass the bar exam: predicting student success using LSAT scores and law school performance. HofstrA l. Rev. **45**, 753 (2016)
5. Bird, S., et al.: Fairlearn: a toolkit for assessing and improving fairness in AI. Tech. Rep. MSR-TR-2020-32, Microsoft, May 2020. https://www.microsoft.com/en-us/research/publication/fairlearn-a-toolkit-for-assessing-and-improving-fairness-in-ai/
6. Calders, T., Karim, A., Kamiran, F., Ali, W., Zhang, X.: Controlling attribute effect in linear regression. In: 2013 IEEE 13th International Conference on Data Mining, pp. 71–00, December 2013. https://doi.org/10.1109/ICDM.2013.114, ISSN: 2374-8486
7. Caton, S., Haas, C.: Fairness in machine learning: a survey. arXiv:2010.04053 [cs, stat] (October 2020), arXiv: 2010.04053
8. Cortez, P., Cerdeira, A., Almeida, F., Matos, T., Reis, J.: Modeling wine preferences by data mining from physicochemical properties. Decis. Supp. Syst. **47**(4), 547–553 (2009)
9. DaliaResearch: The Trump Effect in Europe (2017). https://www.kaggle.com/daliaresearch/trump-effect
10. Domingos, P., Pazzani, M.: On the optimality of the simple Bayesian classifier under zero-one loss. Mach. Learning **29**(2), 103–130 (1997)
11. Dwork, C., Hardt, M., Pitassi, T., Reingold, O., Zemel, R.: Fairness through awareness. In: Proceedings of the 3rd Innovations in Theoretical Computer Science Conference, pp. 214–226. ITCS '12, Association for Computing Machinery, New York, NY, USA, January 2012. https://doi.org/10.1145/2090236.2090255
12. Feldman, M., Friedler, S.A., Moeller, J., Scheidegger, C., Venkatasubramanian, S.: Certifying and removing disparate impact. In: Proceedings of the 21th ACM SIGKDD International Conference on Knowledge Discovery and Data Mining, pp. 259–268. ACM, Sydney NSW Australia, Aug 2015. https://doi.org/10.1145/2783258.2783311
13. Friedler, S.A., Scheidegger, C., Venkatasubramanian, S.: On the (im) possibility of fairness. arXiv preprint arXiv:1609.07236 (2016)
14. Hajian, S., Bonchi, F., Castillo, C.: Algorithmic bias: from discrimination discovery to fairness-aware data mining. In: Proceedings of the 22nd ACM SIGKDD International Conference on Knowledge Discovery and Data Mining, San Francisco, CA, USA, 13–17 August 2016, pp. 2125–2126. ACM (2016)
15. Hardt, M., Price, E., Srebro, N.: Equality of opportunity in supervised learning. Adv. Neural Inf. Process. Syst. **29**, 3315–3323 (2016)
16. Jiang, C., Liu, Y., Ding, Y., Liang, K., Duan, R.: Capturing helpful reviews from social media for product quality improvement: a multi-class classification approach. Int. J. Prod. Res. **55**(12), 3528–3541 (2017)
17. Kamiran, F., Calders, T.: Data preprocessing techniques for classification without discrimination. Knowl. Inf. Syst. **33**(1), 1–33 (2012). https://doi.org/10.1007/s10115-011-0463-8
18. Kohavi, R., et al.: Scaling up the accuracy of naive-Bayes classifiers: a decision-tree hybrid. In: KDD'96: Proceedings of the Second International Conference on Knowledge Discovery and Data Mining, pp. 202–207 (1996)
19. Krishnaswamy, A., Jiang, Z., Wang, K., Cheng, Y., Munagala, K.: Fair for all: best-effort fairness guarantees for classification. In: International Conference on Artificial Intelligence and Statistics, pp. 3259–3267. PMLR (2021)

20. Kusner, M.J., Loftus, J., Russell, C., Silva, R.: Counterfactual fairness. In: Advances in Neural Information Processing Systems. vol. 30. Curran Associates, Inc. (2017)
21. Le, Y., He, C., Chen, M., Wu, Y., He, X., Zhou, B.: Learning to predict charges for legal judgment via self-attentive capsule network. In: ECAI 2020, pp. 1802–1809. IOS Press, Red Hook (2020)
22. Lim, T.S., Loh, W.Y., Shih, Y.S.: A comparison of prediction accuracy, complexity, and training time of thirty-three old and new classification algorithms. Mach. Learn. **40**(3), 203–228 (2000)
23. Mehrabi, N., Morstatter, F., Saxena, N., Lerman, K., Galstyan, A.: A survey on bias and fairness in machine learning. ACM Compu. Surv. **54**(6), 1–35 (2021). https://doi.org/10.1145/3457607
24. Radovanović, S., Petrović, A., Delibašić, B., Suknović, M.: A fair classifier chain for multi-label bank marketing strategy classification. Int. Trans. Oper. Res. (2021). https://doi.org/10.1111/itor.13059, https://onlinelibrary.wiley.com/doi/pdf/10.1111/itor.13059
25. Ratanamahatana, C.A., Gunopulos, D.: Scaling up the naive Bayesian classifier: Using decision trees for feature selection. Appl. Artiff. Intell. **17**(5), 475–487 (2002)
26. Redmond, M., Baveja, A.: A data-driven software tool for enabling cooperative information sharing among police departments. Eur. J. Oper. Res. **141**(3), 660–678 (2002)
27. Refaeilzadeh, P., Tang, L., Liu, H.: Cross-Validation, pp. 1–7. Springer, New York (2016). https://doi.org/10.1007/978-1-4899-7993-3_565-2
28. Rosenfield, G., Fitzpatrick-Lins, K.: A coefficient of agreement as a measure of thematic classification accuracy. Photogram. Eng. Rem. Sen. **52**(2), 223–227 (1986). http://pubs.er.usgs.gov/publication/70014667
29. Sánchez-Morillo, D., López-Gordo, M., León, A.: Novel multiclass classification for home-based diagnosis of sleep apnea hypopnea syndrome. Exp. Syst. Appli. **41**(4), 1654–1662 (2014)
30. Street, W.N., Wolberg, W.H., Mangasarian, O.L.: Nuclear feature extraction for breast tumor diagnosis. In: Biomedical Image Processing and Biomedical Visualization. vol. 1905, pp. 861–870. International Society for Optics and Photonics (1993)
31. Wolpert, D.H.: What does dinner cost? http://www.no-free-lunch.org/coev.pdf

Keyword Recommendation for Fair Search

Harshit Mishra[✉] and Sucheta Soundarajan

Syracuse University, Syracuse, NY 13244, USA
harsh.dsdh@gmail.com, susounda@syr.edu

Abstract. Online search engines are an extremely popular tool for seeking information. However, the results returned sometimes exhibit undesirable or even wrongful forms of bias, such as with respect to gender or race. In this paper, we consider the problem of *fair keyword recommendation*, in which the goal is to suggest keywords that are relevant to a user's search query, but exhibit less (or opposite) bias. We present a multi-objective optimization method that uses word embeddings to suggest alternate keywords for biased keywords present in a search query. We perform a qualitative analysis on pairs of subReddits from Reddit.com (r/Republican vs. r/democrats). Our results demonstrate the efficacy of the proposed method and illustrate subtle linguistic differences between subReddits.

Keywords: search engine · bias · recommender systems

1 Introduction

Online search engines are an extremely popular tool for individuals seeking information. However, as is well known, the results returned by search engines may over- or under-represent results in a way that exhibits undesirable or even wrongful forms of bias [14]. This occurs because search engines commonly use word embeddings to determine the relevance of a document to a search query: e.g., as argued in [2], a hypothetical query for *cmu computer science phd student* may downrank results for female CS PhD students, because male names are closer to the search keywords than are female names in the embedding space. However, in addition to being ethically problematic, this phenomenon may also be unwanted by the user, who may not be aware of the latent bias embedded in their query. In the literature, this problem has been addressed in two main ways: by debiasing a word embedding [2,4] or by re-ranking search results to eliminate such bias [5,18,19].

In this paper, we consider an alternative solution, which we refer to as *fair keyword recommendation*, in which an algorithm suggests less-biased alternatives to a keyword. Our problem was originally motivated by conversations with an academic administration recruiter, who recounted her experiences with searching for job candidates on LinkedIn: when searching for individuals with a particular qualification, she noticed that her search results were primarily white men.

L. Boratto et al. (Eds.): BIAS 2022, CCIS 1610, pp. 130–142, 2022.
https://doi.org/10.1007/978-3-031-09316-6_12

However, because she was active in her field, she knew that there were many good female and minority candidates. When she looked up these female and minority candidates, she noticed that they tended to use different keywords to reflect the same type of qualification. As a hypothetical example, the terms 'secretary' and 'administrative assistant' are often used interchangeably. However, because of sexist connotations [1], men may be unlikely to use the term 'secretary' to refer to themselves; in contrast, the term 'administrative assistant' may be more likely to return less gender-biased results. In such cases, a recruiter searching for 'secretary' may wish to know that 'administrative assistant' is a similar but less biased keyword. Additionally, job candidates selecting keywords for their resumes may wish to know whether their choice of keyword is encoding some sort of bias.

We present FairKR, a novel algorithm for fair keyword recommendation. FairKR works in conjunction with existing search algorithms. FairKR first computes the bias of the results returned in response to a keyword. It then uses a word embedding to identify related terms, and then measures the bias and relevance of those keywords. Finally, it presents a Pareto front of results of varying bias and relevance. Importantly, FairKR does *not* require a debiased word embedding; one can use it with respect to any attribute (e.g., gender, race, political alignment, preferred hobby, etc.), as long as there is some way of measuring the bias of a document set with respect to that attribute.

We demonstrate use of FairKR on a pair of subReddit from reddit.com. In particular, we consider results from r/Republican and r/Democrats. Although the nature of our problem makes it inherently difficult to evaluate results in a quantitative way, we perform a qualitative evaluation across several queries on these subReddits. The results demonstrate the efficacy of FairKR and give interesting insight into subtle differences in language choice between different groups of people.

2   Related Work

To our knowledge, ours is the first work to examine the problem of diverse keyword recommendation. However, there is a recent body of work that has addressed group fairness concerns in rankings. Much of the existing work uses the statistical parity criterion to detect unfairness in the top-k items of a ranking. [12] extends such statistical parity approaches, and introduces a greedy algorithm that attempts to identify a ranking that is fair but optimized for utility. [7] presented a framework for mitigating algorithmic bias for ranking individuals. This work introduced three variations of a greedy algorithm, as well as a feasible algorithm for fairness-aware ranking. [10] observed search bias in rankings, and proposed a framework to measure the bias of the results of a search engine. This framework identifies the extent to which bias in the output is due to the input, and how much is due to the bias in the system itself.

In contrast to these existing works, our paper focuses on generating fair keyword recommendation, as opposed to modifying or auditing the search results directly.

Also related to our work is the problem of debiasing word embeddings, as studied by [2, 15, 20] and [11]. These methods rely on maximizing and minimizing certain sub-vectors of words in a word embedding. [2] examine gender bias, and propose an algorithm that achieves fairness by modifying the underlying data. The algorithm identifies a gender direction for words, and projects neutral words to a subspace orthogonal to this direction.

We were also interested in existing work on diversity in recommender systems. Such systems filter through available data and present the user with a list of relevant information. In online contexts, such systems are used to provide online news feeds on social media sites such as twitter and Facebook and audio, video recommendations on streaming platforms such as YouTube, Netflix and apple/google podcasts. In many cases, it is desirable to maintain a fine balance between providing information that is both relevant and diverse to the end users.

The literature addresses diversity in recommender systems by leveraging existing algorithms to provide different sets of results that can be seen as diverse to the end user. for example, [3] addresses diversity in terms of similarity measures. Such similarity measures can be based on document content- e.g., cosine similarity, document popularity like PageRank, classification similarity etc. They hypothesize that diverse similarity measures can be used to achieve diversity in choices provided to the user.

[16] defines intrinsic diversity in terms of information needs of the user. A diverse result set should strive for novelty while also, covering different information needs of the user. This ends up avoiding redundancy and also provides users a diverse set of results.

3   Objective

This paper's novel contribution is to provide a set of keyword recommendations to the user which are diverse yet relevant to user's original search query, and exhibit less bias.

Assume that one is given a fixed search engine and document database. For a given search query Q, performing query Q using search engine f on database D results in a set of documents $f(Q)$. We define g as a measure of diversity of documents returned from search Engine f for a query Q. We consider a problem of learning a keyword Q' such that

$$g(f(Q')) > g(f(Q)).$$

We also define a relevance function Rel. Ideally, relevance will be measured by click-through rate:

$$CTR(Q) = \frac{no.\ of\ documents\ clicked\ by\ user}{Total\ Documents\ returned\ for\ Q}. \tag{1}$$

However, in practice, click-through rate will not be known ahead of time, and so a more general relevance function must be specified.

Our objective is to solve a multi-objective maximization problem over g and Rel. There are many ways in which this problem can be formulated: for example, maximize g subject to a constraint on Rel (e.g., $Rel(Q') \geq \alpha Rel(Q)$, where $\alpha \in [0, 1]$ is specified by the user), maximize Rel subject to a constraint on g (e.g., $g(Q') \geq \beta$, where β is specified by the user), and others.

As we will describe in the next section, our approach is to provide a set of keywords that are expected to have click-through rate greater than or equal to that of the query keyword and provide results that are more diverse than those provided by the query keyword.

Measuring Diversity: In this paper, we measure diversity in terms of *bias*. Each document returned from the search engine for a keyword Q has a *bias* of either +1 or –1. (These bias scores could be derived from, for instance, bias annotations on the sources of news articles.) The bias for a keyword Q is simply the average of the *bias* scores of the returned documents. A low *bias* means most of the documents returned were from different sets leading to high diversity and vice versa.

Measuring Relevance: We define *relevance* as a similarity measure to capture similarity between two set of documents. There are various similarity measures that can be used such as Euclidean distance, Manhattan distance, Cosine similarity, Jaccard similarity, and others. In this work, we use a method based on Cosine similarity, in which for each document in the two sets, we find the most similar document in the other set, and so define a mean Cosine similarity for each set. The overall similarity is then the harmonic mean of these two values (this is akin to F1-score).

4 Proposed Method

In this paper, we explore the *fair keyword recommendation* problem. In this problem, a user enters a keyword into a search engine, which may return results that are biased with respect to some attribute. These attributes may be those traditionally considered 'protected', such as gender or race; or may be other attributes of interest, such as political alignment. For example, as we will see later, the keyword 'privilege' gives results that are disproportionately from a Republican party-associated subreddit. In contrast to existing methods, which re-rank search results to obtain fairness or balance, the goal of our problem is to suggest less-biased alternatives to the original keyword. For example, the keyword 'protections' returns results that are from both Republican and Democratic party subreddits.

Fair keyword recommendation has similar high-level goals as debiasing search rankings: reducing 'bubbles' and echo chambers, which can create a divide between people with different views [6,9,13]. However, it provides a 'gentler' approach than directly re-ranking results, in that the user may choose whether to accept a recommended keyword.

We propose `FairKR`, a multi-objective optimization algorithm framework that uses word embeddings to suggest alternate keywords for a user's search query.

By using a word embedding, FairKR creates a list of candidate words for the original search query, and scores words in this list based on relevance and bias to create a set of suggested words which can be used in place of a biased word to achieve a more diverse set of recommendations.

4.1 Problem Setup

FairKR is a general framework for fair keyword recommendation, and can be instantiated with the user's choice of relevance and bias measures. FairKR is intended to supplement an existing search engine, and does not itself perform searches.

In this paper, we will refer to the user's input query as the *query keyword*. A query is performed on a *dataset* consisting of a set of text documents. As discussed in Sect. 3, we assume that the user provides a way to measure the relevance and bias of a particular document with respect to the query. A natural relevance function would be the function used by the search engine itself. The bias function could be one of those described in Sect. 2: for example, if interested in gender bias, the work on gender bias in word embeddings would be a natural candidate.

The output of FairKR is a set of keywords that, ideally, have high relevance to the query keyword but are more diverse/less biased (for example, if the query keyword produced results with a strong male bias, the alternatives should be less so). FairKR uses no prior information about the dataset and therefore can be used alone or as part of a larger architecture to reduce biases present in social media.

4.2 The FairKR Framework and Implementation

Denote the query keyword as Q and the dataset as D. As described before, FairKR works in conjunction with an existing search engine/algorithm, which is used to perform the keyword searches. Denote this search algorithm as S. $S_Q(D, n)$ denotes the top-n results returned by S applied to D. Let $B(d)$ be the bias of document d with respect to an attribute of interest, and (overloading the notation), let $B(D)$ represent the average bias of document set D. We assume $B(d)$ (the bias of an individual document) is binary (as is appropriate for our dataset), but this can easily be changed if desired. Similarly, let $r_Q(d)$ be the relevance of document d to keyword Q, and $r_Q(D)$ be the relevance of a document set D to Q. Denote the word embedding used by FairKR as W (W need not be debiased in any way).

At a high level, FairKR performs the following steps.

(1) As a pre-processing step, FairKR removes stop words and tokenizes each word in each document $d \in D$.
(2) Next, given keyword Q, FairKR applies the search algorithm S to D and fetches $S_Q(D, n)$, the top-n most relevant documents from D.
(3) FairKR then performs an iterative process in which it identifies the k alternative keywords $A_1, ..., A_k$ nearest to Q in the embedding space defined by W (the choice of k depends on the termination criteria). It then uses S to

perform a search of each A_i using search algorithm S applied to D to obtain set $S_{A_i}(D, n)$. For each of these i sets, FairKR computes the bias and relevance of those sets with respect to the *original* keyword Q. Using these values, FairKR produces a Pareto front along the bias-relevance axes. This Pareto front contains an alternative keyword A_i if A_i is not dominated by any of the other alternatives or by Q itself. A keyword is non-dominated if there is no other keyword whose search results have both a lower bias and higher relevance score. (As discussed in Sect. 4.2, it may sometimes be more appropriate to use a 'pseudo'-Pareto front that allows for keywords that are highly biased, but in the opposite direction.)

(4) FairKR repeats the above step until a satisfactory Pareto front has been defined, and outputs the Pareto front (or a desired subset) to the user. In our experiments we continue until 10 recommended keywords are found, or no more are available. In our analysis, we highlight both the Pareto front (computed using the scalar version of bias), as well as high-relevance words with opposing bias.

Through this process, the end user is made aware that by using an alternate keyword she can still get relevant results, but from a different point of view.

Table 1. Collective Inputs and Outputs of Algorithm

Inputs	
	Q: Input keyword
	A: Alternative keyword
	d, D: Document, set of documents
	S: Search algorithm
	$S_Q(D, n)$: Top-n most relevant documents to keyword Q from document set D, as found by algorithm S
	$B(d), B(D)$: Bias of a document d or document set D
	$r_Q(d), r_Q(D)$: Relevance of a document d or document set D to query keyword Q
	W: Word embedding

Measuring Relevance. We compute relevance using a cosine similarity-based approach that compares the documents returned for A_i to those returned for Q. In this approach, we compute a variant of F1 by measuring the precision and recall as follows: First, for each document $d' \in S_{A_i}(D, n)$ (the top-n documents returned in response to A_i), we compute the greatest similarity between d' and a document $d \in S_Q(D, n)$ (the top-n documents returned in response to Q). This similarity is measured using cosine similarity between the bag-of-words corresponding to the documents. The *precision* is then the average of these maximum similarities. *Recall* is computed similarly, but in the other direction (i.e., finding the closest document from $S_{A_i}(D, n)$ to each document in $S_Q(D, n)$). Then the F1-score, or relevance, is the harmonic mean of precision and recall.

Algorithm 1. Fair keyword recommendation

1: Q = original query keyword
2: k = number of desired keywords, n = number of returned documents
3: max_iter = maximum number of iterations, $num\_iters = 0$
4: D_A = documents (posts) from subReddit A
5: D_B = documents (posts) from subReddit B
6: $D = D_A \cup D_B$
7: $S_Q(D, n)$ = top-n relevant documents from D for Q
8: $S_A = S_Q(D, n) \cap D_A$
9: $S_B = S_Q(D, n) \cap D_B$
10: $Bias_Q = |S_A| - |S_B|$
11: sim = list of k most similar words from word embedding
12: $recs = \{Q\}$
13: **while** $|num\_iters| < max\_iter$ and $|recs| < k$ **do**
14:     **for** each word w' in sim **do**
15:         $S_{w'}(D, n)$ = top-n relevant documents from D for w'
16:         $S'_A = S_{w'}(D, n) \cap D_A$
17:         $S'_B = S_{w'}(D, n) \cap D_B$
18:         $Bias_{w'} = |S'_A| - |S'_B|$
19:         $Rel(w')$ = F1-score between $S_{w'}(D, n)$ and $S_Q(D, n)$
20:         **if** w' is not dominated by any word in $recs$ **then**
21:             Add w' to $recs$
22:             Remove words from $recs$ that are dominated by w'
23:         **end if**
24:     **end for**
25:     sim = {next most similar word from word embedding}
26:     $num\_iters + +$
27: **end while**
28: Return $recs$

Measuring Bias. In our dataset (described in Sect. 5), we obtain posts from Reddit.com. We consider posts (documents) from pairs of subReddits in which each subReddit corresponds to a particular group (e.g., Republican vs. Democrats). In this case, the bias function follows directly from the dataset. For a given document/post, that document has bias of either $+1$ (indicating that it was posted in one subReddit) or -1 (indicating that it was posted in the other). This can be adapted for, e.g., queries for news articles, by using pre-annotated biases of news sources.

The bias of a set of documents D is simply the average of the biases of the individual documents.

Termination. We find the top-k closest keywords based on the word embedding. In our experiments, we set $k = 10$: this appeared empirically to be sufficient to identify alternative keywords. In our analysis, we highlight both the Pareto front (computed using the scalar version of bias), as well as high-relevance words with opposing bias. Also, It is possible that in certain situations no alternative keywords are found and in those cases, no alternative keywords are returned.

4.3 Limitations

Our current framework has a few important limitations. First, as explored in other works, word embeddings learned from collections of data often demonstrate a significant level of biases [8]. When these embeddings are used in low-level NLP tasks, it often amplifies the bias. Thus, it is quite likely that the GloVE embedding that we use is itself biased, reducing the efficacy of FairKR. However, debiasing word embeddings is a challenging problem and is the subject of much active research, and is outside the scope of this paper. FairKR is not inherently tied to any particular word embedding, and if less biased or unbiased word embeddings are created, they can easily be used.

Second, FairKR only accommodates single-world queries. Adapting to longer queries is not trivial, but is possible. One possibility is to compute bias separately for each keyword in the query and then aggregate. The relevance measurement would remain same. One challenge in this problem would be in identifying alternative multi-words queries to the end user. This could be solved using existing techniques for keyword recommendation: first for each keyword in the query, identify candidate keywords, and then score them using bias/relevance. We can suggest recommended candidate keywords to the end user and let them decide how they want to frame the new query.

Third, FairKR only supports bias computations along one axis. In many cases, a query is biased along multiple dimensions. Dealing with this is challenging, but one solution is to define bias in a multidimensional space. For each candidate keyword, we can then calculate the final bias by finding the L2 norm of bias in this multidimensional space with respect to the original bias distribution of the dataset.

We plan to address the second and third limitations in our future work.

5 Experimental Setup

Here, we discuss our datasets as well as the simple search engine that we implemented to demonstrate FairKR.[1]

5.1 Data

Given that there is no ground truth for which keywords 'should' be returned, we perform a qualitative analysis in which we demonstrate the use of FairKR on real data. For our analysis, we compare pairs of contrasting subReddits from Reddit.com. Using the Python PRAW package, we crawled 'top' posts from the following pair: (r/Republican, r/Democrats). We collected a roughly equal

---

[1] https://github.com/harshdsdh/fairKR.

number of posts from each subReddit in a pair. Dataset statistics- the number of posts collected and the total number of members of each subReddit- are shown in Table 2. Because we have roughly the same number of posts from each subReddit in a pair, FairKR does not need to account for size differences in its bias computation. Due to space limitations, we only present full results for the Republican/Democrats pair, but briefly discuss interesting observations for other pairs.

Next, we used data from Google trends [17] to create a list of keywords based on top trending queries. Most of these words did not appear in the dataset or did not show substantial bias. For each pair of subReddits, we manually identified some keywords that showed interesting differences between the two subReddits.

Table 2. Dataset properties.

subReddit	Posts Collected	Members
r/democrats	2445	143K
r/Republican	2262	147K

5.2 Search Engine

To demonstrate FairKR, we implement a simple search engine algorithm. For a given query word Q, we compute the tf-idf score of each document with respect to Q, and return the 20 highest scoring documents (or fewer, if fewer than 20 documents use that word). Obviously, real-world search engines are much more sophisticated than this, and FairKR can work with any existing search algorithm.

6 Analysis and Discussion

Here, we discuss the results of FairKR on the Republicans/Democrats pair of subReddits. Results presented here use the document similarity-based relevance calculation, as discussed in Sect. 4.2. A bias of $\pm p$ indicates the sum of the document biases, divided by the total number of documents. A bias of 0 thus indicates that an equal number of documents from each subReddit were returned. A bias of ± 1 indicates that all results were from one subReddit. In all plots, the original query is shown in boldface. This query, naturally, always has a relevance of 1 to itself. The Pareto front, computed by treating bias as a scalar (direction-less) is circled in green, and includes the original keyword. We additionally note high-relevance words that are biased in the opposite direction. Depending on the application, FairKR may be implemented to return just the Pareto front, or the Pareto front plus the high-relevance, opposite-biased words.

Although our implementation of FairKR considers the 10 words closest to the original keyword (using the GloVe word embedding), in some cases, some of these words occurred 0 times in the dataset and do not appear in plots.

For the political subReddits (r/Democrats, r/Republican), we considered the query keywords 'rioting' and 'privilege'. On these plots, a positive bias (right side of plots) indicates a bias towards r/Democrats, and a negative bias (left side of plots) indicates a bias towards r/Republican. Results for each of these keywords are shown in Fig. 1. Results for the query 'rioting' are shown in Fig. 1a. The keyword itself returns results disproportionately from the Republicans subReddit (by a 4:1 ratio, giving a bias of $\frac{1-4}{5} = -0.6$). When considering words that are highly relevant, we observed that 'unrest' returns results disproportionately from the Democratic subReddit (by a 3:1 ratio, for a bias of 0.5), and 'riots' returns results biased towards Republicans subReddit (with no results from the Democratic subReddit). Interestingly, almost all related keywords are either neutral or Republican-biased: the only related word with a Democratic bias is 'unrest'. This could indicate the extent to which riots have been discussed by Redditors from each political party (for instance, Democrats may instead choose to discuss factors leading to riots or protests, rather than the riots or protests themselves). The keyword returned by FairKR on the Pareto front is 'looting', as this returns documents that are evenly balanced between the subReddits. If desired, FairKR can also return 'unrest' to provide a Democratic counterbalance to the original keyword. Here, we also observe that FairKR returns a neutral alternative keyword ('looting') along with keywords which are less biased or biased in the opposite direction ('unrest').

For the 'rioting' keyword specifically, we were curious to see if there has been any change the above analysis after the January 6th, 2021 insurrection. To answer this, we re-collected data and performed the analysis again. Earlier data shows that people in the Democratic party subReddit tended to use words such as 'unrest' instead of 'rioting', while individuals in the Republican subReddit were using words such as 'rioters' and 'riots'. However, results from January 2021 show that people in the Democratic subReddit use words such as 'protests' and 'mobs' when referring to this concept. People in the Republican subReddit still use words such as 'rioters' and 'riots', but there is a significant reduction in the bias of these words.

Results for the query 'discrimination' are shown in Fig. 1b. The keyword returns results which are slightly biased towards Republicans (by a 4:3 ratio). When considering words that are highly relevant, we observed that 'harassment' and 'gender' are neutral in terms of bias while 'racism' is biased towards Republican subReddit (by a 4:1 ratio). The keyword returned by FairKR on the Pareto front is 'harassment' as an alternative with less biased and relevant results.

Results for the query 'privilege' are shown in Fig. 1c. The keyword returns results which are biased towards Republicans (by a 5:0 ratio). When considering words that are highly relevant, we observed that 'immunity' is also biased towards Republican subReddit (by a 3:0 ratio), 'protections' is biased towards Democratic subReddit (by a 9:2 ratio). The keyword returned by FairKR on the Pareto front are 'protections' and 'privileges' as alternatives which are relevant and biased in the opposite direction.

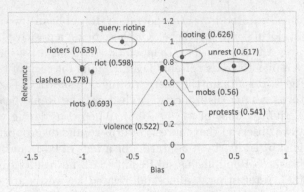

(a) Results for original query 'rioting'.

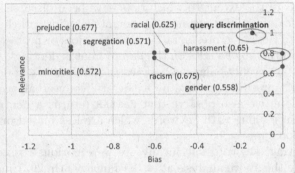

(b) Results for original query 'discrimination'.

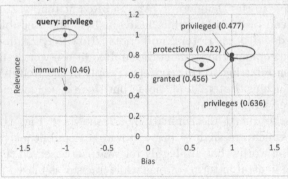

(c)Results for original query 'privilege'.

Fig. 1. Potential keyword recommendations for queries on political subReddits. Along the x-axis, positive values represent bias towards the r/democrats subReddit, while negative values represent bias towards the r/Republican subReddit. Words on the Pareto front (where bias is a scalar) are circled in green. High-relevance words with opposite bias are circled in red. (Color figure online)

For the original keyword 'loneliness' the keyword returns results disproportionately from the r/AskMen (bias of 0.25). When considering words that are
highly relevant, we observed that 'sadness' and 'anguish' were also biased towards
r/AskMen, while 'boredom' was biased towards r/AskWomen (by a 2:1 ratio,
for a bias of -0.33). The keywords returned by FairKR on the Pareto front are
'grief' 'loneliness', and 'anxiety'. Potential candidates with opposite bias include
'boredom' and 'longing', both of which are extremely relevant to 'loneliness'.

As another example, consider the query 'government'. The keyword returns
results disproportionately from the British subReddit (by a 3:2 ratio). The
Pareto front contains the word 'public', which is still biased towards r/AskABrit,
but less so (an 11:9 ratio), and is highly relevant. On the opposite side, the
word 'governments' gives results exclusively from r/AskAnAmerican. The word
'administration' shows strong bias towards r/AskAnAmerican, and is also highly
relevant to 'government'.

7   Conclusion and Future Work

In this paper, we considered the problem of *fair keyword recommendation*, and
we proposed FairKR, an algorithmic framework for identifying highly-relevant
but less-biased keyword alternatives. A major application of this problem is on
web search, where fair keyword recommendation can be a step in addressing
problems caused by echo chambers or filter bubbles. Search engines can leverage
FairKR as a post-processing method using it to recommend less biased query
alternatives to the end user. It can also be used as a plugin to any web browser.

We also hope that it will be useful on career-related social media sites (like
LinkedIn), where recruiters may struggle to find a diverse applicant pool simply
because of the keywords that they are using, and applicants may struggle to be
found because of how they have written their profiles. In our future work, we
plan to extend this algorithm to propose alternatives to a complete search query,
not just an individual keyword. We are also considering the problem of dealing
with bias along multiple axes.

In our future work, we will analyse how results vary with different word
embeddings and different datasets and how it compares to other debiasing and
re ranking approaches. We also plan to conduct a survey to evaluate the efficacy
of FairKR.

Acknowledgements. S. Soundarajan is supported by NSF #2047224.

References

1. Blaubergs, M.S.: Changing the sexist language: the theory behind the practice.
   Psychol. Women Q. **2**(3) (1978)
2. Bolukbasi, T., Chang, K.W., Zou, J.Y., Saligrama, V., Kalai, A.T.: Man is to
   computer programmer as woman is to homemaker? Debiasing word embeddings.
   In: Advances in Neural Information Processing Systems, pp. 4349–4357 (2016)

3. Candillier, L., Chevalier, M., Dudognon, D., Mothe, J.: Diversity in recommender systems. In: Proceedings of the Fourth International Conference on Advances in Human-oriented and Personalized Mechanisms, Technologies, and Services. CEN-TRIC, pp. 23–29 (2011)
4. Dev, S., Li, T., Phillips, J.M., Srikumar, V.: On measuring and mitigating biased inferences of word embeddings. In: AAAI, pp. 7659–7666 (2020)
5. Dutta, R.: System, method, and program for ranking search results using user category weighting. US Patent App. 09/737,995, 20 June 2002
6. Flaxman, S., Goel, S., Rao, J.M.: Filter bubbles, echo chambers, and online news consumption. Public Opin. Q. **80**(S1), 298–320 (2016)
7. Geyik, S.C., Ambler, S., Kenthapadi, K.: Fairness-aware ranking in search & recommendation systems with application to Linkedin talent search. In: Proceedings of the 25th ACM SIGKDD International Conference on Knowledge Discovery & Data Mining, pp. 2221–2231 (2019)
8. Gonen, H., Goldberg, Y.: Lipstick on a pig: debiasing methods cover up systematic gender biases in word embeddings but do not remove them. arXiv preprint arXiv:1903.03862 (2019)
9. Himelboim, I., McCreery, S., Smith, M.: Birds of a feather tweet together: Integrating network and content analyses to examine cross-ideology exposure on twitter. J. Comput.-Mediat. Commun. **18**(2), 154–174 (2013)
10. Juhi Kulshrestha, Muhammad B. Zafar, M.E.S.G.J.M., Gummadi, K.P.: Quantifying search bias: investigating sources of bias for political searches in social media (2017). https://arxiv.org/pdf/1704.01347.pdf
11. Kaneko, M., Bollegala, D.: Gender-preserving debiasing for pre-trained word embeddings. In: Proceedings of the 57th Annual Meeting of the Association for Computational Linguistics (ACL) (2019)
12. Zehlike, M., Bonchi, F., Castillo, C., Hajian, S., Megahed, M., Baeza-Yates, R.: Fa*ir: a fair top-k ranking algorithm (2018). https://arxiv.org/pdf/1706.06368.pdf
13. Nguyen, C.T.: Echo chambers and epistemic bubbles. Episteme **17**(2), 141–161 (2020)
14. Noble, S.U.: Algorithms of Oppression: How Search Engines Reinforce Racism. NYU Press, New York (2018)
15. Pennington, J., Socher, R., Manning, C.: GloVe: global vectors for word representation. In: Proceedings of the 2014 Conference on Empirical Methods in Natural Language Processing (EMNLP), pp. 1532–1543. Association for Computational Linguistics, Doha, Qatar, October 2014. https://doi.org/10.3115/v1/D14-1162, https://www.aclweb.org/anthology/D14-1162
16. Radlinski, F., Bennett, P.N., Carterette, B., Joachims, T.: Redundancy, diversity and interdependent document relevance. In: ACM SIGIR Forum, vol. 43, pp. 46–52. ACM New York, NY, USA (2009)
17. Trends, G.: (2021). https://trends.google.com/trends/?geo=US
18. Zehlike, M., Castillo, C.: Reducing disparate exposure in ranking: a learning to rank approach. In: Proceedings of The Web Conference 2020, pp. 2849–2855 (2020)
19. Zehlike, M., Sühr, T., Castillo, C., Kitanovski, I.: Fairsearch: a tool for fairness in ranked search results. In: Companion Proceedings of the Web Conference 2020, pp. 172–175 (2020)
20. Zhao, J., Zhou, Y., Li, Z., Wang, W., Chang, K.: Learning gender-neutral word embeddings. CoRR abs/1809.01496 (2018). http://arxiv.org/abs/1809.01496

FARGO: A Fair, Context-AwaRe, Group RecOmmender System

Davide Azzalini[1]([✉]), Elisa Quintarelli[2], Emanuele Rabosio[1], and Letizia Tanca[1]

[1] Politecnico di Milano, Milan, Italy
{davide.azzalini,emanuele.rabosio,letizia.tanca}@polimi.it
[2] University of Verona, Verona, Italy
elisa.quintarelli@univr.it

Abstract. Lots of activities, like watching a movie or going to the restaurant, are intrinsically group-based. To recommend such activities to groups, traditional single-user recommendation techniques cannot be adopted, as a consequence, over the years, a number of group recommender systems have been developed. Recommending to groups items to be enjoyed together poses many ethical challenges, in fact, a system whose unique objective is to achieve the best recommendation accuracy possible, might learn to disadvantage submissive users in favor of more aggressive ones. In this work we investigate the ethical challenges of context-aware group recommendations, in the more general case of ephemeral groups (i.e., groups where the members might be together for the first time), using a method that can recommend also items that are new in the system. We show the goodness of our method on two real-world datasets. The first one is a very large dataset containing the personal and group choices regarding TV programs of 7,921 users w.r.t. sixteen contexts of viewing. The second one, which has been collected specifically for this work and that is made publicly available as one of the contributions of this article, gathers the musical preferences (both individual and in groups) of 280 real users w.r.t. two contexts of listening. We compare the results of our approach with seven other group recommender systems specifically developed to be fair. We evaluate the goodness of our recommendations using recall, while their fairness is assessed using two measures found in the literature, namely, score disparity and recommendation disparity. Our extensive experiments show that our method always manages to obtain the highest recall while delivering ethical guarantees in line with the other fair group recommender systems tested.

Keywords: group recommender systems · context-aware recommender systems · computer ethics · fairness

DA is supported by the ABB-Politecnico di Milano Joint Research Center, which provided financial support.

L. Boratto et al. (Eds.): BIAS 2022, CCIS 1610, pp. 143–154, 2022.
https://doi.org/10.1007/978-3-031-09316-6_13

1   Introduction

Several everyday activities are intrinsically group-based, thus recent research concentrates also on systems that suggest activities that can be performed together with other people and are typically social. The group recommendation problem introduces further challenges with respect to the traditional single-user recommendations: *(i)* the group members may have different preferences, and finding items that meet the tastes of everyone may be impossible; *(ii)* a group may be formed by people who happen to be together for the first time, and, in this case, not being available any history of the group's preferences, the recommendation can only be computed on the basis of those known for the group members combined by means of some aggregation function; *(iii)* last but not least, people, when in a group, may exhibit different behaviors with respect to when they are alone, and therefore their individual preferences sometimes might not be a reliable source of information.

This last observation introduces an unfairness problem, in fact, if the recommender system learns to consider the preferences of some users as more relevant than those of the others, the overall satisfaction of the users belonging to a group may not be optimal. This unbalance in the negotiation power that the system learns to assign to different users with the purpose of obtaining the best possible recommendation accuracy may be the result of unfair dynamics, such as some users being more aggressive and some others not feeling confident enough to stand up for themselves.

In this work we extend a state-of-the-art system for context-aware recommendations to ephemeral groups based on the concept of contextual influence [1,2] to account also for fairness.

Experiments on two real-world datasets show that the proposed approach outperforms seven other fair group recommender systems by achieving a consistently better recall while providing similar ethical guarantees.

The main original contributions of this article are: *(i)* a novel technique for providing fair, context-aware recommendations to ephemeral groups able to recommend also items that are new in the system; *(ii)* an extensive experimental campaign on two real-world datasets which demonstrates the goodness of our technique both in terms of accuracy and fairness of the recommendations produced; *(iii)* the first publicly available real-world dataset with both individual and group context-aware preferences. The dataset can be downloaded at https:// github.com/azzada/FARGO.

2   Related Work

In this section, works related to the one presented in this paper are reviewed. After a brief general introduction to recommender systems, context-awareness, and group recommendation techniques, a thorough discussion of fairness in group recommender systems is presented.

Recommender Systems are software tools and techniques providing suggestions for items to be of use to a user [3].

Context-Aware Recommender Systems. The majority of the existing approaches to Recommender Systems do not take into consideration any contextual information, however, in many applications, it may not be sufficient to consider only users and items [4]. Recent studies have shown that Context-Aware Recommender Systems can generate a very high increase in performance [5].

Group Recommender Systems. Group Recommender Systems are systems which produce a recommendation for a group of users [6]. Group recommendations works usually address two kinds of groups, *persistent* and *ephemeral* [7]. Persistent groups have a previous significant history of activities together, while ephemeral groups are formed by people who may happen to be together for the first time. In the case of persistent groups, classical recommendation techniques can be used since the group can be considered as a single user; whereas in the case of ephemeral groups, recommendations must be computed on the basis of those known for the members of the group. A number of different aggregation strategies for the individual preferences have been proposed over the years. The most common examples are: plurality voting (which uses the 'first past the post' principle: repetitively, the item with the most votes is chosen), average (averages individual ratings), additive (sums individual ratings), multiplicative (multiplies individual ratings), Borda count (points are assigned to items based on their ranking, then the item with the most points is chosen), approval voting (counts how many individuals have rating above an approval threshold for a certain item), least misery (takes the minimum of individual ratings), maximum satisfaction (takes the maximum of individual ratings) and most respected person (uses the rating of the most respected individual) [6].

Most of the aggregation strategies just described clearly violate the fairness principles. For instance, *maximum satisfaction*, used in [8–13], chooses the items for which the greatest value among the preferences of the group members is the highest with the risk of ignoring the satisfaction of most of the users in a group. Another clear example of unfair recommender systems are works such as [14–16], which assign a different power to group members depending on their expertise.

Fairness in Recommender Systems. In single-user Recommender Systems fairness is usually assessed with regard to sensitive attributes which are generally prone to discrimination (e.g., gender, ethnicity or social belonging) by verifying the presence of a discriminated class within the user set [17,18]. When fairness is evaluated considering Group Recommender Systems, it should be computed within groups. Since the groups we consider in this work are composed of few users, evaluating fairness in the way just described is not a suitable solution. Instead of detecting unfairness towards a protected group of users, we aim to detect and prevent unfairness towards single users within a group whose desires are not taken into consideration when forming a recommendation for the whole group.

Fairness in Group Recommender Systems. Some aggregation strategies, that despite not having been developed to explicitly address ethical issues, exist that aggregate individual preferences in a way that resembles fairness. *Least misery*, used in [7–13, 19–23], chooses the items for which the lowest value among the preferences of the group members is the greatest. The authors in [24] introduce an aggregation function which tries to maximize the satisfaction of the group components, while, at the same time tries to minimize the *disagreement* among them. The authors in [25] investigate the role played by context in the design of a system that recommends sequences of activities to groups of users as a multi-objective optimization problem, where the satisfaction of the group and the available time interval are two of the functions to be optimized. In particular, their findings suggest that the dynamic evolution of a group can be the key contextual feature that has to be considered to produce fair suggestions. *Average*, used in [8–14, 19, 20, 23, 26, 27], computes the group preference for an item as the arithmetic mean of the individual scores. Lastly, some recent works try to explicitly target the aim of producing fair group recommendations. In [28] the preferences of individual users are combined with a measure of fairness, to guarantee that all the users are somehow satisfied. In [29, 30] two aggregation strategies are proposed, one is based on the idea of proportionality, while the other one is based on the idea envy-freeness. In [31] the authors formalize the notion of rank-sensitive balance (i.e., an ordered set of recommended items is considered fair to a group if the relevance of the items in the top-N is balanced across the group membes for each prefix of the top-N) and propose a greedy algorithm to achieve it. In our experiments we compare our approach against all the aggregation strategies mentioned in this last subsection.

3   The Proposed Method

In this section a review of the approach presented in [1, 2], *CtxInfl*, will be given. Then, our contribution to make *CtxInfl* more fair will be presented. The resulting method is named *FARGO*.

3.1   CtxInfl

It is considered a set of items I and a set of users U, from which any group $G \in \wp(U)$ can be extracted. C is the set of possible contexts in the given scenario, where a context c is the conjunction of a set of dimension/value pairs (e.g., for the TV dataset, a context might be $c = \langle time\_slot = primetime \wedge day = weekend \rangle$). It is assumed the availability of a log $\mathcal{L}$ recording the history of the items previously chosen by groups formed in the past, where each element of $\mathcal{L}$ is a 4-ple (t_j, c_j, G_j, i_j) where t_j is the time instant in which the item $i_j \in I$ has been chosen by the group $G_j \in \wp(U)$ in the context $c_j \in C$. A contextual scoring function $score(u, i, c)$, with $u \in U$, $i \in I$, $c \in C$, assigning to each user a score given to the items in the various contexts is computed offline on the basis of the log of the past individual choices and on the basis of the items descriptions in terms of their attributes using any context-aware recommender system for single users from the literature. $TopK(u, c, t)$ is the function which returns the list of the K items preferred by user u in context c, according to the values of $score(u, i, c)$ for each $i \in I$ available at instant t. Given a target group $G \in \wp(U)$, a context $c \in C$ and a time instant t, the group recommendation is obtained by recommending to the users in G a list (i.e., an ordered set) of K items, considered interesting in context c, from those items in I that are available at time instant t according to the following procedure:

Influence Computation. The group preference for an item is obtained by aggregating the individual preferences of the group members on the basis of their influence. In each context c, the influence $infl(u, c)$ of a given user u is derived offline by comparing the behavior of u when alone (i.e., u's individual preferences) with u's behaviors in groups (i.e., the interactions contained in the log $\mathcal{L}$). Basically, the influence of u tells how many times the groups containing u have selected one of u's favorite items. Let $TopK(u, c, t)$ be the list of the K items preferred by user u in context c, according to the values of $score(u, i, c)$ for each $i \in I$ available at instant t. The contextual influence is defined as follows:

$$infl(u, c) = \frac{|l_j \in \mathcal{L} : c = c_j \wedge u \in G_j \wedge i_j \in TopK(u, c, t_j)|}{|l_j \in \mathcal{L} : c = c_j \wedge u \in G_j|} \qquad (1)$$

The value of $infl(u, c)$ quantifies the ability of user u to direct the group's decision towards u's own tastes while in context c.

Top-K Group Recommendation Computation. Top-K recommendations are computed online, when a group of users requires that the system suggests some interesting items to be enjoyed together. The system must compute the group preferences for the items, and then determine the K items with the highest scores. Given a group $G \in \wp(U)$, its preference $score(G, i, c)$ for $i \in I$ in the context $c \in C$ is computed as the average of the preferences of its members weighed on the basis of each member's influence (Eq. 1) in context c:

$$score(G, i, c) = \frac{\sum_{u \in G} infl(u, c) \cdot score(u, i, c)}{\sum_{u \in G} infl(u, c)} \qquad (2)$$

Then, the top-K list of items preferred by a certain group G in context c at time instant t is determined by retrieving the K items with the greatest scores among those available at time t.

3.2   FARGO

Being *CtxInfl* based on the concept of influence, it inevitably privileges the preferences of the most influential users. As a consequence, the results of the recommendation process are biased towards the preference of one user or few users of the group which can be considered as the leaders, or, using a more contemporary

word, "influencers". Following the definition of ethics and fairness provided in
[32], it is easily understandable that this kind of aggregation strategy doesn't
follow any of the fairness principles. Our aim is to add an element of fairness to
CtxInfl while maintaining its general structure, which already proved to be very
efficient and scalable [2]. Among the various phases (i.e., individual preferences
computation, influence computation, and Top-K group recommendations computation) of *CtxInfl*, the last one is the most suitable for introducing a fairness
element since it is the only one which acts on groups. Following this intuition,
we propose to add a fairness factor to the computation of the score for each item
(Eq. 2), in order to modify the order of the items in the Top-K list produced
so that items which would represent unfair recommendations will not appear
on top. This is further motivated by the fact that when people make decisions
in groups, they do not always follow the decision of a leader, as assumed by
CtxInfl. In some cases people may take decisions trying to satisfy every group
member as much as possible. This means that considering only the influence
factor may not be a complete strategy even if we put aside our ethical concerns.
In order to maintain the computation of Eq. 2 scalable and lightweight we decide
to build our fairness element using just the individual contextual scores, which
are already needed to compute Eq. 2. We call *consensus* the metric that quantifies how much the individual preferences of the group members agree on the
evaluation of an item. The *consensus* of a group G on an item i in a context c
is defined as *one* minus the variance of the group members' scores for item i in
context c:

$$consensus(G, i, c) = 1 - \frac{\sum_{u \in G} \left(score(u, i, c) - \overline{score}(u, i, c) \right)^2}{|G|} \tag{3}$$

The *consensus* for an item for which users gave a similar evaluation will be close
to 1, while it will reach its minimum when very discording scores are considered.
According to the formula of the maximum variance:

$$\sigma_{max}^2 = \left(\frac{max\big(score(u, i, c)\big) - min\big(score(u, i, c)\big)}{2} \right)^2 = 0.25,$$

$consensus \in [0.75, 1]$, as $score(u, i, c) \in [0, 1]$. After having defined *consensus*,
we propose to integrate it in Eq. 2 in the following way:

$$fair\_score(G, i, c) = \frac{\sum_{u \in G} infl(u, c) \cdot score(u, i, c)}{\sum_{u \in G} infl(u, c)} \cdot consensus(G, i, c)^{|G|} \tag{4}$$

We exponentiate *consensus* to the group size (which has the effect of further
reducing the overall score) according to the intuition that the magnitude of the
problem of unfairness in group recommendations is proportional to the group
size. In fact, the bigger is the group, the bigger is the potential harm produced
by recommending solely taking into consideration the leader/influencer's will.
As an example, given a context $c = $"*daytime*", an item i available at the time
of the recommendation, and a group $G = \{u_1, u_2\}$ composed of two users u_1

and u_2 with contextual influences $infl(u_1, c) = 1$ and $infl(u_2, c) = 0.333$, let's consider the following two cases:

$$
\begin{aligned}
&score(u_1, i, c) = 0.9, \ \ score(u_2, i, c) = 0.2 \\
&score(G, i, c) = \frac{1 \cdot 0.9 + 0.333 \cdot 0.2}{1 + 0.333} = 0.725 \\
&consensus(G, i, c) = 1 - \frac{(0.9 - 0.55)^2 + (0.2 - 0.55)^2}{2} = 0.8775 \\
&fair\_score(G, i, c) = 0.725 \cdot 0.8775^2 = 0.558
\end{aligned}
$$

$$
\begin{aligned}
&score(u_1, i, c) = 0.7, \ \ score(u_2, i, c) = 0.8 \\
&score(G, i, c) = \frac{1 \cdot 0.7 + 0.333 \cdot 0.8}{1 + 0.333} = 0.725 \\
&consensus(G, i, c) = 1 - \frac{(0.7 - 0.75)^2 + (0.8 - 0.75)^2}{2} = 0.9975 \\
&fair\_score(G, i, c) = 0.725 \cdot 0.9975^2 = 0.721
\end{aligned}
$$

It can be noted how, even though *CtxInfl* assigns the same group score in both cases, in the case above just the influencer (i.e., u_1) would be truly satisfied with the recommendation. Note also how, in the case below, in which both users like item i, the *consensus* has a minimal impact in the computation of $fair\_score$.

4   Experimental Results

In this section we present the results obtained by applying the proposed approach to two different real-world datasets. To evaluate the recommendation performance we use the *recall*. Let i be an item in the test set, i_t the starting time of availability for i, i_G the group of users that chose the item, i_i the item chosen and i_c the context in which the item was chosen. $TopK(G, c, t)$ indicates the set of top-K items for the group G in context c among those available at time instant t, determined using the recommendation methodology to be evaluated. Recall@K is computed as follows:

$$
Recall@K = \frac{|i \in TestSet : i_i \in TopK(i_G, i_c, i_t)|}{|i \in TestSet|}
$$

We consider values of K (number of items to be recommended) of 1, 2 and 3.

To evaluate the ethical properties of our method we used the two metrics proposed in [33] for estimating user discrimination, namely, *score disparity* and *recommendation disparity*, which we adapt to our needs.

The first one, called *score disparity*, is computed as the Gini coefficient of user satisfaction (i.e., the relative gain achieved by the user due to the actual recommendation with respect to the optimal recommendation strategy from the user perspective). Firstly, the user satisfaction for a user u is defined as: $\mathcal{A}(u, c, t) = \frac{\sum_{j \in TopK(G, c, t)} score(u, j, c)}{\sum_{j \in TopK(u, c, t)} score(u, j, c)}$, then, *score disparity* is defined as:

$$
D_S(G, c, t) = \frac{\sum_{u_1, u_2 \in G} |\mathcal{A}(u_1, c, t) - \mathcal{A}(u_2, c, t)|}{2n \sum_{u \in G} \mathcal{A}(u, c, t)},
$$

where n is the number of users.

The second one, called *recommendation disparity*, is computed as the Gini coefficient of user gains (i.e., how many of the the recommended items match the user Top-K items). After computing the user gain with the following formula: $sim(u, c, t) = \frac{|TopK(G,c,t) \cap TopK(u,c,t)|}{K}$, the *recommendation disparity*, is obtained as:

$$D_R(G, c, t) = \frac{\sum_{u_1, u_2 \in G} |sim(u_1, c, t) - sim(u_2, c, t)|}{2n \sum_{u \in G} sim(u, c, t)}.$$

The choice of these specific metrics for quantifying fairness relies on the fact that they have been proposed to specifically consider the disparate impacts of recommendations on different users.

We compare our approach to the following methods: average (**AVG**) [8–14, 19, 20, 23, 26, 27], **Fair Lin** [28], **Fair Prop** [29, 30], **Envy Free** [29, 30], minimum disagreement (**Dis**) [24], least misery (**LM**) [7–13, 19–23] and **GFAR** [31]. The choice of these specific methods is motivated by the fact that they are either very well-known and broadly adopted baselines (e.g., AVG, LM) or represent recent state-of-the-art approaches for fair group recommendations (e.g., Fair Lin, Fair Prop, Envy Free, GFAR).

4.1   TV Dataset

This dataset contains TV viewing information related to 7,921 users and 119 channels, broadcasted both over the air and by satellite. The dataset is composed of an electronic program guide (EPG) containing the description of 21,194 distinct programs, and a log containing both individual and group viewings performed by the users. The log spans from December 2012 to March 2013 and contains 4,968,231 entries, among which we retained just the syntonizations longer than three minutes. 3,519,167 viewings are performed by individual users, which are used to compute the individual preferences of the group members. The remaining 1,449,064 viewings have been done by more than one person. The two context dimensions considered in the experiments are *day of the week* (weekday vs. weekend) and the *time slot*. The available values for the time slot are: graveyard slot (from 02:00 to 07:00), early morning (from 07:00 to 09:00), morning (from 09:00 to 12:00), daytime (from 12:00 to 15:00), early fringe (from 15:00 to 17:00), prime access (from 18:00 to 20:30), primetime (from 20:30 to 22:30), and late fringe (from 22:30 to 02:00). Group viewings are split into a training set (1,210,316 entries), and a test set (238,748 entries) with a 80%–20% ratio. This way of splitting the dataset is selected in order to maintain the usual Recommender System literature splitting percentage: 80% training set, 20% test set. Results are reported in Table 1 considering $K = 1$, $K = 2$ and $K = 3$.

The superiority of our method recall-wise is very pronounced. For what regards the ethical guarantees, *FARGO*, delivers a very good *score disparity*, while, for what regards the *recommendation disparity*, it seems to perform generally worse than the other methods (except for $k = 1$, for which its performance

Table 1. Comparison with other fair methods on TV dataset

	K=1			K=2			K=3		
	Recall	D_S	D_R	Recall	D_S	D_R	Recall	D_S	D_R
FARGO	**37.94%**	7.61%	17.85%	**54.08%**	**1.85%**	12.69%	**64.20%**	0.89%	10.08%
AVG	33.914%	7.07%	18.15%	51.56%	2.93%	8.78%	62.91%	1.36%	7.53%
Fair Lin	33.22%	8.83%	18.25%	50.80%	3.59%	7.46%	61.21%	1.61%	**7.01%**
Fair Prop	32.99%	8.83%	13.45%	50.55%	4.25%	8.90%	62.03%	1.79%	7.70%
Envy Free	29.33%	10.43%	13.81%	47.37%	4.23%	10.87%	58.67%	1.89%	8.72%
Dis	33.57%	6.67%	17.45%	51.95%	2.76%	8.97%	63.26%	1.30%	7.61%
LM	30.35%	**5.69%**	**12.42%**	47.10%	2.58%	10.11%	58.27%	1.25%	8.18%
GFAR	30.47%	-	18.28%	44.48%	-	**5.59%**	55.19%	-	7.41%

Table 2. Comparison with other fair methods on Music dataset

	K=1			K=2			K=3		
	Recall	D_S	D_R	Recall	D_S	D_R	Recall	D_S	D_R
FARGO	**25.00%**	2.19%	**1.62%**	**40.28%**	0.87%	2.03%	**49.31%**	0.53%	2.40%
AVG	12.50%	0.81%	3.24%	25.00%	0.39%	2.91%	34.72%	**0.25%**	2.71%
Fair Lin	11.11%	2.19%	4.17%	23.61%	0.81%	2.14%	31.94%	0.48%	**1.81%**
Fair Prop	13.19%	**0.66%**	2.55%	20.83%	0.38%	3.24%	29.86%	0.37%	3.00%
Envy Free	12.50%	0.81%	3.24%	25.00%	0.39%	2.95%	34.72%	**0.25%**	2.71%
Dis	22.92%	0.74%	3.41%	34.72%	0.43%	2.83%	41.67%	0.32%	2.49%
LM	13.89%	1.14%	3.76%	25.00%	**0.35%**	3.13%	34.72%	0.28%	1.99%
GFAR	6.06%	-	8.73%	24.24%	-	**1.88%**	33.33%	-	6.24%

is on par with the other methods). Please note that for GFAR it is not possible to compute the score disparity as the method does not involve the computation of group scores for the items.

4.2 Music Dataset

This dataset has been created by asking participants to fill in two different forms: an *individual form* collecting demographic data (i.e., age and gender) and contextual individual preferences about music artists, and a *group form* to be filled in groups asking for a collective choice of a music artist that was available at the time of the choice in a particular context. The following two listening contexts have been selected considering that both are common situations users can relate to both when alone and when with other people, and that users' preferences would likely be different in each of them: *during a car trip* and *at dinner as background music*. We defined a list of 30 music artists well-known in Italy covering most of the music genres available. The metric used to evaluate preferences is a number between 0 and 4 reflecting the following list:

0. user would not listen to it or user does not know it
1. user would listen to it very seldom

2. user would listen to it sometimes
3. user would listen to it often
4. user would always listen to it

The dataset obtained contains data gathered from 280 users. The user set is composed by 57 females and 223 males, the age of the users is between 18 and 60. Since the forms have been proposed mostly to university students the users' average age is in the interval 18–30. For each user, preferences regarding both the car trip and dinner contexts are gathered. From the group forms, 498 context-aware collective preferences have been gathered. Of this, 272 groups were composed of 2 users, 158 of 3 users, 32 of 4 users and 36 of 5 users. As for the previous dataset, we used a 80%-20% split for training and test sets. This dataset has been collected specifically for this work and is made publicly available as one of the contributions of this article. The dataset can be downloaded at https://github.com/azzada/FARGO.

Results are reported in Table 2. Also in this case *FARGO* delivers the best recall. Contrarily to the previous dataset, in this case our method achieves a very good *recommendation disparity*. For what regards the *score disparity*, all methods provide very low (i.e., good) values.

5   Conclusions

In this paper we have introduced FARGO, a new method for providing fair, context-aware recommendations to ephemeral groups, which is also able to recommend items that are new in the system. If we consider both recall and fairness, it is not possible to identify a best overall method across all datasets and values of K. Even if we ignored recall, a clear winner fairness-wise is not evident (all of tested methods, except for *Dis*, perform best fairness-wise for at least a value of K in at least one of the two datasets). We argue that the relationship between fairness and recommendation accuracy should be seen as a tradeoff. On both datasets of our experiments, FARGO provides the best solution to such tradeoff by achieving the best recall across all values of K while delivering similar ethical guarantees to the other fair methods tested. Contrarily to what one might think, *LM* is not the best method fairness-wise, this implies that the problem of maximizing both recall and fairness is not a simple one. This is a complex problem that deserves further investigations, as recall and fairness seem not to be inversely correlated in a trivial manner. Although there may be some combinations of individual preference scores that would lead FARGO to violate the principle of social choice (imagine that there are three users, A, B and C and two items i and j; if the individual scores for i are 0.4, 0.4 and 0.4, while those for j are 0.4, 0.4 and 0.6, then the proposed method, depending also on the influences, may suggest item i, which has a higher consensus, despite the fact that clearly item j would make all users equally or better satisfied), it turns out that this is actually not a problem in practice as by filtering out at runtime dominated items (and hence respecting the social choice principle) both recall and fairness metrics worsen significantly. This may suggest that in reality groups tend to choose items that make everyone equally happy.

Future works include better investigating the reasons why the two fairness measures are somewhat unstable between the two datasets (e.g., investigating why *FARGO* delivers a better score disparity for the TV dataset, while, for the Music dataset, it delivers a better recommendation disparity), as well as finding alternatives to the consensus as a fairness element to be integrated in *CtxInfl*.

References

1. Quintarelli, E., Rabosio, E., Tanca, L.: Recommending new items to ephemeral groups using contextual user influence. In: Proceedings of the RecSys, pp. 285–292 (2016)
2. Quintarelli, E., Rabosio, E., Tanca, L.: Efficiently using contextual influence to recommend new items to ephemeral groups. Inf. Syst. **84**, 197–213 (2019)
3. Ricci, F., Rolach, L., Shapira, B., Kantor, P.B.: Recommender Systems Handbook. Springer, New York (2011). https://doi.org/10.1007/978-0-387-85820-3
4. Adomavicius, G., Tuzhilin, A.: Context-aware recommender systems. In: Ricci, F., Rokach, L., Shapira, B., Kantor, P.B. (eds.) Recommender Systems Handbook, pp. 217–253. Springer, Boston (2011). https://doi.org/10.1007/978-0-387-85820-3_7
5. Verbert, K., et al.: Context-aware recommender systems for learning: a survey and future challenges. IEEE Trans. Learn. Technol. **5**(4), 318–335 (2012)
6. Masthoff, J.: Group recommender systems: combining individual models. In: Ricci, F., Rokach, L., Shapira, B., Kantor, P.B. (eds.) Recommender Systems Handbook, pp. 677–702. Springer, Boston (2011). https://doi.org/10.1007/978-0-387-85820-3_21
7. O'Connor, M., Cosley, D., Konstan, J.A., Riedl, J.: PolyLens: a recommender system for groups of users. In: Prinz, W., Jarke, M., Rogers, Y., Schmidt, K., Wulf, V. (eds.) ECSCW 2001, pp. 199–218. Springer, Dordrecht (2001). https://doi.org/10.1007/0-306-48019-0_11
8. Masthoff, J.: Group modeling: selecting a sequence of television items to suit a group of viewers. In: Masthoff, J. (ed.) Personalized Digital Television. HCIS, vol. 6, pp. 93–141. Springer, Dordrecht (2004). https://doi.org/10.1007/1-4020-2164-X_5
9. Bourke, S., McCarthy, K., Smyth, B.: Using social ties in group recommendation. In: Proceedings of the 22nd Irish Conference on Artificial Intelligence and Cognitive Science (AICS) (2011)
10. Ntoutsi, E., Stefanidis, K., Nørvåg, K., Kriegel, H.-P.: Fast group recommendations by applying user clustering. In: Atzeni, P., Cheung, D., Ram, S. (eds.) ER 2012. LNCS, vol. 7532, pp. 126–140. Springer, Heidelberg (2012). https://doi.org/10.1007/978-3-642-34002-4_10
11. Chaney, A.J.B., et al.: A large-scale exploration of group viewing patterns. In: Proceedings of the TVX, pp. 31–38 (2014)
12. De Pessemier, T., Dooms, S., Martens, L.: Comparison of group recommendation algorithms. Multimedia Tools Appl. **72**(3), 2497–2541 (2013). https://doi.org/10.1007/s11042-013-1563-0
13. Kim, N., Lee, J.-H.: Group recommendation system: focusing on home group user in TV domain. In: Proceedings of the SCIS, pp. 985–988 (2014)
14. Ali, I., Kim, S.-W.: Group recommendations: approaches and evaluation. In: Proceedings of the IMCOM, pp. 1–6 (2015)

15. Gartrell, M., et al.: Enhancing group recommendation by incorporating social relationship interactions. In: Proceedings of the GROUP, pp. 97–106 (2010)

16. Berkovsky, S., Freyne, J.: Group-based recipe recommendations: analysis of data aggregation strategies. In: Proceedings of the RecSys, pp. 111–118 (2010)

17. Yao, S., Huang, B.: New fairness metrics for recommendation that embrace differences. CoRR, abs/1706.09838 (2017)

18. Li, Y., Ge, Y., Zhang, Y.: Tutorial on fairness of machine learning in recommender systems. In: Proceedings of the SIGIR, pp. 2654–2657 (2021)

19. Baltrunas, L., Makcinskas, T., Ricci, F.: Group recommendations with rank aggregation and collaborative filtering. In: Proceedings of the RecSys, pp. 119–126 (2010)

20. Senot, C., Kostadinov, D., Bouzid, M., Picault, J., Aghasaryan, A., Bernier, C.: Analysis of strategies for building group profiles. In: De Bra, P., Kobsa, A., Chin, D. (eds.) UMAP 2010. LNCS, vol. 6075, pp. 40–51. Springer, Heidelberg (2010). https://doi.org/10.1007/978-3-642-13470-8_6

21. Van Deventer, O., De Wit, J., Vanattenhoven, J., Gualbahar, M.: Group recommendation in a hybrid broadcast broadband television context. In: Group Recommender Systems: Concepts, Technology, Evaluation, vol. 997, pp. 12–18 (2013)

22. Gorla, J., Lathia, N., Robertson, S., Wang, J.: Probabilistic group recommendation via information matching. In: Proceedings of the WWW, pp. 495–504 (2013)

23. Ghazarian, S., Nematbakhsh, M.A.: Enhancing memory-based collaborative filtering for group recommender systems. Expert Syst. Appl. 42(7), 3801–3812 (2015)

24. Amer-Yahia, S., Roy, S.B., Chawlat, A., Das, G., Yu, C.: Group recommendation: semantics and efficiency. In: Proceedings of the VLDB, pp. 754–765 (2009)

25. Migliorini, S., Quintarelli, E., Carra, D., Belussi, A.: What is the role of context in fair group recommendations? In: Proceedings of the PIE@CAiSE (2019)

26. Zhiwen, Yu., Zhou, X., Hao, Y., Jianhua, G.: TV program recommendation for multiple viewers based on user profile merging. User Model. User-Adapt. Inter. 16(1), 63–82 (2006). https://doi.org/10.1007/s11257-006-9005-6

27. Shin, C., Woo, W.: Socially aware TV program recommender for multiple viewers. IEEE Trans. Consum. Electron. 55(2), 927–932 (2009)

28. Xiao, L., Min, Z., Yongfeng, Z., Zhaoquan, G., Yiqun, L., Shaoping, M.: Fairness-aware group recommendation with pareto-efficiency. In: Proceedings of the RecSys, pp. 107–115 (2017)

29. Qi, S., Mamoulis, N., Pitoura, E., Tsaparas, P.: Recommending packages to groups. In: Proceedings of the ICDM, pp. 449–458 (2016)

30. Serbos, D., Qi, S., Mamoulis, N., Pitoura, E., Tsaparas, P.: Fairness in package-to-group recommendations. In: Proceedings of the WWW, pp. 371–379 (2017)

31. Kaya, M., Bridge, D., Tintarev, N.: Ensuring fairness in group recommendations by rank-sensitive balancing of relevance. In: Proceedings of the RecSys, pp. 101–110 (2020)

32. Dwork, C., Hardt, M., Pitassi, T., Reingold, O., Zemel, R.: Fairness through awareness. In: Proceedings of the ITCS, pp. 214–226 (2012)

33. Leonhardt, J., Anand, A., Khosla, M.: User fairness in recommender systems. In: Proceedings of the WWW, pp. 101–102 (2018)

Author Index

Printed in the United States
by Baker & Taylor Publisher Services

Printed in the United States
by Baker & Taylor Publisher Services